Using Portfolios
in the
English Classroom

Credits

Every effort has been made to contact copyright holders for permission to reproduce borrowed material where necessary. We apologize for any oversights and would be happy to rectify them in future printings.

All student work contained within is used with permission

Chapter Twelve: Using Portfolios to negotiate a Rhetorical Community by Marian Galbraith, John Hennelly, and Alan C. Purves. Preparation of this chapter was supported by the National Research Center on Literature Teaching and Learning under Grant number R117G10015 from the Office of Education Research and Improvement, U.S. Department of Education. The findings and opinions expressed here do not reflect the position or policies of the sponsoring agency.

Christopher-Gordon Publishers, Inc.
480 Washington Street
Norwood, MA 02062

Printed in the United States of America

10 9 8 7 6 5 4 3 2 1   02 01 00 99 98 97

ISBN: 0-926842-62-5

ACKNOWLEDGMENTS

As is the case with any anthology, a list of those who in some way contributed to the writing of the chapters in this volume could run many pages in length. As editors, however, we would be remiss if we failed to acknowledge the key roles certain people and organizations have played in the development of this project.

Our greatest amount of thanks goes, of course, to the teachers in the Portfolio Project—Rochelle L. Abelson, Deane Beverly, Marsha Casey, Nicole Elbert, Nancy Lester Elitzer, Maria Fusco, Marian Galbraith, Richard Harris, John Hennelly, Suzanne Heyd, Gertrude Karabas, Pamela Kiniry, Anne Kuthy, Carole Mackin, Carol Mohrmann, Charles Phelps, Joseph Quattrini, Deborah Stence, Jeanne Stendardo, and Christine Sullivan. Their contributions and enthusiasm in their classrooms, as well as at the monthly meetings of project teachers in Stockbridge, Massachusetts, were key elements toward making the project a success and this volume a possibility. We would also like to thank Kathleen Sims and Ellen Mainwaring, our colleagues at the National Research Center for Literature Teaching and Learning, for coordinating and facilitating those monthly meetings, and the Red Lion Inn at Stockbridge for the pleasant facilities it afforded.

The project would not have been possible at all without the support of the National Research Center on Literature Teaching and Learning at the University at Albany State University of New York, which was itself supported by the Educational Research and Development Programs as administered by the Office of Educational Research and Improvement, United States Department of Education, Grant R-117G10015. We would also like to thank Kate Blossom, the Centers Assistant Director for Outreach, for her work in developing and promoting LitNet, a computer network that allowed those working in the project to correspond and communicate through E-mail and electronic bulletin boards.

It almost goes without saying that without the support of their administrators and fellow teachers, the work of the teachers in this project would not have been possible. Finally, we would also like to thank Roseanne DeFabio of the New York State Department of Education and Joan Baron of the Connecticut State Education Department for helping to select the teachers. As this volume indicates, they did a marvelous job.

TABLE OF CONTENTS

Chapter 2: Building the Portfolio Structure....................27
by Deane A. Beverly, Carole Mackin, and Marian Galbraith

Chapter 3: Creating the Final Portfolio.......................53
by Maria Fusco

Chapter 4: Designing the Showcase Portfolio.................63
by Rochelle L. Abelson

Chapter 5: Finding Our Way: Authenticity and Transformation in the Use of Portfolios.....................69
by Mary Sawyer and Suzanne Heyd

Chapter 6: CD Portfolios: A Multimedia Approach..............81
by Jeanne Stendardo

INTRODUCTION

Alan C. Purves

This volume is the collaborative work of a group of middle- and high-school teachers who, from 1992 to 1995, were involved in a project examining the implementation of portfolios in the literature classroom, grades 6-12. The project was conducted through the National Research Center on Literature Teaching and Learning at the University at Albany, State University of New York. The editors were the project coordinators.

The project grew out of my interest in the assessment of learning in literature and my earlier research on the appalling quality of tests and examinations in English literature. I was interested in what ways the states, which were often charged with examining the performance of students in English, including literature, were working to improve the quality of assessment. At that time, there was a burgeoning interest in portfolios, particularly the writing portfolio. In the early 1990s portfolios seemed the great panacea. Never sure about panaceas, I first got the National Research Center on Literature Teaching and Learning to do a survey of how states were handling portfolios, particularly for literature. It turned out that none were actively engaged in literature portfolios for state assessment. However, two neighboring states, Connecticut and New York, were among those exploring possibilities. After some talk with the state supervisors, and a workshop with some of the experts on portfolios, we decided to enlist the cooperation of several middle schools and high schools. We needed to work within a fairly confined geographic range, and we wanted a mix of schools and districts.

Upon consultation with the state supervisors, we found one rural district

(Canajoharie, New York), three urban districts (Danbury and Groton, Connecticut and Schenectady, New York), and two suburban districts (Colonie, New York and Old Saybrook, Connecticut). The teacher in Old Saybrook, John Hennelly, later moved to another district, West Hartford; and a teacher in Groton moved her project to Berlin, Connecticut, a suburban district. In the second year, we added Mechanicville, New York, which is a small city surrounded by farms, and Bayard Rustin School in Manhattan. The teachers who were nominated were considered experienced teachers, many of them were leaders in their district or region, and they were committed to staying with the project for three years.

We began the study with no preconceptions about what portfolios should be, but as we worked together and shared our experiences with different forms of experimentation, some principles began to emerge. What follow are some personal reflections on what I have seen and heard from the teachers and students.

We concluded early on in the project that portfolio assessment is not just a frill or an assessment but a key part of a whole approach to the teaching of English and literature. From talking with students and teachers and observing classrooms, we emerged with a set of principles that hold beyond our local circumstances and apply broadly. Let me start with a summary of these seven principles and then follow with an elaboration of each one:[1]

1. A portfolio is meant to present the student to the outside world.

2. A portfolio should seek to reflect the breadth of the student's accomplishments.

3. A portfolio should seek to justify the particular course or curriculum that the student has undertaken.

4. A portfolio should be the responsibility of the student.

5. A portfolio has a rhetorical purpose: to inform and to persuade.

6. Creating a portfolio is formative evaluation; the portfolio, summative evaluation.

7. The portfolio has nothing to do with state or national assessment.

1. A portfolio is meant to present the student to the outside world. In the professional world, a portfolio is what an artist or a business person takes to a prospective employer or client. It may have papers and pictures; it may be on videotape or a CD-ROM. Whatever the medium, it is the first glimpse that many people have of that person. A portfolio is an amplified résumé. It seeks to show the person off to the world by example, to say, "Look, here is what I have done that may serve as an indicator of what I can do." It usually includes things that the person has created or helped to create, and it may contain comments on or reviews of those artifacts.

In a school setting, the portfolio is not a mere collection of tests, scores, papers, or drafts of papers. It is not an internal document for the student, teacher, and administrator. It should seek to contain those items that best represent the accomplishments of the student to a broader world. Some may be things that have been assigned, but some may be freely chosen. What the teachers and students in the project developed was a clear sense of the importance of the portfolio. For both, it was a demonstration of young people's performance as students of literature—that is, their performance as readers, viewers, writers, talkers, dramatizers, and artists in their own right. It showed what they knew, what they could do, and what they did on their own—sometimes not even as part of class or school work.

One of the items that some teachers had heard should be in a student's portfolio is a succession of drafts. It's as if a series of rehearsals were necessary as part of the performance. As we discussed the matter, many said they could tell that the person had rehearsed or not rehearsed by the performance itself. So what were the drafts supposed to tell us? How closely should we examine the changes? What would we learn from such a study? Whether the student did the work without help? Not really. Whether the student understood the feedback? Perhaps. That the teacher encouraged revision? Probably. That the student cares about the quality of the writing? Yes, but that can be seen just as well in the final version.

The issue of drafts raised a distinction in the purpose the portfolio serves. It brought us to separate the working portfolio from the presentation portfolio. The first serves a formative function and remains a document internal to the class, to be gone over by students and teachers. It should contain drafts, notes, and comments, and it can be messy because only students and teachers see it. The presentation portfolio, however, serves a summative purpose, providing evidence to the outside world of the accomplishments of students and the class (and by implication the teacher). It should be crafted, polished, and definitely not messy. An actor does not display his or her dressing room—important as it may be to his or her craft.

As the later chapters show, the portfolio can be thought of as a portrait. Any portrait is taken from an angle, and the angle of the portrait may vary from student to student and from class to class. We have a number of different portraits represented in this volume. One kind of portrait is a portrait of mastery, proving to the students and the world that they are indeed competent individuals. This appears in the Danbury and Canajoharie schools, to name but two. Another kind of portrait appears in the classes where mastery is not an issue (the Advanced Placement class, for example); there the portrait may be one to show the student as a thoughtful, sensitive reader with a catholic taste, as Nancy Lester Elitzer describes. John Hennelly poses the students as writers, adept at their craft. In other classes, the angle of the portrait is that of growth and change over a period of time, as in Groton and Schenectady. In still others it is a portrait of the student as a member of an intellectual or interpretive community, as in Hartford. In all of the classes, however, it is a portrait of the student as a responsible human being.

2. A portfolio should seek to reflect the breadth of the student's accomplishments. The English and literature curricula, however conceived (whether as courses focusing on genres, themes, or periods; whether dominated by literary analysis, dramatization, or reader response approaches; whether focusing on writing over reading), include three major components that should probably be represented in a portfolio: knowledge, practice, and habits. The precise mix depends upon the approach and the goals of the particular program. The curriculum in English does demand, however, that the students do something, produce something, be other than passive. What they produce tells what they have learned about, what they have learned to do, and who they have learned to be.

Knowledge in literature can be divided into knowledge of that which is contained in texts (such as allusions to myths and folktales) and knowledge about the world surrounding the writing and criticism of texts (such as literary terms, still a staple of the middle-school curriculum). Any portfolio should include some demonstration of what students know, which can include evidence of what they have read, what concepts about literature they have learned, and what they have gained as general knowledge from having explored a theme or pursued a research project. It may go beyond literature to language, history, society, or a new culture.

Practice can be divided into two parts: *responding*, which covers reading, watching, and listening; and *articulating*, which covers speaking and writing about individual texts or about literature in general. *Responding* includes decoding or making out the plain sense of the text or film, and particularly coming to some whole impression—a re-creation of what is read—and then presenting this in a journal, report, or summary. But response is not enough; too often it is simply what the teachers in the project refer to as *plot vomit*. Most students are good at this, and plot vomit is not what is meant by response. There is a complex set of possible intellectual strategies that emerge in talk or writing. For this reason, most teachers in the project used the response journal as part of their teaching strategy. It was central in the working portfolios of many classes.

Articulating covers a wide variety of ways by which students let people know what their response is. This is the key to the contemporary literature classroom in many ways. It is not just reading in a closet but bringing an impression of what is read out into the open. Like any school subject, literature involves public acts in which the student must be more articulate about procedures and strategies as well as conclusions than might be true outside of school. Proofs are not necessary in mathematical applications outside of school; essays about one's reading of a text are not required after reading every library book. A portfolio needs to contain evidence of articulated, extended responses, such as essays, transcripts of discussions, or recordings of oral interpretations. These may be individual or group responses. In one school, a class that had studied *Julius Caesar* prepared versions of each act. One group made a rap version of Act One, another transformed Act Three into a modern trial. The performances were videotaped and copies of the tapes formed part of each student's portfolio.

Habits refer broadly to the set of attitudes, stances, and beliefs encouraged through formal or informal instruction. It should be seen as emerging from knowledge and practice, since it involves the establishment in students' minds of the preferred kinds of knowledge and ways of doing. Individuals do some things as a matter of conscious volition; other things they do by habit. They are disposed to do them, and school and other educational institutions reinforce and direct those dispositions.

The school reader of literature exists in a field of school reading that consciously seeks to develop in that reader a set of habits of mind about how to read and how to talk about what has been read. Habits are a necessary part of our having an educational system and of our being a society. They are what constitute us as a culture of readers; they are not to be attacked in the name of individualism. They enable us to participate in a variety of groups with ease and confidence. I have argued for several years that we should be more conscious about these habits that we teach than we have been, and that we should take pride in our success as well as raise our own concerns about what we are doing.

Our students practice and learn how to perform a particular kind of reading and they are encouraged to read this way voluntarily. They do this through being encouraged to talk about certain facets of the text and their experience of it and not to talk about others. They are encouraged to see themselves as the makers of meaning and that meaning is what they negotiate with the teacher and with the authority that resides in the text and its critical history. Above all, they are encouraged to talk and write about the text; they cannot remain mute. The curriculum, then, seeks to promote habits of mind in reading and writing, and these should be seen in the portfolio, which means that there must be multiple samples of student responses in order to see what aspects of them have become habitual. In fact, that is why we need a portfolio in the first place. A single essay or a single test does not tell us enough about the habits of the minds of our students; only a portfolio can do that.

Another set of these habits we seek to inculcate is less obvious: it concerns the aesthetic judgments students make about the various texts they read and how they justify these judgments publicly. Literature education is supposed to develop something called *taste* or the love of *good literature*; thus, the curriculum looks beyond being able to read and write to wanting to read and write what the school values. It may be very specific in developing a love of the *best*. It may also include the development of a tolerance for the variety of literature, of a willingness to acknowledge that many different kinds and styles of work can be thought of as literature, and of an acceptance that just because we do not like a certain poem does not mean that it is not good. The development of such habits of mind should lead students to the acceptance of cultural diversity in literature and, by extension, in society. These are often cited as parts of the curriculum in school literature, but they loom less large in the minds of students and teachers because they are not part of the assessed curriculum; in addition, we know less how to handle the student who is recalcitrant in these habits. We do not know how best to capture these in a portfolio (or any other form of assessment). But the teachers use reading logs and other reports as indirect evidence of habits.

The school curriculum can also lead students to develop a taste based on an awareness of the meretricious or the shoddy use of sentiment or language. Experienced readers of literature can see that they are being tricked by a book or a film even when the trickery is going on—and they can enjoy the experience. Like advertising and propaganda, literature manipulates the reader or viewer. The conscious student can be aware of such manipulation and value the craft at the same time as discerning the motives that lie behind it. One aspect of the literature portfolio can be the record or log of what has been read by the student. This can be described and even rated by a teacher or some other person for what is reported as well as the quality of the report's presentation. The problem, of course, is that of not imposing an adult taste on an adolescent or a taste of an intellectual on a person who is discovering fiction through *Sweet Valley High* or the comics. Too narrow a view may have the wrong result. The judge must be careful to describe the taste and to note not only what is read but what sorts of comments emerge on what has been read.

3. A portfolio should seek to justify the particular course or curriculum that the student has undertaken. The portfolio should seek to capture all of those aspects of a literature curriculum and the performance of students in school literature as they reflect the aims and standards set by the community, the school, and the class. I do not think they should seek to represent a set of national or international standards or some state-ordained checklist. Such will serve only to trivialize the learning and turn teachers and students into hypocrites. A portfolio must be a comprehensive record of the student in the context of the school and the class, a portrait including many facets. I do not think portfolios can serve assessment purposes beyond the classroom and particularly not some state or national assessment purpose. Portfolios represent the curriculum in practice, in a real place with real people, not a set of abstractions. To make what I have outlined concrete, teachers should ask themselves, and perhaps go over with their class, the following questions: (1) What do I look for in student reading and response? in student writing and performance? (2) What do I accept as evidence ? (3) What do I see as being better? as being older or more mature? (4) What do I want to communicate about the students and the class? to whom? The answers must be particular to the individual class to have any validity at all.

A portfolio should not be a collection of scores on commercial tests nor items on a behavioral checklist provided by a commercial or state agency. It should, I think, contain a statement of the goals and aims of the course and the school. This way, anyone looking at the portfolio should be able to reconstruct the literature program that the student has had and should know what its objectives and criteria were. It may well also include a listing of the opportunities provided by the school for students to participate in activities related to literature—a student magazine or a school play, for example. This might appear as a standard insert in each student's portfolio.

4. A portfolio should be the responsibility of the student. This is the opposite side of the tenet I just set forth, and it is equally simple: A portfolio should be created by the students. It may have guidelines from the school or teacher about the kinds of things that might be included (or must be included), such as a number of kinds of writing, a self-evaluation, a list of books read, or a number of original compositions or performances (e.g., film, music, writing). But the decision as to what specific pieces should be included and how they should be included should be made by each student. Students must also work out how best to put group work into the portfolio. If it is a project that involves the building of a model, they might have to use photographs. If there is a dramatization, there must be an audiotape or a videotape. If there is a really good discussion, they must figure out how to put that into the portfolio to show why it is good and what part they took in it. Many of the students in the project had to add a comment on their role in group work. The teachers decided it was not fair to give each member of a group a blanket grade.

With portfolios, the students are laying themselves on the line before the whole school or perhaps before a jury of teachers. It is their choice as to whether they should be seen as uncaring slobs or as people who take pride in their work. Teachers cannot do this for them. By taking responsibility for what they show of themselves to the world, they have a new power that they don't have when they are simply handing things in and getting grades. It takes time for them to realize that they are not helpless—that they earn the grade or the rating, you do not give it to them. We have also found that they become quite good at judging their own worth. There are a few who don't get the point, who think that just because they did it they deserve a good grade. Most come to see a difference between doing it and doing it for a portfolio, which is a public document.

One technique the teachers in the project used to encourage this responsibility was the technique of *grouping*. This is a form of reflection that has been used in other contexts and that works in schools. It depends upon having the members of the group use the same format each time they meet. The format is usually one of questions about how the members of the group are progressing toward a set of goals that they have defined. The group members share their answers to those questions each time, talk with each other about them, and encourage each other. It is a time of sharing and reflection, generally not one of admonition or assessment (other than self-assessment). What goes on in the group is confidential. It works in an English class this way: The students divide into groups of three (the group would remain together for the year). Every two weeks the three would get together for a half-hour and share their answers to the following questions:

- What do I know now that I didn't know?

- What can I do now that I couldn't do?

- What do I do now that I didn't do?

With respect to each question, the students should be encouraged to make an individual or a collective plan and refer their answers to that plan. The grouping is among the students. The teacher does not participate or even know what the plan of the groups might be. That should come out in the portfolio itself. In Christine Sullivan's class, which is not reported on here, I observed the students in a group session. Many times there was encouragement and support. Grouping is a way of having the students look at themselves and learn how they can take responsibility for their own learning. It is simple, and it works.

5. A portfolio has a rhetorical purpose: to inform and to persuade. Again this point sums up much of what we have gone over before. The portfolio should inform the observer as to what students have done in the particular literature course. It should reflect the breadth and depth of the course and the experiences it contains. Since it is public, it should seek to be understandable to the outside world, and perhaps it should conform to principles I have set up in the earlier points:

First, the presentation portfolio should reflect the curriculum of a class and of the school as well as reflect the broader interests of the student. It need not do this chronologically, although that is often a possible organization. It might be organized by groups or classes of activity (papers, discussions, dramatizations).

Second, the portfolio should convey to the observer the value of what the student has done. It should also seek to show why it is important to have done what was done, to have included what was included, to have been judged by the standards that have been established. For these reasons, it should have some sort of introduction and commentary, certainly by the student, perhaps by the class, and perhaps even by some outside juror if the portfolio is to go beyond the class.

Third, the portfolio should convey the distinct quality of the individual student. The portfolio should attempt to show that this particular student has done as well as he or she has by saying something about change, growth, breadth, mastery, or knowledge. It should explain why this particular student is worth noticing.

One thing that these three principles suggest is that a portfolio cannot be slapped together. It should make a good first impression as well as reinforce a strong second and third impression. One thing the students and teachers in the project quickly discovered was how important the cover is. It is what the audience or jury first sees and it can set the image of the student. Many classes worked on covers extensively. Like any composition, a portfolio is known by its content, its arrangement, and its style. A portfolio is to a composition as a book is to a chapter or a hypertext to any of its components. And a portfolio takes time; it is not the work of the night before. It will probably take most of a week once every quarter to review portfolios with students. But don't begrudge the time, for the students will have gained in the depth of understanding what they might have lost in the one short story that might have been covered superficially.

6. Creating a portfolio is formative evaluation; the portfolio itself, summative evaluation. This is a tricky point, perhaps the most difficult for students and teachers, and one I alluded to earlier. During the course of our teaching literature and other aspects of English, we act as the coach, the person who encourages the students to bring out their best, which may come out in discussions and conferences, in drafts of papers, or in rehearsals of various sorts. In this role, we are generally friendly creatures, like the helpful beasts in the traditional quest stories. But, gradually we must let go of our control so as to be ready for the time when we must drop that helpful role, when the students are showing their stuff for real, when they have to confront the dragon, and we are the dragon-judge. This is hard for many of us and for our students. But it is a shift in role that we must acknowledge in ourselves and explain to our students so that they can stand on their own. To do this, we should be brutally honest about our criteria. That is the first step. There must be no surprises about what we are looking for and what our criteria for success might be. We must announce these the first day of class. Then we must tell the students that they must assume responsibility for meeting those criteria. We must appeal to their self-pride and their desire to *look good*, and we must slowly let them know that them—not we—are the ones who are responsible for their performance.

We can then be the judge (unless we can get someone else to take on that role); we can be the expert who can describe the performance of students and hold it up against standards that are agreed upon by teacher and student. We have to cast off our mantle of friendliness and look through the lens of the critic or the judge. This is not an inhumane act at all; it is an act of love, and we should try to help our students understand it. We can no longer be the parent/advocate, the attorney for the defense. We cannot rationalize our students' work; it must stand on its own, for we will disappear from their lives.

That is the point at which our students become independent of us, and it is a point toward which we must lead them so that they can be free of us and autonomous. I think it is the hardest part of teaching, but it is probably the most important. We are seeking to help our students to become independent responsible human beings who no longer need us. To effect this end, we need to balance our tendency to do things for the students with our tendency to serve as the judge. This duality is the crux of the portfolio approach, I think; it is also the crux of what it means to be a teacher. The fact of portfolios encourages us to face ourselves as teachers and as human beings responsible for the education (the leading out away from childhood and into the world) of our students.

7. The portfolio has nothing to do with state, large-scale district, or national assessment. This seems like a harsh statement, but it comes from both our experience in this project and my many years in large-scale assessment. Despite where we started—a concern with state measures of individual or school performance—we all came to realize a number of things, one of which is that the political nature of state and national governments and testing agencies is a mercurial one. The goals and aims and even the practices can shift at the click of a ballot. To be caught up in one form of assessment and then switch to another is usually not a matter of rational decision but of reaction and counterreaction.

Portfolios are too valuable to be caught in the maelstrom of state assessment politics. The portfolio is not simply a device by which students can be sorted and ranked. It is a way of making school meaningful to each student as an individual. It is all that we have said in the first six principles. That being so, the portfolio should not be subjected to the vagaries of large-scale assessment and to matters of validity, reliability, and comparability. A student's portfolio is designed to show the student as an individual, not to reduce him or her to a decile or a deviation from a norm.

I realize that this last position may, as one critic has charged, make the portfolio simply a nice thing. But as the writers of this volume have shown, portfolios are more than just a gimmick, they are a way of making a whole philosophy of instruction and curriculum come to life. They are a way of enabling teachers and students to chart their own destinies and see themselves as valued human beings. Besides, they are fun.

Endnotes

1. Different versions of these principles have been presented elsewhere (see, e.g., Galbraith, Hennelly, and Purves, 1994; Purves, Quattrini, and Sullivan, 1995). I apologize if they are familiar to some readers; however, they remain cardinal principles of the project.

References

Galbraith, M., J. Hennelly, and A.C. Purves (1994). *Using portfolios to negotiate a rhetorical community* (Report Series 3.10). Albany, NY: National Research Center on Literature Teaching and Learning, University at Albany—SUNY.

Purves, A. C., J. A. Quattrini, and C. I. Sullivan (1995). *Creating the writing portfolio.* Instructors manual. Lincolnwood, IL: NTC.

PART 1
REFLECTIONS ON PRACTICE

Introduction

The essays in this section are primarily the stories of teachers in the class-room, describing the impact portfolios have had on their teaching styles and ideas. The section begins with a dialogue between two teachers, Rich Harris and Deborah Stence. Harris was with the project from the beginning: he is the voice of experience in the dialogue. Stence is the newcomer to portfolios: she is the novice, the questioner. Their dialogue took place on a computer disk, which was passed back and forth between the two and on which each would comment upon the other's reflections. Rich and Debbie discuss possible problems in implement-ing portfolios in the classroom, as well as how portfolios demand student self-evaluation without making the teacher relinquish his or her own evaluative role. This conversation brings up many of the questions teachers have about portfolios. It is a real conversation, giving a feeling of an on-going faculty-room dialogue. It is interesting to note that many teachers throughout the book write about their conversations with other teachers.

The next chapter is also a conversation. The three authors work together in Groton, Connecticut: Deane Beverly teaches a group of students in the sixth grade, Carole Mackin teaches the same students in the seventh grade, and Marian Galbraith teaches them in the eighth grade. These three have worked together to create a series of portfolios that provide students with a bridge between teachers and school years. All three stress the need for creating standards in the classroom: Beverly offers advice for the portfolio neophyte, with a focus on the students' need for self-evaluation and their ability to set goals; Mackin focuses on student growth; and Galbraith explains how she helps students to create a "reader's profile" and to see their work as evidence of learning that they can carry with them to high school or other parts of their lives.

Exploring portfolios in the middle-school classroom is continued by Rochelle Abelson and Maria Fusco, who teach seventh and eighth grades, respectively, in Mechanicville, New York. This school district has long had a history of asking students to create a scrapbook, which is not the same as a portfolio because students do not assess their own work. The idea of a portfolio as a final project proves problematic for Fusco, who, after a very successful first year, finds that she must *reinvent the wheel* during the second year after Abelson's students arrive in her classroom already familiar with the idea of the portfolio. Like Abelson, she finds that a combination of art and writing make the portfolio *special*.

The tone shifts with the next chapter by Mary Sawyer and Suzanne Heyd. This chapter has a more formal voice, and it is an explanation of the need for portfolios. In the chapter following, Jeanne Stendardo discusses the creation of the multimedia CD-ROM portfolio, offering a concrete explanation of what a state-of-the-art computer lab should look like, as well as a helpful definition for the computer-leery. Her essay begs the question that most teachers end up asking: But when will I find the *time* for all this stuff? This is a question inherent to portfolios and underlies most of the stories in this volume, many of which offer suggestions for managing time in the portfolio classroom.

In contrast to Stendardo, with her belief that students should be given a wide range of media from which to demonstrate literacy, Nancy Lester Elitzer believes in developing students as readers, and uses her chapter to describe the process of creating an *autobiography of a reader*. For Lester, reading is a practice and a love; books must be explored and discussed and owned.

If colleagues are the people teachers work with, then students are a teacher's colleagues, and teachers must help students *turn pro* to acknowledge that they have become professionals in the area of language use. In their chapter, Joe Quattrini and his students Melissa DiVisconti, Sarah Leonard, and Austin Willoughby offer ten rules for doing so. In the final chapter of this part of the book, Marsha Casey and Nicole Elbert focus on initiating students who are "less able and more disinterested" into portfolio practice. Much of their chapter is a collection of handouts and letters used to give learning power and authority back to their students.

Chapter 1

A Dialogue
Introducing Portfolios

Richard A. Harris
Deborah Stence
Danbury High School

Getting Started

Rich: Portfolios—What is their value? Why have one? How do I start one? These questions constantly run through my mind as I begin the process of gathering data. This year I will be using an American Studies group as fellow researchers. I know that the idea of self-assessment is valid, but how do I get students to see that value? How do I get them to see that learning can take place when they reflect on their own work and that they can, in fact, place worth on what they have done. I know that for some the idea of becoming one's own teacher strikes a terrifying note. I also know that, for some, once the power of self-assessment becomes known, I will not be able to hold them back. But it's worth the effort.

This year I will share my frustrations and my joys with another teacher. That may be a way to give justification to this whole idea.

Debbie: I have looked forward to introducing the portfolio for the past couple of years. I must confess, however, that the concept of self-assessment scares the wits out of me. I listened as young students from other schools discussed their self-directed experiences and wondered if it might ever be a remote possibility for the students who work in Room D164. Regardless of the outcome, I guess that this year will be a revelation for me. And I know now why the disciples were sent out "two by two" to spread the good word; without a team to cheer her on, support her, remind her of her goals and to keep passing and moving toward the win, a player could forget to believe, much less to spread that belief. I know that I am committed to seeing my students develop their portfolios this year, and I sincerely trust them to turn out quality.

In all honesty, however, I do not trust them with the task of self-assessment. Perhaps I have set myself up for this anxiety by the group work we completed last week with a theme paper. When teams of four and five had submitted their collaborative thesis papers discussing the many and varied themes in *To Kill a Mockingbird*, I invited them to respond with a self-assessment of their team's effort, strengths, and weaknesses, as well as their own effort, along with an assessment of the value of their group's paper. The values they assigned were so inflated and unrealistic that I am scared to turn these evaluators loose with their individual work.

About That Grade Inflation

Rich: Grade inflation is a problem that I have had to deal with, but in the opposite manner. When I first asked students to assess individual work, they balked—I was flooded with questions and comments that truly showed a sense of anxiety: "What do you mean? I can't do that. You're the teacher. Grade me." It was clear to me that in order to get this task accomplished, I would have to teach how to assess. This proved to be a problem at first because assessment for me is a skill that I have acquired over twenty-plus years of teaching. I realized that what I had asked was indeed a monstrous task, not something that could be accomplished overnight. I went back to my lessons to see what it was that I had expected the students to learn. This gave me a picture of my intent. I looked at my assessments to see if the students had shown this to me. The jury is still out on that one. What I realized was that students cannot be asked to assess work—their own or someone else's—unless there is a set of standards to be followed. The way to develop this is wide open.

Debbie: So it sounds to me as though I have bit off far more than I expected to chew. In reality, it is the self-assessment that is the *real* target here, at least for me as the facilitator. So tell me, Rich, when this concept or plan is introduced to the class, which is discussed first? The product or the process? Oh my. I remember hearing that phrase used in the workshop. I don't mean to sound so naïve, but it truly is the way I feel at this stage. I never considered the height and breadth of this scheme before I decided to build. It is intimidating, yet I suppose, as with all other units and projects, it will depend upon the enthusiasm and commitment with which it is introduced.

Rich: I have learned that the process must come first. However, the end result must not only be the process. We have gone that way in writing. We get caught up in the process and we never seem to finish anything.

Debbie: Speaking of never finishing anything, I have spent the last couple of days in reflection of this forthcoming project. My theme has been "Why jump into another new venture when I have not yet established consistent success with my last great undertaking, the writing process?" What worked with one group bombed miserably the next year. There's a part of my conscience that whispers, "Finish what you've already started!" while another voice cries, "You'll be more successful at that once you've introduced this dimension." I know that the Connecticut Writing Project's Workshop on Revision is becoming a timely piece of my solution. Revision has been my weak link both personally and with my students. And certainly it will be a cornerstone to this portfolio experience. I became a convert to revision theology at the summer writing project, but I seem to have lost my vision. Any great advice here?

Rich: Part of the problem is that teaching occurs in isolation. One of the goals of the project was to get converts so that the feeling of isolation is lessened. Remember that the writing process is not the sum total of the student's knowledge—it may only help the student to voice his or her knowledge in a clear consistent form. One can never master that process because it is by definition a process.

My best advice is not to double up—use the process when it applies, and then include the drafts and/or the finished works in the portfolio so that the student can assess the learning.

Dust Off Your Red Pen

Rich: Related to this is the idea of correction. Where has the role of the teacher gone? Students become so used to work that is *great*, that shows feeling or emotion, that they become used to inflated grades. The red pen has become an object of scorn both to students and other so-called educators who place value on output with little concern for correctness—political or otherwise. For myself, the red pen is back. I feel compelled to indicate where writing can be improved. I was shocked to read a paper from a student of mine. He had turned this paper in to a history teacher, one of my colleagues, and he had received a B+ grade. That was not so bad until I turned to the last page. "Good command of English structure." The very first sentence was not even a sentence.

Debbie: This conversation does my heart good. It's not so much that I needed validation as it is that I can now bring my red pens out of hiding. This is the first year for red pens. I had, for a season or two, bought into the theory that the student's self-confidence would be destroyed by my red-handed comments. After several years of self-restraint on my part, I have become totally convinced that it was indeed a grievous neglect on my part to fail to correct individually. I was allowing and encouraging my students to avoid necessary correction. I became an accomplice and a co-conspirator to mediocrity. I was annoyed that my students didn't want to be bothered to strive for improvement when I, the person in charge, had purposely avoided correction. My conscience as an educator kicked in. I had failed my students and lowered my expectations for them and for myself. So I am back to redlining in a big way and it is good to know that while I may betray colleagues who still stand behind the hands-off doctrine, I have at least one ally who sees correction as more than trendy. I suppose part of this is self-awareness as well: it doesn't take me as long to be convinced that my student feels unthreatened by what I might think or suggest. Come to think of it, I seem to remember Mr. Cassles, my eighth-grade English teacher, taking lots of time to point out what needed fixing. And he is the very person who saw the writer in me and helped me to declare English as my favorite subject. I always looked forward to the red pen all over my papers when he handed them back; those remarks led to consistent improvement on my behalf.

Don't I owe my students as much?

Rich: The portfolio can be used as the correcting device that is available to all students all the time. If used efficiently, the portfolio contains all levels of writing and understanding. Students can trace thought development through drafts as well as through finished pieces of work. The portfolio becomes the red pen. Students can trace writing development by reviewing their own work and by critiquing the work of others. When listening in on students as they work on the review of other students, I am amazed at the number of times I hear "I like the way that you said that." Students take those examples back to their own writing. The red pens go off in their heads and the better form becomes a part of the learning. The portfolio becomes a spell check, a grammar check, and a logic check. Even with no *red* marks on the work, the corrections are made. This is why the reflective process is so important to the development of the portfolio as well as to the learning for the individual. Portfolios allow the moment to be frozen in time but not finished: they allow the return to past experiences. Assignments are completed but they are not finished; learning can come from the previous assignment. Correction is a very important part of the process, but by using a portfolio, this process becomes internalized; allowing the student to grow in responsibility and develop a strong sense of self-concept. Students can become more comfortable with their learning because they finally have a chance to reflect on their knowledge based on the evidence they have created.

Allowing the Learning to Happen

Debbie: I am thrilled to have a live demonstration to report this morning! I've run into just the visible proof to which you have referred. A young man in my study hall this year was my student two years ago during Sophomore Composition and Literature. I had some great expectations for him, based upon seeds from his personal writing journal. He had lost his dad, faced that loss and other major transitions, and, through his sharing, I spotted what could become some meaningful memoirs on the far horizon. My dreams on his behalf never materialized. He failed to "go there" as my kids would say. I was disappointed, yet I knew that there were pieces that would no doubt surface later.

I am pleased to report that during study hall he has been eager to share and to discuss the portfolio that came about last year when he studied with another teacher. There was the memory piece that I had envisioned *by faith*. It had to wait for his timing. I saw the process as you describe it by being on hand to plant seeds and then to celebrate post-harvest. As the television character Ralph Cramden would have remarked, "This thing is bigger than both of us, Alice." To be able to see the tangible grow with the thinker/learner was a privilege, and it was certainly one that I desire to experience more often. I see what you mean, *finally*, that the process was far more significant than the piece of paper that verifies it, and that the relationship with that paper is necessary to encourage that process along its path.

Rich: This process that you speak of is so obvious that it seems we miss it just because of that fact. For years we have been taught that knowledge is the key—but the key to what? Without the ability to flex those mind muscles, the possession of knowledge is useless. We have to be willing *and able* to let students learn and to let them understand how they learn. I am convinced that if the proper framework is established, students will constantly amaze, entertain, and astound you. Proper assessment should show growth over time, and that time may be one week, but it also may be five years. Implementation of the portfolio, or at least a variation of the portfolio, allows for this type of learning to take place. This is not to say that we cannot guide and foster learning—quite the opposite. What this allows the teacher to do is give the student skills that are beneficial in the (I hate to say it) *real world*. Not all learning can be tested, but all learning can be assessed. It does mean giving up some authority, but the respect you gain and give is well worth risking the security of the grade book.

Control Issues and the Grade Book

Debbie: There you go mentioning that grade book. So tell me how you personally convert the assessment (self- and teacher-driven) into corresponding grades for *the book*? By what criterion do you initiate the process?

Rich: Self-assessment, I believe, is impossible to evaluate from the outside. A way to include the reflective process used in the portfolio system is to develop the portfolio and the corresponding assessment as a part of a participation grade. All work should be included in the portfolio—at first—graded and other. The real learning takes place when the student goes back and looks at the body of evidence developed and makes some personal evaluations on what is there. This way the assessment itself is not graded. No one except that student has to know about the weaknesses; however, those weaknesses have to be acknowledged and addressed.

First Things First

Debbie: I must write this down, lest I lose the Kodak moment that evolved today: In anticipation of parent conferences this evening, and as a foreshadowing (or forewarning) of portfolios on the far horizon, I invited all students to write a self-assessment of their first-quarter learning experiences, both ups and downs. I requested a second paragraph to address personal needs, personal goals, and a setting of sights for the months ahead.

I am humbled to report that the experience has borne fruit—a respectable percentage from each student group made an honest, reliable statement of where they have been and how far they have come, and cited a target for where they personally would like to go this year.

A Word of Caution

Rich: I bring good news. Not only are we in the mainstream of portfolio exploration and use, but we are at the head. I was astounded by some of the practices out there in public education. The idea of the portfolio has indeed come into its own. My concern is that the textbook publishers will get too involved. Soon we will be seeing textbooks telling us how to create a perfect portfolio. For the portfolio to be successful, it has to come from within. Guidelines may be drawn, but the individual classroom teacher and the students must create the elements of the portfolio. I witnessed several accounts of states becoming involved with the portfolio as a tool to evaluate students, and what I saw was a standardization of the portfolio. For me, this is a serious problem. Teachers have to shun the quick fix and *create*.

Debbie: I see that often in other areas. We feel insecure about trying new things and think that trying something that worked in someone else's classroom can just be duplicated in our own. As a fairly new teacher, I am always eager to see how things are being done, but then I have to wrestle with it to fit it into my own teaching style and to accommodate that particular group of students with their individual needs. When I suggested the portfolio to the groups who will share this process with me this year, I paved the way gently with advice from you and a sense of tried-and-true guidelines. Your guidelines, though, will only lead me elsewhere to establish mine. By the way, I presume that you establish these directives as a group. Do you find that they have varied very much from one group to the next?

Guidelines Depend upon the Group

Rich: For each group not only are the directives different, but so also are the elements that become the body of evidence within the assessment. As an example: given the directive to demonstrate growth in understanding of SAT vocabulary, some students may point to proficiency in the typical quiz or test, while others may show the words in context in other assignments. There is no way to get away from a set of standards within a class structure. What the portfolio with its connected reflection allows is the opportunity for the student to show learning in a variety of ways. It also allows that student the time to assess real learning without the idea of failure hanging overhead.

There's That Grade Book Again

Rich: This idea of grading is one that keeps rearing its ugly head. Where do you go with this? I wonder if the way of authentic assessment will be able to clear this up. For example, the process begins with establishing standards (the buzz word of the nineties). If we begin with the course content, add the expectations, and develop the challenges, we should be able to *grade* the student's work. What gets in the way is the idea that there is a right and a wrong answer for all questions. Performance has counted not enough, and the process of learning has not even seemed to enter into the procedure that we call *evaluation*. It seems to me that the portfolio begs the question, "What about life-long learning?" Assessment of this builds skills that are real and necessary. Without these items there is little difference. For a school, or a department for that matter, we need to develop a sense of sharing. We need to stop allowing everyone to be completely independent. We need to set the standards for all to follow, and we need to work at them. If we base the course of study on the skills to be acquired, then we do not need to control the items used, as long as the standards and the skills are adhered to. Most people need to know what is expected, and we as teachers are no different. The standards for the assessment of the portfolio must be developed from within. There are already too many *experts* out there who are far too willing to tell us what the standards are.

Bringing People Aboard

Debbie: It relieves me to hear you say this. Conversations among portfolio advocates are always so vague, as if the actual standards are secrets that cannot be shared between teachers. I think that this exclusion has held me back. I never wanted to duplicate the exact guidelines of my colleagues, but I did want to get some specific idea of what has worked as well as to know what cautions need to be taken. Why should we all reinvent the wheel when so many have been sent to prepare the way on our behalf as well as their own?

Rich: At meetings, these ideas have to be spoken about and addressed. They cannot be talked *at*, they must be talked *about*. Some people will have to listen, and they will be uncomfortable because we will be talking about uniform standards that will have to be applied to all students and, ultimately, to all teachers!

Say Hello to Authentic Assessment

Rich: The idea of authentic assessment keeps entering the conversations here at Danbury High School. I wonder if it means that people are ready to hear that the way we look at student learning is about to change. I am convinced that in order to use the portfolio correctly to assess student learning we must be willing to let go of the safety blankets. Report cards as we know them must either be changed or dropped altogether. If assessment is to be used as a learning tool then the results of that assessment must be accessible to the students in a form that is understood and in a form that is usable. That information must also be in a form that documents growth. It should also identify strengths and weaknesses in a way that allows students to improve. There goes that old growth over time song again.

It has taken me two and one-half years to get to this point, but now that I am here I find it hard to return. It is not easy to give up the power, but for the development of real learning it is crucial. This is a risky business—one that is well worth it. It seems that all teachers embrace the concept of getting students to learn, but when they are offered the chance to really implement this the challenges are either too much or not what we *really* want to do.

Debbie: This is so ironic . . . that after such an interval since our last correspondence, I should find you right on my wavelength. It was this morning as I filled out interim reports (and had to rely on quiz scores for criteria) that I heard myself say, "Thank goodness that they will have the portfolio to prove their strong areas this quarter. Otherwise they are going on record as being remembered for their reluctance to read and resistance to retain what they've read." I was thinking also about the day I introduced the portfolio concept, inviting them to include their *best* quiz or test scores. On second thought, when you have two zeros, one 17, a 53, and three perfect 100s among your scores, then it would be appropriate to show who you are on the days when you prepare and the days when you were noncommittal about English class. A complete portfolio should celebrate the total student, don't you think?

And one young man, who seems to always be within the *behavior hampers learning* segment of my period-four population, shared with excitement about the fishing tournament in which he won six hundred dollars last weekend. I heard myself asking him to write it up and bring in photos so that he will celebrate a real happening as it relates to his own expertise. That may well turn out to be his highlight—and if that's where he's learning about himself, then isn't it critical that he should have the freedom to highlight that experience? Or am I carrying this a bit too far?

Here Goes: Changes in the Wind

Rich: To begin a class centered around portfolio assessment, the teacher has to relinquish the total control for the learning of the classroom. This is not to say that control is lost; on the contrary, the class control becomes more pronounced because everyone now shares responsibility for learning and, in fact, everyone becomes a learner. Part of the responsibility of learning is the evaluation of what is learned and, even more so, the way in which it is learned. A portfolio invites the student to revisit. It allows for the growth that has taken place to be implemented. It does not eliminate deadlines, but it makes them less important than the learning. Adapting to this for the process of evaluation has to cause a dramatic change in the way student learning is documented. Report cards will need to be changed. It is difficult to see how the current system of recording grades can be adapted. I believe that the system must be recreated from the beginning. If the portfolio is to be a valid method by which to assess students, then the report card must mirror that learning. Numerical or alphabetic grades don't do that, and they should not be morphed so that it appears they do.

Debbie: So now what we are getting into is a ripple effect that has no boundaries within (or even outside of) the school systems that have stepped innocently into the portfolio bed. This splashes over into other departments, onto entire grading systems, and so on. Seems like we must get into the business of indoctrinating the higher-ups if we are to offer this as a better quality of life and measurement. Otherwise, aren't we compromising and limiting what might be accomplished by starting it in the first place? How long does a new process have to be here before it may be recognized as more than another mere trend? On the other hand, aren't we putting the new idea at risk when we strive to gain its acceptance by making it *official?* And whose job is that, anyway?

This Is More Than a Trend

Rich: If *official* makes one think *important,* then it is necessary for that to happen. The time for the risk has come, and if we do not act it may pass. The publishers and seminar people are already out there just waiting to get administrators to buy the package. Let's beat them to the portfolio!

Debbie: So then, once again, the teacher and the student lose ownership of the idea and of the direction it must take. Isn't that another compromise when the publishing industry sets the pace and the climate for what began as a classroom experience? How can we remain true to this as a process and a promise for the learning it documents if someone is peddling it as a *kit* or some easy package of answers. I wish that there were such a magic tool. I could feel less anxious about this coming quarter, where it's about to come together for some of my own while it falls apart for the others who haven't saved their potential treasures.

Rich: If the portfolio is to be part of the assessment process then a procedure should be set up that makes the student assessment part of the final grade. For example, make the student assessment based on the portfolio part of a final exam. That way the students are strongly encouraged not only to look at their learning but to evaluate it, and as a result of that looking and evaluating make a grade. In a college-level course, that assessment may be equal to 60 percent of a final examination. It would depend on where you, as the teacher, are in the process and on where the students are in the process as well. I think that when this is given a chance, the teacher is amazed at the level to which the students rise. I know I was!

Yes! I Am Looking for a Handout

Debbie: Perhaps at this point you could advise me as to the printed instruction that you distribute on portfolio assignment. We have been saving our souvenirs for two quarters now in anticipation of this experience. Monday begins the quarter where we pull it all together to analyze, to make selections and considerations, and to labor over revisions and documents that will celebrate the learning that has taken place. But a few tips as to your successful accomplishments would help me out here! A tangible compass, if you will.

Rich: The ways to assess the growth of learning need to be redefined. The current methods of recording the *grade* of a student need to be adapted to show skills, depth of understanding, and application. What has to be in place is a procedure for the student to record the assessment. That assessment also has to have validity and power. The development of rubrics or scales must be a collective process from the beginning. If everyone has a commitment, success is almost guaranteed.

Run with It

Debbie: Now about that issue of commitment. . . . We are in the stage of searching through the *Save Your Stuff* file and at first I was fearful for those who never saved enough to work with. But now that we have been in the computer lab, we have come up with new ideas for creative assignments to compensate for their missing trophies. So while some students are committing their oldies to print, the others are creating new masterpieces on the spot so that they too will have revision possibilities as we move down to the wire for this—my original portfolio-moves-into-the-classroom experience. The actual assignment was a great idea, if I do say so myself. I casually said, "If you haven't enough creative possibilities for your portfolio, take your research paper or your thesis paper from *Of Mice and Men* and design a fictional story that demonstrates the theme that you chose for your thesis or for the topic that you addressed in your research paper." Some began immediately while others couldn't make the transition directly into fiction, so they opted to tell real-life occurrences to demonstrate the themes in question. So they are assessing even before they begin assessment, aren't they?

You Can Survive

Rich: *Yes*. What has to be done now is reinforcement. The process becomes almost natural if it is not stifled. The fears of losing control disappear. Control of the learning and the evaluation does not change. As the classroom teacher, you can become even more aware of the ability of the students.

Debbie: I have had the good fortune this semester to implement the portfolio with my adult evening-school students before I attempt a similar expectation with my ninth graders. The introduction to self-assessment turned out to be the most captivating discussion of the semester. Of course, I started it backwards since this is my first go-around with it, and I decided after the semester started that we should try it. But I have to say that students were excited at the prospect of expressing what has gone on in their learning experiences in all of their courses, and they felt validated that someone even wants to give audience to the areas of weakness in an effort to expect them to address their own shortcomings. I even presented it that way with a preface: "Where else can you earn credit for expressing your explanations of why you didn't fulfill class expectations? Your honest assessment offers you the freedom and also the responsibility to reflect not just upon the victories and skills mastered, but also to admit to yourself and to plan to correct your shortcomings and the areas that you have postponed or denied." The shy members of the group (recent immigrants, English as a Second Language students who just cannot yet take the risk of reading their work aloud or even sharing their ideas) looked up with smiles. They felt so liberated—as if they had just discovered that someone knows that they can be their own worst obstacle and forgives them for it. After that they began to share pieces of their work that they had been reluctant to pull out.

Rich: The feeling of liberation is not only focused for the students, it becomes infectious. The classroom teacher is also given this feeling because it allows for the idea of not having to always be right, to always be there with the correct answer to every question at any given moment. It allows for the skill to develop after an understanding of the need for the skill exists. Portfolios allow for the student to admit to weaknesses because they also allow for those weaknesses to be corrected before assessment takes place. Even without the correction, the idea that the student is aware of the weakness helps with the learning and with the assessment. Awareness is very important; portfolios help to create awareness.

Debbie: That is where I have fallen short in this, my debut. Because I thought that we needed the full semester to fill up our files, I am afraid that I didn't leave them time to compensate for the shortcomings. I would plan differently next year so that there is post-portfolio time to do some restoration work.

On the Horizon

Rich: Looking to next year, what can be said of the portfolio as an assessment tool? For myself, I am convinced that, as a tool for both the assessment of learning and as a way to reflect on the business of teaching, the portfolio provides insights for teacher and student alike.

For me and for my students, it works.

Building Upon Success

Debbie: I guess that I can now make the same claim. We are in the final stages of portfolio creation for the sake of an alternative assessment as our final. The results are marvelous. Revision is happening almost by accident now that they are word processing final pieces and creating their assessments for each piece. You were right—these processes are so interwoven that when they do kick in, they all work together. I am seeing so much more from them than I expected. And the assessments are exhibiting much more proof of learning than I would have expected. Letting go has been the key, exactly as you predicted. It has not been as difficult for me as I had feared. But again, you were right. I had to make the decisions as to whom to trust and where to draw lines. My sophomores were not taking themselves as seriously as my freshmen; therefore, I didn't try it with them. But next year it will be a way of life in my classrooms even from the first weeks of school. I have made that promise to myself after seeing the results of this year's self-assessments. This has been a complete conversion experience for me—and for the majority of my students. It has become a key to success that transcends all grade levels and ability levels.

Chapter 2

BUILDING THE PORTFOLIO STRUCTURE

Deane A. Beverly
Carole V. Mackin
Marian Galbraith
West Side Middle School

When a builder is putting together the plans for a new project, one of the first things he or she thinks of is the foundation. Without a strong, well-constructed foundation, the builder, to say the least, will be on *shaky* ground. This is also important when a language arts teacher begins thinking about using portfolios as a tool to assess the growth of students. As with the builder, the teacher who is at the beginning stages of the portfolio must plan and create a strong, well-constructed foundation. Once the foundation is laid, the structure can be built, design elements incorporated, and finishing touches added.

The school from which the following ideas and sample student selections have been taken is a middle school serving grades 6, 7, and 8. Classes are heterogeneously grouped so that there is a wide range of reading abilities. The basic philosophy of the reading program is to develop lifetime learners. Students are allowed to choose books that they want to read and are asked to react or respond to those books in a response journal, or literary log. Through both in-class activities and responses to written entries, we work to move students away from story retelling and toward personal reactions and reasoned responses to their reading.

Each of us began this project on the same footing—as neophytes with students who had no prior experience with portfolios. Each year has presented us with new levels of student awareness and new dimensions to explore. The result has been a three-year journey through portfolio development. The process of laying the foundation to framing the structure to adding finishing touches is one that has occurred not only within each of our classrooms but across them as well, as each of us has built on the prior successes of students and colleagues.

Deane Beverly: Laying the Foundation

The first question that all of us had when we were asked to begin portfolio assessment was "Where do we start?" As a teacher on the sixth-grade team, my first thought was to begin reading all that was available to me from educational journals so that I could become aware of what others were doing in this area. This should be something every teacher should do before jumping into portfolio assessment, because it is a slow process, one that takes many twists and turns along the way.

Once I read and talked with colleagues about portfolio assessment, I was ready to jump in. The first year of our portfolio project was one of trial and error. My colleagues and I began by purchasing hanging folders and containers in which to store the materials we planned to collect. The one thing we kept hearing over and over was that the portfolio should center on student-generated materials, not simply on the traditional worksheets and teacher-generated work usually found in student folders. That became our primary focus. We began by looking at students setting goals in reading for the first quarter and the self-assessment of those goals as they proceeded throughout that first year. As we progressed through the project, we found that many new ideas were generated, and we began to get a clearer picture of what we wanted to include in the portfolios.

I want to point out some of the ideas, philosophies, and results that we have reached now that we have used portfolio assessment for three years. One of the things I feel is very important as I greet a new class in September is that I always need to find out where they are in their portfolios, what they know about the reading process, and what they are bringing with them. I have come to realize that many students coming from the elementary grades do not always have the literary background that we will expect them to build on. I, therefore, always begin the process by asking the incoming sixth graders to write me a letter in June to tell me about themselves as readers—what they read; what they like to read—as well as to introduce themselves to me. I try to answer all letters over the summer so that I have a personal contact before the new year begins. I have discovered over the years that this is a very easy way to get to know these students in a general way. When the new class arrives for the start of school, one of the first things I do is to give them a reading survey. This is the first thing that will be placed in their portfolio. I have found that a simple, short-answer type of survey is most useful because the students are not sure about what I am doing this for and therefore are often reluctant to answer in great detail. A sample of questions I ask would be:

- My opinion of reading is: _____ OK _____ Love it _____ No way
- Why do people read?
- What makes a good reader?
- What is your favorite book?
- Who is your favorite author?
- What do you find hardest about reading?

After I read the surveys I feel that I know where the students are coming from and what I need to do to develop better readers who can appreciate literature for what it can give back to them.

The next process that I feel is an intricate part of the portfolio is the setting of goals for the first quarter. Setting goals is usually a very new idea for students. I explain the concept that setting goals gives them something to focus on during the quarter and can act as a guide for them. I usually set examples of very simple, easily attainable goals for the first quarter, such as:

- I will read every night for at least twenty minutes.
- I will finish my journal on time.
- I will read at least three books this term.

While this simple idea of setting goals is the ideal place for some students to start, other students are already setting more involved goals. For instance, one student wrote:

> *My first quarter goal is to meet all deadlines of reading. I will do everything I need to do for reading. I want to read more and respond to what I am reading.*

A second student wrote for a second-quarter goal:

> *My second quarter goal is to read and respond to two Newbery or Caldecott Medal-winning books. I would like to do this because I would like to read some no-junk books and also to possibly develop a better taste for varied literature.*

These examples of goals set by sixth graders show that they are beginning to realize that they can take charge of their learning and will be responsible for what they do.

I have found that by starting simply the students will see that they are able to accomplish something right away. For many of these students it is the first time that they have had to be accountable to themselves rather than just having to please a teacher. I try to emphasize this idea throughout the year: that this is their portfolio, not mine, and it is supposed to show them what they are accomplishing.

When we reach the halfway point of the first quarter, I ask the students to look at the goals they set at the beginning of the quarter and to assess their progress to this point. I call this "Where Am I As a Reader?" I ask them to be honest in their answers because this is their goal and they need to be the ones who push themselves to fulfill that goal by the end of the quarter. At the end of the quarter, I ask each student to evaluate his or her goal and to tell me if the goal was completed and how it helped in his or her reading process. I have found that most students feel that they have accomplished their goals and that they are doing great. However, there are those students who have matured early on to see that they must be honest with themselves, and they have stated quite frankly that they did not accomplish their goals and that they need to begin to work harder next quarter. This is the glimmer of hope that I begin to see that tells me that portfolio assessment works.

Once I have established the setting of goals in the first quarter, I try to guide students to be more exact in their goal setting and to take a closer look at what they really need to focus upon. I find that by the third quarter most students have begun to set more exact, more strict goals for themselves and to feel pride in what they are accomplishing.

An aspect of the portfolio that I find really beneficial to the students is that they are able to tell me how they feel about what they are reading without feeling the pressure of having to answer questions about the reading. This is a slow process, much like the goal setting, but it does begin to improve by the second quarter for most of the students. I am always amazed at the honesty of most students when they react to a book they are reading, whether it is positive or negative.

There are many pieces of writing that can be included in a portfolio. As I said earlier in this chapter, I am concentrating on the reading portfolio. I have, over the years, developed a number of ideas that I feel will help the individual student show where he or she is as a reader. This includes the use of a reading log that shows the books read, book summaries both for oral and written presentations, ideas for book talks, and many ideas for journal writing and responses to books. One thing that I have found to be very true is that "Rome wasn't built in a day"; likewise, a portfolio assessment program isn't built and completed in three years. If you want instant gratification and validation for your teaching, portfolio assessment is not the way to go. It is an ever-changing process: what works one year will not necessarily be successful the next. You must be willing to constantly change your focus and be able to come up with new ideas to show students that they are always good at something and that you value them as students. The self-evaluation component of the portfolio is invaluable to you as the year progresses, and you will find that parents will begin to see what their child is doing in your class when conferences are held and the portfolio is shown.

One of the most gratifying ideas that I have been able to develop came in the third year of the project. I borrowed the title from S. E. Hinton's novel *That Was Then, This is Now* to enable students to prepare for the next level by writing a self-assessment of their year in reading from September to June. I asked them to look at themselves as readers and learners and to be honest with themselves as to what changes have occurred during the year and how those changes have affected them. It was one of the best results I have had from any class. I would like to share some of those results and try to give some idea of the students' backgrounds to show you that they truly represent a wide range of abilities and backgrounds.

The first examples I would like to share come from three students who were not *readers* when the year started. The first is a student who receives help with English as a second language. He reads quite well, but at the beginning of the year he had difficulty expressing his ideas in writing. He made great strides, as shown in this excerpt:

> *I think I have changed in reading because I've been reading more books. I've found that sometimes you can read instead of sitting and watching TV. I also found that there are good authors like R. L. Stine. He keeps me reading the book because I want to know what's going to happen next. . . . I learned a lot in these past months in reading. I think that it is good that there is a reading class in this school.*

The second student was one who from the beginning did not consider deadlines and seldom completed assignments on time. He was constantly late with work and usually read only one genre, horror. His reflection of his progress shows clearly what portfolios can do for students:

> *I think that I have improved in many ways. I have read different kinds of authors and different kinds of books. Instead of reading just R. L. Stine books, I have read books by Gary Paulsen. Instead of reading horror stories I read more biographies, mysteries, and adventure. In September, I had no idea how to react in my journal. Now I can do it with ease. I'm glad I learned so much. This will help me a lot in life.*

The third example is probably the one that makes me sure that this works. This student was not failing, but was very close in the first three marking periods. For some reason, his fourth quarter was a 180-degree turnabout. While he didn't become an A student, he finally realized what he could do, and he did it!

> *I think I've changed as a reader a lot. I've been reading more and more and I've been reading a lot more than I was in September. I'm caught up in my work unlike in September. I think something inside of me wanted to succeed; that, and my parents getting after me about my grades.*

I feel that these three self-assessments point out what students can do if they are allowed to be put in charge of their learning.

In contrast to the three assessments above, I want to include three students who from the beginning were avid readers and good students but did not set goals and realize they were responsible for their learning. I am including these with no further explanation except to say that they represent the gratifying results of portfolio assessment:

> *In September, I came as a very nonaggressive reader. As I came along, reading got more interesting. . . . Now I read all the time. How do I feel about all this? Well, I feel great inside because I know I've made a change. I've made an improvement as a reader. That makes me feel important.*

> *I think that from the time I came to West Side in September and where I am now, I've changed my reading habits. My ideas and habits about reading have drastically improved. When I first came here I read, but not that much. I think having to read three or more books for each marking period has really gotten me to read more fluently. By reading more I think I've developed a higher reading level for myself.*

> *When I came to West Side in September, I was excited with the prospect of having a class period for reading. This has not changed throughout the year. I feel that I have greatly matured as a reader this school year. I no longer read only books by my favorite authors and I am no longer hesitant to read books of different genres. Rather than just reading books, I have learned to look deeper, finding hidden meanings and parts of the story that I may have missed otherwise.*

Portfolios are not overnight successes. They require much time and planning and if you are going to be successful with your endeavor in portfolios, you need to realize that it takes time. Jump in, but don't be discouraged if your first effort is not what you wanted it to be. Go back to the drawing board and come up with a new plan. Remember that a good foundation is the key to a good portfolio program. You will find success, believe me.

Carole Mackin: Framing the Structure

Christmas in June—what an enchanting prospect! It has, fortunately, happened to me. For the last three years, Deane, minus the Santa Claus suit and beard, has arrived in my classroom on the last day of school bearing gifts. He and his entourage of elves deliver one hundred or more sixth graders' portfolios. Some are thick, some are thin, but each one represents a child's developing efforts, talents, and interests throughout the sixth grade.

In our pre-portfolio days, Deane, Marian, and I had established a June activity in which we asked our incoming students to write to us about themselves, their interests, and their thoughts about reading. Over the summer, we read each student's letter and wrote an individual letter of response, which was either mailed to the student's home or delivered personally on the first day of school. Writing one hundred or so letters obviously demanded great amounts of time, but we felt that the benefits were significant.

A fundamental belief underlying all that we do is that each student is special, with unique talents, abilities, and needs, and that a key component of our reading program is encouraging and validating each reader's response and voice. Our students' letters offer us important pieces of personal information and our letters to them provide an opportunity to establish the beginning of a dialogue, which is integral to our student-teacher relationships.

As that first year of portfolios drew to a close, Deane, Marian, and I followed our usual procedure and asked our incoming students to write their letters of introduction. But this time Marian and I also asked them to present their portfolios through their letters. We did not realize then the full significance of what we were initiating. Previously, our thoughts regarding individual students—and, consequently, our letters to them—were based solely on the contents of their letters. But now, our emerging student portraits were not based on a single letter, a slice of time. Instead, Marian and I had individual portfolios to carefully peruse. There were student-selected goals, personal reflections and assessments, best work, and lists of books read and favorite authors. We had an unprecedented opportunity to become acquainted with each of our new students as we spent hours reading through the contents of individual portfolios. Our letters to them became even more personal and relevant, based as they were on multifaceted contents of their portfolios.

Since the advent of our portfolios, each September I do not welcome new seventh graders, but rather I greet old acquaintances. Before the first day of school I already know each student's previous year's reading history, which affords me the opportunity to quickly move beyond the "let's get to know one another" phase and begin assisting each one to build on that unique history. The benefits of this knowledge are numerous, but of equal significance is what has occurred for the last two years on the first day of school.

Each began as a typical first day of school and quickly became one of those never-to-be-forgotten, serendipitous moments in the classroom. As students in my first-period class received their sixth-grade portfolios with the letters I had written to them over the summer, an immediate hush swept the room. Each student began by reading my letter and then immediately started reading through his or her portfolio. Individual reactions quickly followed—smiles, nods, chuckles—and then, for some, whispered shadings of portfolios. Students asked, "Did you really read everything in my portfolio?" "Can I take it home? I promise I'll bring it back tomorrow!" The period had ended, students from the next class crowded the doorway, and some were still reluctant to stop reading and put their portfolios away. The day finally came to an end and there were some uninterrupted moments to reflect on this event which, through no personal assistance, repeated itself like a scripted scenario in my four other reading classes. As I puzzled through the *what, why, how,* and *can-I-get-this-to-happen-again* questions, I began to sense that in some way the portfolios were helping my students address an important developmental need.

Middle-school students, particularly seventh and eighth graders, live in a seemingly constant state of change. It is during these years that they move from childhood to the generally adult-dreaded, infamous teen years. Physical changes abound and emotions ride a wildly careening roller coaster. Throughout it all, these early teens are very focused—on themselves. Much of their thought and agonizing are inner-directed as the same questions play on an endless tape: "Who am I?" "Does anyone like me?" "How do I look?" "Does anyone like me?" "Who will I be?" "Does anyone like me?" Difficult as it seems at times to move them from these self-focused questions to matters of a more academic nature, it is possible, and the portfolio provides the means to do that as well as address these questions of self.

As my students interacted with their portfolios those first days of school, I was struck by the similarity between those reactions and the responses of most people to old family pictures. The old photograph album captures special moments, brings to a level of reality memories of important people, places, and events that help us define who we are. For the child as well as the emerging teen, those pictures provide some answers to that endless tape of nagging questions. In much the same way, it seems to me the portfolio does the same thing. It offers an array of snapshots, a longitudinal look at this unique individual. Not only does it provide us with that person's special history, but it also offers guidance on future directions and possibilities.

Since most seventh graders during the course of that year chronologically leave childhood and enter their teens, it seemed logical and inevitable that a focus on self-awareness and self-reflection would be developmentally sound. Questions then were designed to provide students with both guidance and a framework for conducting their *inner* journeys. These questions (with variations) formed the basis of the students' portfolio engagement, in both written work for possible inclusion and for student-teacher conferences:

- "Who am I as a reader and a learner?"
- "What have I learned about myself, about others, about . . . ?"
- "What have I accomplished?"
- "How have I changed?"
- "Why do I think these changes have happened?"
- "What do I want to do next?"

In addition to these guiding questions, I determined that it was important for seventh graders to understand the relevance of curricular goals to their efforts throughout the year. Working with the district's K8 Integrated Language Arts Curriculum, I extrapolated the seventh-grade reading goals, presented them to my students, and asked that they select a goal to work on for the first quarter. This was far from a success because the educational jargon required too much explanation and the students, although accustomed to setting personal reading goals in the sixth grade, were not familiar with curriculum-based goals. After attempting several modifications, the present method, instituted this year, has provided the most success.

At the beginning of the first quarter this year, students chose a personal reading goal, which they assessed at the end of that period. This provided them with a high comfort/success level since it enabled them to continue with the goal-setting method initiated in sixth grade. Throughout the quarter, in mini-lessons or in my responses to students' journal entries, I referred to curricular reading goals whenever appropriate.

At the end of the first quarter, following the self-assessments of personal reading goals, the students and I worked on *Reflections of a Seventh-Grade Reader* (form 2.1). This portfolio piece, the result of various adaptations, presents seventh-grade reading goals in kid-friendly language and provides the student and teacher with an ongoing, year-long means to assess how that student is changing and improving as a reader. *Reflections of a Seventh-Grade Reader* not only helps the student focus on the successes and goals achieved, but it also clearly identifies those goals that still require attention. This self-assessment and the self-reflection questions previously listed usually form the basis for end-of-quarter student/teacher conferences. Part of the *Reflections of a Seventh Grader* format used this year is given in form 2.1.

Each quarter, students have the opportunity to consider what has been learned and done, to reflect on progress, to establish new goals (both curricular and personal), and to choose work that documents and proves their self-assessments. As the school year progresses, portfolios thicken with students' self-reflections, assessments of goals, as well as extrapolations and/or full-length selections of best work.

For the first two years of our portfolio project, as summer vacation shimmered in the near future, I asked my students to respond to Marian's letter by writing letters in which they presented themselves through their portfolios. Although this was a very successful way both to close this school year and to open the new one, I decided to try something a little different this past year: a showcase portfolio.

In September the students and I talked about and compared what could be in a working portfolio with what might be in a showcase portfolio. Throughout the year, each time we discussed or worked with portfolios, the terms were incorporated so that students developed a deepening understanding of the distinction. My intent was to have students so thoroughly understand the concept of a showcase portfolio that creating their own at the end of the seventh grade would be both easy and exciting.

To help them accomplish this, each student received, about two weeks before the close of school, an eight-item checklist entitled *Formatting Your Showcase Portfolio*. As part of that checklist, students were asked to review their working portfolios, journals, library cards, etc., and to decide what to put in their showcase portfolios. Once those materials were selected, they were asked to do the following:

> Make a list that shows what you have learned and done this year and
> how you think you've changed and grown as a reader and a learner.

Each student created an informal graphic organizer based on the contents of the
showcase and used that to complete the next checklist item. Then they were
given the following instructions:

> Use the list you made to help you write a paper for your showcase-
> portfolio. This paper is your opportunity to *sell yourself* as a reader
> and a learner to the people who see your showcase portfolio. It's okay
> to brag about yourself, about how you've changed and improved as a
> reader and a learner this year. You can include excerpts from journal
> responses, projects, portfolio items, etc., to prove what you've done
> and learned. Your paper should have your name, the date, and this
> heading: *Reflections of a Seventh (Almost Eighth) Grader*.

This opportunity to create a showcase portfolio was a real success and far
exceeded my expectations for enthusiasm and engagement. Many seventh
graders are usually less than thrilled when asked to produce quality work in the
hot, humid days preceding summer vacation, but this project sparked their attention. Perhaps it was the chance to brag, or the tangible collection of representative work, or the knowledge of what had been learned and accomplished.
Perhaps it was all of this as well as the opportunity to reflect on their own
two-year chronology. Whatever precipitated this level of excitement engendered
outstanding student understanding and engagement. The following are selections from just a few of the showcase portfolios. The students' voices speak far
more eloquently than I ever could.

In his *Reflections of a Seventh (Almost Eighth) Grader*, Clark wrote:

> Some of the things I did this year were reading books, reading and
> making poems, making book covers, writing nonfiction responses and
> biographies about authors, and creating the Changes project. From
> doing these things I learned about new authors I like, how to express
> my feelings in a different way, how to design a book cover, how to read
> and write true stories about people and the things that affect their
> lives, and how to summarize nonfiction material. I learned about an
> author's whole life and what influences an author. I also learned how
> to notice the development of characters in a book, how to notice
> changes in the feelings of a character as different events take place, and
> how to notice why an author chooses to take and write from a certain
> point of view.

In a response to *Scorpions* by Walter Dean Myers, which he excerpted for his
showcase, Clark wrote:

This book is excellent because the author keeps the same style of writing throughout the whole book. Sometimes I can put myself in some of the characters' spots such as when Tito tries to stop Jamal from doing something. I can put myself into his spot. When Jamal feels that he should ignore somebody but just can't, it reminds me of everyday life. I'll be reading a certain part of the book and will think to myself, that just happened to me the other day. I always have a picture in my mind of what's going on and can put myself into the character's spot.

Sabrina began her reflection piece by stating:

> *I feel I have grown a lot as a reader this year. RED (Reaction, Explanation, Detail) taught me how to write a response and not a book report.*

Sabrina included in her portfolio part of a response she wrote to Lurlene McDaniel's book, *Mother Help Me Live*:

> *The climax of this book was so interesting I could barely put it down. At first, when Sarah found her birth mother (Janelle) and Janelle was so mean to her, I couldn't believe it. I knew, though, that Janelle would come back. I thought it was so sad when Sarah had to leave and she would never see Janelle again because it meant that Sarah didn't have a bone marrow donor. I guess for a book like the ones that Lurlene McDaniel writes finding the birth mother and having her have the compatible bone marrow would be too easy. Probably the reason for this being so difficult to find compatible marrow is so the book keeps your attention. It works.*

Another excerpt Sabrina included was from a response to a newspaper article concerning the notorious drowning of Susan Smith's two boys:

> *I think this whole story is so sad. Of course now we know the mother killed them. I think that is absolutely horrible. I don't know how anyone could do that to her child or children. In a way I think that Susan Smith should be put through the same thing she put her children through, but I am against killing as a punishment for killing. I think everyone should just rot in prison if they kill someone. To me, killing someone who has killed is like telling children not to hit their siblings, and then hitting them as a punishment. What have you taught them? Nothing. You tell them not to kill, and you kill them. Brilliant.*

In his reflections piece, Sam discussed the poetry project that we worked on for about four weeks. When I introduced this project to my students I saw so many furrowed brows and wrinkled noses that I decided to ask who enjoyed reading and/or writing poetry. Only a few indicated even lukewarm enthusiasm; most were quick to offer what they didn't like about poetry. By the end of the first week, as we read poems of dedication and tribute by poets such as Sakae Roberson, Langston Hughes, Alice Walker, Nikki Giovanni, Duane Big Eagle, and Gary Soto, students were excited participants. By the time we arrived at the point for students to write their poems, many already had drafts to share. One of Sam's poems, entitled *Tea Bags*, was part of his portfolio:

> *An old woman lives in Brooklyn, New York.*
> *She sits at her kitchen table squeezing*
> *soggy tea bags that are pale from being used over*
> *and over into an off-white porcelain mug.*
> *Her grandchildren live upstairs, but she is still*
> *lonely. They don't visit anymore.*
> *Her hair is curly and white with the wisdom*
> *and knowledge of many years.*
> *She has seen the world at war, twice, and*
> *lived past two husbands.*
> *Her shelves are full of Jumbo Crossword*
> *Puzzles that have been done twice or three times.*
> *She glances out the windows as she envisions*
> *herself young again playing in the street.*
> *She looks forward to being visited by her*
> *great-grandson so every few months I go to*
> *New York.*

Sam also included excerpts from responses he wrote. In this one for Avi's *Wolf Rider*, he presents his ideas about a book's lead:

> *I think the lead in this story is fantastic. By the time you've finished with the first page, you're hooked. There can be a downside to that. The book is so good that you read it in a day and a half. I like it when books last longer. Leads are very important. If you don't have a good lead people might not want to read your story. Avi's leads usually are very good. That is why his books are such a hit.*

One of things Sam learned about himself this year is that he loves reading fantasy, especially the works of C. S. Lewis. This excerpt is from a response to *The Voyage of the Dawn Treader:*

> *Yet again Mr. Lewis has amazed me. This book was fantastic. The detail allowed me to be aboard the Dawn Treader for the whole trip. I am excited to continue reading C. S. Lewis' series. Whenever I finish reading one I think the next one won't be as good as the one before, but it is. . . . A*

> *friend told me that Lewis was a very religious man and that his stories are based on Bible stories with just names and creatures changed. I can relate to that in* The Lion, the Witch, and the Wardrobe *when the white witch (the devil) kills Aslan (Jesus) and then Aslan rises from the dead. He also talks about the lord over the seas which I think is God.*

While reading *Sweet Illusions* by Walter Dean Myers, Michele explored her own beliefs and ideas, as this excerpt from her journal shows:

> Sweet Illusions' *theme focuses on teen pregnancy. This is a very important subject. This book has caused me to think very carefully about my future and to plan ahead. These teens seem tough, and they are all growing up in the ghettos. All the emotions expressed in the book are so real to me. Most of my teenage cousins have children. . . . When my cousins were increasing the population, as they joke, I was thinking about the future. Children out of wedlock are okay if you're smart and responsible. But if you have a drug problem or not enough money and you're pregnant, you must seriously consider your alternatives. This book really gives you a glimpse into the life of a teen in the same situations as my cousins. It stabs your heart because it's so sad. You can actually feel what they are going through. You feel that it's your baby. You cry when they cry, and you hate when they hate. This book is tough on your heart. These girls are irresponsible and they're paying. Some wanted kids for love, and I think that's the wrong reason for having kids.*

In January the seventh graders began a favorite authors project. Each student was asked to identify a favorite, living author whose books had been read this year. Biographical materials that focus on young-adult/adult authors were gathered from various libraries and media centers so that students could thoroughly research their favorite writers. Students were responsible for writing research papers as well as letters to their authors based on their research and the novel(s) read. Although everyone knew that busy, popular authors seldom have the luxury of responding to the numerous letters they receive from their readers, the project was eagerly embraced, especially as students shared their growing understanding of the ways in which authors' books are influenced by the courses of their personal lives. Michele chose to write to Stella Pevsner; in part of her one-and-a-half page letter she stated:

> *I read* How Could You Do It, Diane? *and enjoyed it very much. The subject was very thought provoking. I could emphasize with Bethany because I lost my grandmother in May of 1994. It was a very sad time and hard for me to deal with. Because Bethany was the same age group as me, she experienced the same feelings about death.*
>
> *I thought your book was phenomenal and that you have incredible talent as a writer because you made me feel like I was part of the book and going through the same things as Bethany and her family. An example of this would be when Bethany's father found out about Diane's other*

attempt at suicide. When I read the book, I had an impulse to read more of your books. When I went to read more, all I could find were comical books of a less serious nature.

It disappointed me because How Could You Do It, Diane? *was so intense and about a very important topic. I thought you were a serious author, and as I mentioned, all I could find were comical books. Another thing was that the book was so real, like real people had lived it, because you created such strong emotions, personalities, and values for the characters. People can be like that in real life. When Bethany found the bloody paper towels and the shattered glass, her questions were powerful, and it was one of the most emotional parts of the book. I hope that you continue to write books about provocative subjects like suicide. If you don't, I still think you are a phenomenal writer.*

A month after Michele mailed her letter, she received a one-page handwritten letter from Stella Pevsner. In one part of her letter she wrote:

Thank you for your very thoughtful and insightful letter. It's a particular pleasure to hear from readers like you.

I'm sorry you lost your grandmother. You must have been very close. I hope the good memories will console you.

Yes the *Diane* book was more serious than my others, but *And You Give Me a Pain, Elaine* also had quite a sad event. Usually, I try to look at the brighter side of life and try to inject upbeat attitudes in my books. All lives have problems, but they can be solved, or at least dealt with most of the time.

The final major interdisciplinary project for seventh graders was *Changes*. Students were immersed in this theme in their five core classes. The project included writing comparative autobiographies; studying the dissension and conflicts that occurred before and during the Civil War; growing, observing, and charting Wisconsin Fast Plants; reading together *A Family Apart*, the first book in the *Orphan Train Adventures* series by Joan Lowery Nixon; and analyzing the changes and development of the main character in a self-selected novel. Michele included in her portfolio her complete project on Scarlett O'Hara, the larger-than-life character in Margaret Mitchell's *Gone With the Wind*. The following is an excerpt from her conclusion:

At the end of the novel she was like an old woman in a slightly young body. She had many hardships but also good triumphs too. She never lost control of what she was or who she was, and she did what she had to do, even if it was extreme, short of selling her soul to the Devil. . . . You are aware of how much she is changing even when she isn't. When she was with Rhett in her later life, she was like a child again, defiant and rebellious. She was already so set in her rut that Rhett wasn't going to stop her from accomplishing whatever she wanted to get done. Even though it's rotten to say, I believe that her misfortune helped her to realize what a spoiled brat she was and how to improve herself. I really admire her for that.

These are a small sample of what students have chosen to include in their showcase portfolios to portray who they are and what they have learned and accomplished. Each time I look at a student's portfolio I am once again reminded of the power it has to provide its readers with a multidimensional, in-depth, longitudinal analysis of a unique individual, much as the structure of a building both embodies an architect's designs and displays them to the outside world.

Deane, Marian, and I have had the very good fortune of developing and implementing portfolios with our students for the last three years. In that period of time my understanding and perception of portfolios has changed significantly. When I began, I was as concerned and nervous and excited as a new student on the first day of school, and my seventh graders were completely baffled as I grappled with the *how, what,* and *when* of involving us with portfolios. Yet, as I struggled to find my way, to refine and adapt my efforts, to reach a level of comfort and familiarity, something wonderful happened. My students got there before me.

They experienced the portfolio's power whenever they perused its contents, reflecting time and again on all the dimensions of self that the portfolio provided. The power of the portfolio is its ability to help each individual develop a deepening, more fulfilling level of self-understanding and self-awareness. Without a true understanding and awareness of self—who I am, where I have been, and where I want to be—all else is moot. As an educator, I had not previously found and incorporated into my classroom any significant, sustained method to do this. Now, however, I do have the means. My students and their efforts to learn and grow are valued, and the portfolio is a framework that allows them—and their parents and teachers—the opportunity to celebrate the process and honor the participants.

Marian Galbraith: Finishing Touches . . . Almost

In the eighth grade at West Side Middle School, the nature of portfolio development has changed enormously over the past three years. This is not so much a result of my own efforts but those of my colleagues. Due to the experiences they have provided in earlier grades, eighth-grade students now enter their last year in the middle school accustomed to assessing their own learning and proud to showcase that learning through their portfolios.

This has resulted in a change in the way the eighth-grade students develop their portfolios. In the first year of the project, my work resembled that of my sixth-grade colleague, Deane Beverly. Because the students and I had never worked with portfolios before, we concentrated on the first fledgling attempts to look at their work reflectively and to take responsibility for a portion of their learning. For the first time, students set goals, and for the first time they began to assess themselves as readers.

The students who entered eighth grade during the second year of the project came with one year's experience with portfolios. This allowed us to add another facet to the portfolio. That year's efforts provided the opportunity to strengthen habits of self-reflection and to add to those the notion of a portfolio as a show-case. The portfolio became both internal reflection and external presentation.

Eighth graders in the third year were the first to use portfolios in all three years of middle school. These students expected to examine their own work periodically and to take stock of what they had learned. They were not at all surprised to be greeted on the first day with a letter from their teacher that responded to their portfolio. Where then would we focus our efforts during the third year of portfolio development? The answer, of course, was in the portfolios the students sent from seventh grade.

Determining the Focus

Like Carole, I spend a portion of my summer responding to the portfolios of incoming students. Each year, those portfolios are my first real encounter with my students as learners. They also suggest the paths we'll travel with portfolios during the following year.

The portfolios I received this year were denser, thicker, richer with resources. Here were two years of development and an opportunity for me to see what students had accomplished in both sixth and seventh grade. One of the things that occurred to me was that not only had their reading and responding matured during the two years, but more importantly there had been a change in the nature of their reflective discourse. As I read, I focused my attention on the ways students talked about themselves.

It didn't take long to discover that these students, while writing with pride about the pieces they had chosen for their portfolios, were still unaware of many of the things these pieces showed about them as readers and responders. I found it easy to write to these students because of the rich material they had chosen, but I also found there were many things I noticed about them as readers and responders of which they seemed unaware. I filled my letters with these things, praising one student for his keen attention to an author's descriptive language, another for her tendency to use books to make sense of the world, yet another for being able to understand a character so well that she could write diary entries in the character's voice.

Those letters set the tone for the student-teacher dialogue that was to continue throughout this year. During this third year of portfolio development, we would concentrate on developing the reflective voice, strengthening the student's ability to see herself in her own work, and making the language of reflection part of the student's working vocabulary.

The First Day

For eighth graders the first day of school began with two things—the return of their portfolios, which now included my letter of response, and the start of a new eighth-grade portfolio, which included a *Reader's Profile*. Students were anxious to read the letters I had written, and as they did, they began to look back through their portfolios. Because they knew I had no other way of knowing them, they looked at the pieces I mentioned to see what had *given them away*. Soon they were pointing at pieces of evidence and nodding their heads. This was a critical moment. It was the first opportunity I would have to encourage these incoming students to dig deeper into their own pieces and recognize the wealth of information they presented.

I capitalized on the moment by asking them to use their portfolios to complete a Reader's Profile. The Reader's Profile is a self-assessment tool that students use to measure themselves against the goals of the eighth-grade reading curriculum. It asks students to determine whether they rarely, sometimes, or usually practice certain behaviors related to larger curriculum goal areas. Because the summer months had put a distance between them and their last self-assessments, they needed to rely on their portfolios to find evidence of their learning.

Completing the survey was a time-consuming and difficult process for the students. As I moved through the room I answered student questions by pointing out places in their own portfolios where they might have exhibited one of the behaviors. I gave examples from previous students. Gradually, lights began to dawn and students began to recognize these behaviors themselves. They were proud of how many *eighth-grade things* they could already do, and they recognized instantly the areas with which they were unfamiliar. By the end of the second day, the students had not only taken a closer look at what they had already achieved, but they had also identified their possible goals for the eighth grade. These goals were written in the back of their literary logs, where we could frequently refer to them as the quarter unfolded. (A segment of the Reader's Profile is provided in form 2.2.)

Using *Real* Writing

During the first quarter I continued the dialogue that I had begun in those summer letters. I responded to the students' work, both verbally and in writing, by pointing out what I was seeing in their responses to reading. I would, for instance, tell a student when I noticed a shift in her writing from always responding to the events in the story to an emerging tendency to respond to what the book meant to her as a reader. I would suggest to a student the opportunity a book offered for him to work toward his goal. I referred to the goals and descriptors in the Reader's Profile. I didn't neglect opportunities to discuss the contents of student entries or discussions, but I coupled that with observations about their changing reading habits.

The end of the quarter presented the first new opportunity to reflect on their learning to date. In the past I had used forms to prompt student thinking in the direction I wanted it to take. I had never been satisfied with the results. The students' writing was an answer to a question or the completion to a starter rather than an in-depth reflection on their learning.

The question "What did you learn this quarter?" yielded responses something like this:

> *This quarter I learned about how an author creates a character. In my entries I wrote about the character and what I thought of the character. I noticed how an author uses dialogue to create a character. I also noticed that you can tell about a character from the way he acts.*

In previous years I had asked students to choose pieces of evidence and describe what they showed about them as readers. In labeling a piece of evidence a student might complete a starter in this way:

> I chose this piece of evidence because it shows: *what I learned and because I got a good grade on it.*

This type of self-assessment made no connection between the evidence and the learning. Although there is evidence, it is difficult to see what was important about the piece. A student like this is aware of growth, can identify it, but is unable to elaborate on it. I concluded that it was the fault of the form. It simply didn't provide students with an opportunity to develop fluency in self-reflection.

In the third year I abandoned forms and instead relied on the types of nonfiction writing we were practicing in class. In the first quarter, I asked students to write an expository piece in which they detailed what they had learned because they had set a goal. In providing guidance for the goal piece I asked them

- to describe their goal and why they had chosen it,
- to consider what they had learned from the goal, and
- to detail a piece of evidence that would illustrate what they had learned.

Borrowing from Purves, Quattrini, and Sullivan (1995), as well as from discussions with Alan Purves, I defined *learning* as:

- what they could do now that they couldn't do before,
- what they knew now that they didn't know before, and
- what they did now in the normal course of their reading and responding that they didn't do before.

This time the responses came closer to the mark. Kristine wrote:

> *My first quarter goal was to write better and more detailed journal responses. I planned to try to use more details in responding to the books I read. I chose this goal because in the past my responses were not very detailed.*
> *During this quarter I worked on my goal by trying to use more details in my reactions. Because of my goal I learned that I needed to use more description and less storytelling. My evidence for this are my journal entries for 9/8/94 and 9/15/94 on the book* The Fog *by Caroline Cooney (on the preceding page). I chose this [entry] because it shows how my entry*

changed from a short nondescriptive paragraph to almost a full page of the descriptive reactions.

Although Kristine is certainly addressing the issues raised in the guidelines, she is not writing an answer. Instead, she is reflecting on what she has learned from a goal she identified and for which she took responsibility. She is able to connect her learning with work she has produced.

I was pleased with the result but not yet satisfied. I wanted students to examine all of their learning, to see the learning I was seeing in classroom activities. I hoped that students would develop fluency and coherence as they wrote about themselves and their learning.

Finding a Format

At the end of the second quarter I asked students to sit with other students, look through their notebooks, their literary logs, and their completed class projects, and make a list of what they had learned, using the same definition as before. Using those lists, the students would compile evidence to record and document their learning. The results were gratifying. The students' lists were long and plentiful, and when I asked them to find pieces of evidence to substantiate their claims, they were able to do so easily. Now I needed to find a format that would allow them to adequately discuss what they had found.

I discovered that format in a cover letter that would accompany attached evidence (see form 2.3). This cover letter creates a link between curriculum content and the portfolio process. Because our high-school English classes rely heavily on the five-paragraph essay as a primary mode of discourse, I try at appropriate points throughout the year to help students acquire this tool for success. The cover letter could be used to practice this form of writing. The essay adapts well to the portfolio process and helps students to focus their thoughts on what they have learned. Several students have used the cover letter itself as evidence of learning.

This assignment yielded responses like this cover letter from Sean, a student whose reading, writing, and reflective skills were developing simultaneously:

> *This quarter you have filled my head with wonderful stuff. I have learned about the Depression this quarter. I also have learned how to talk in a fireside chat (small group discussion) and I now think about the conflict in a book all the time.*
>
> *I know a lot of things because of your teaching me and my learning. I now know what a fireside chat is. I can also hold up a good conversation about my understanding of books in a fireside chat. My proof is a good work award that I got from you after my fireside chat. Also a picture of my group and I interviewing Mrs. Smith in a fireside chat proves that I have learned to learn from an interview.*
>
> *I can do a considerable amount of skills this quarter because of this learning. I can now write an essay which I couldn't do before. To show this I have more than one item of proof. As you are reading this you're reading*

my evidence and proof of my ability to write an essay. My other piece of evidence is from the last essay I wrote. I also learned about theme. I can spot a theme in a book. I know that a theme is the issue that a book raises.

I have one more thing to show you and tell you about my learning this quarter. I have changed greatly as a reader because of my 1/10 and also my 4/12 entries. They show that I understand that a book can really touch a person's heart and that the book, Teacup Full of Roses, *really touched my heart.*

So, this quarter I have learned about the Depression, fireside chats, how to write an essay, and also how a book can touch a person's heart. The one thing I think about the most and that I will always remember, is how a book can touch a person's heart. Teacup Full of Roses *touched my heart in a way that no other book has ever done.*

What a difference! Sean has a great deal to say about himself. He is clearly aware of himself as a reader, is able to organize his ideas, and is able to point to evidence of his accomplishment. Though his writing and reading skills may lag behind some of his peers, his thinking does not. He has changed as a reader during the quarter and his portfolio has allowed him the opportunity to proudly record his individual growth.

Developing the Language of Reflection

The cover letter made apparent an awkwardness in self-reflection. Students stumbled over words, finding it difficult to find the right words to describe their learning. I wanted to help students to develop the language of self-reflection, to become comfortable with the vocabulary that would allow them to talk not only naturally about their learning but also more precisely. As the third quarter went on, we used this vocabulary in class discussion and as we wrote back and forth in the literary logs. I asked students to use literary terms as they explored new concepts in their responses.

I noticed over the course of the third quarter that terms that students had known for some time began to crop up unsolicited in their class discussions. Even the vocabulary for new concepts we were learning in class was finding its way to paper, albeit awkwardly. I held my breath and waited for the next set of cover letters that would accompany the portfolios.

I was rewarded with cover letters that were fluent and clear, made good use of evidence to back up a claim of learning, and made effective use of vocabulary to describe learning. The following is just a portion of Sarah's cover letter:

This quarter I learned many things. From reading books of different cultural points of view, I learned about many different cultures and customs. I also learned how to back up the predictions I make with evidence and the reason I made the prediction. I learned how to respond to different features of the book such as the lead, rising action, climax, connections, etc. I also learned how to write and put together a newspaper.

I learned about many different cultures and customs from reading books of different cultural points of view. The cultures I learned about were Indian, Jewish, and Sameness. I learned that [some] Jewish holidays are for remembering all that the Jews had to go through in the Holocaust and to keep the traditions alive. I learned that although the culture Sameness isn't a real culture, it is a culture [in The Giver*]. I learned that in Sameness everything is carefully controlled and decided for you so that things will be safer. I also learned that the Indian culture is a very peaceful one. They believe very much in family. Evidence that I have learned about these cultures is in my second February entry from* White Hare's Horses *and my March 16, 1995, entry from* The Giver.

Another thing I learned was how to make predictions and back them up. Making predictions helps you use what you already know from the past to think about what might happen in the future. This is also a very good method to use for problem solving. By backing up your prediction you give a reason or evidence about why you think your prediction might happen. This makes things clearer for anyone else who may be reading or listening to your predictions. Proof that I learned how to make predictions and back them up are in my first February one-third entry from White Hare's Horses *and my March 5, 1995, chapter 1 entry from* The Devil's Arithmetic.

Something else I learned from my third quarter reading goal was to respond to different features of the book like lead, climax, rising action, connections, irony, conflicts, etc. Doing this helps you recognize and better understand these features. Through this I learned that the climax usually comes when there are many conflicts built up in the book that need to be solved. The rising action comes before the climax and starts when the conflicts begin to accumulate. I also learned that the falling action comes when the conflicts begin to get resolved. I also learned that authors present their conflicts in many different ways such as through flashbacks, the character, or through actions. Evidence that I learned how to respond to features of the book are in my last entry from The Devil's Arithmetic *and the March 16, 1995, entry from* The Giver.

The letter goes on to describe what she had learned about newspaper and play writing. What is evident from this segment is that this student, like many others, could speak effectively about her learning. Her cover letter was rich with detail and was accompanied by exemplary pieces of evidence. She had become fluent in the language of reflection.

Wrapping Up

As the final act of the portfolio year, students were asked to examine their portfolios to discover how they had grown as readers and writers during their three years of portfolio use. Unlike the letters they wrote at the end of the sixth or seventh grades, the students had no specific audience. Students from our school attend too many different high schools for us to be able to know who might be their next teacher. I have never found these letters as rich and detailed as the letters that accompany each quarter's work, but even these letters showed a growth in the ways they were able to relate themselves to the work showcased in their portfolios.

In order to appreciate this growth it is perhaps best to compare a letter written at the end of seventh grade with one written at the end of eighth grade. Consider this letter from Darrell, an incoming eighth grader. Although he was asked to write about his portfolio and about himself as a learner, he totally neglected that part of the letter, preferring to write about himself as a student:

> *Dear Mrs. Galbraith,*
>
> *I'm looking forward to seeing you next year. I found out that most reading teachers are different and they all make you write journal entries different. I'm not saying that it's bad, but I get used to one way and then the teachers tell you to write them another way.*

His letter goes on to describe the new addition to the building.

By the end of the year Darrell, too, had developed the words to describe himself as a reader. Asked once again to read his portfolio and describe his growth over three years, he wrote:

> *How I've grown as a reader? That is a good question. I think that I've grown a lot as a reader. I went from reading easy books like* My Side of the Mountain *to reading books like* The Catcher in the Rye. *Compare those two books and then I guess you can see that I've changed as a reader.*
>
> *I'm not really sure if my taste in books has changed, but I think they did. Well, I'm almost certain they did. I started off in sixth grade just liking sports and adventure books, and now in eighth grade I read books like* A Separate Peace. *Don't get me wrong, I still like sports and adventure books, but I've added coming of age books. I have changed my tastes in a big way.*
>
> *In the past three years I haven't really noticed changes in my reading practices. I've always read thirty minutes everyday since sixth grade and even during the summer. I really don't think I've changed my practices at all.*
>
> *I think that I am a pretty strong reader because I can figure out different things about the book. I can realize how a character develops, I can predict the ends of books, and I can set a goal for reading a book. In sixth grade probably the only thing out of those three that I could do was predict. I guess that means I got stronger since sixth grade. I don't think I have any weaknesses.*
>
> *I think that reading has helped me become the person I am today. If I didn't read then I wouldn't have a good personality or vocabulary. I probably wouldn't even be able to talk. So I guess that is how reading has helped me, but I don't know if it has taught me anything about the world around me.*

This student has grown in many more ways than he is able to give himself credit for, but he can use a portfolio to develop his vision of himself as a reader.

His letter, though, reminds me of something I have learned in three years of portfolio development. Although I can look back over three years and see great changes in both my own work and that of my students, there is far more to be realized, far more to be accomplished with portfolios. Standing as I am at the end of a continually evolving three-year line, I can only look forward to next year's portfolios to discover the new paths we will travel.

Finishing Touches?

A builder completes his or her construction by providing the finishing touches. But any homeowner knows that the finishing touches are never done. Students in the eighth grade learn to elaborate on their self-reflection, to refine the ways they talk about themselves as learners—in other words, to provide finishing touches to the portfolio they are constructing. But the portfolio is a house that is never completely finished. With luck it has created a habit of self-examination, a way of thinking about themselves and their learning that students will never be done with.

The same is true for the portfolio process we have tried to develop over the past three years. It is a house we have not finished building. We have grown accustomed to yearly renovations and we are already beginning to add an addition.

Because of the excitement this process has generated, the portfolio is spreading beyond the walls of the Reading/Language Arts classroom. It began with the students themselves. Their increased self-awareness brought to light the ways they were using reading and writing in other classes. As this learning was brought into the reading portfolio, the reaction rippled through our teams. We shared student remarks with our team colleagues, and soon portfolio cover letters and evidence were being shared as well.

Next year reading portfolios will become team portfolios. For one week of each quarter students will return to a home base to create their portfolios. Their cover letters and evidence will be based on learning from each of the core subjects. They will carry their goals with them from room to room, from subject to subject. Soon all of their teachers will be reminding students of evidence, stretching their ability to see themselves in their work. And we will begin building again—a new construction from the ground up, a new room for learning.

References

Purves, A. C., J.A. Quattrini, and C.I. Sullivan (1995). *Creating the writing portfolio*. Lincolnwood, IL: NTC.

Form 2.1

REFLECTIONS OF A SEVENTH-GRADE READER

First Quarter (FSQ) Reflection:

Second Quarter (SQ) Reflection:

Third Quarter (TQ) Reflection:

Fourth Quarter (FQ) Reflection:

Think about yourself as a reader. Consider the ways you think about books and how you respond to them. Read each question on this page and decide if you seldom, sometimes, or frequently do what each question asks. Write FSQ, SQ, TQ, or FQ in the appropriate column, depending on which quarter you are reflecting upon.

Then, in the appropriate row above, write a comment or reflection on your reading experiences and set a goal for the quarter. When you are choosing your new reading goal, look at the goals you marked as seldom or sometimes. Your new goal should be one of those.

As the school year progresses, these quarterly reflections will give you an opportunity to see how you are changing and improving as a reader.

STRETCHING YOUR READING EXPERIENCE:

Do you . . .	Seldom	Sometimes	Frequently
Read books that challenge you with more difficult, complex material?	_____	_____	_____
Read a variety of authors?	_____	_____	_____
Read different genres?	_____	_____	_____

USING PERSONAL EXPERIENCES TO IMPROVE YOUR READING:

Do you . . .	Seldom	Sometimes	Frequently
Compare your experiences to those of the characters in your books?	_____	_____	_____
Use what you already know about books to understand other books?	_____	_____	_____
Make and revise predictions as you read?	_____	_____	_____

Form 2.2.

THE READER'S PROFILE

Think about yourself as a reader. Think about the ways you think about books and respond to them in your literary log entries. Check each of the items below to better understand yourself as a reader.

1 = rarely

2 = sometimes

3 = usually

UNDERSTANDING HOW STORIES DEVELOP:

Do you:

Notice how the plot unfolds: exposition, rising action, climax, resolution?	1 2 3
Recognize the conflict and know about different kinds of conflicts?	1 2 3
Think about the theme of the book?	1 2 3
Notice how characters develop and change?	1 2 3

NOTICING THE WAY AN AUTHOR WRITES:

Do you:

Think about what an author accomplishes in the lead?	1 2 3
Think about how the author's ending affects the meaning of the book?	1 2 3
Understand how an author creates a character?	1 2 3
Notice how an author builds suspense or creates humor?	1 2 3
Note the author's use of language—vivid description, imagery, dialect?	1 2 3
Think about why an author chooses to write from a particular point of view?	1 2 3
Have an idea of why an author uses flashback?	1 2 3
Understand an author's use of symbolism?	1 2 3
Get ideas for your own writing as you read?	1 2 3
Recognize cultural perspectives in books?	1 2 3
Ever think about how a filmmaker makes a movie? Why the filmmaker uses certain camera angles, music, lighting, or editing?	1 2 3

Form 2.3.

ASSEMBLING THE PORTFOLIO

Name _____

1.   What have you learned this quarter? Begin your portfolio by reviewing what you have done this quarter and what you have learned. You might want to start with columns like this:

What I Know That	What I Can Do That	How My Reading
I Didn't Know Before	I Couldn't Do Before	Habits Have Changed

This list won't go in your portfolio, but it will help you to collect your evidence and to write your cover letter. You might want to review your second-quarter work to remind yourself where you were. Then look at your literary log, in your three-ring binder, and to your partners for ideas.

2.   Collect Your Evidence. Find at least three pieces of evidence that you would like to put in your portfolio to show the kinds of learning you listed in Question 1. Because you read and use your knowledge of reading, books, and authors in other places, you may want to use pieces of evidence from your reading class, from other classes, or from your personal work.

       Be sure to proofread and prepare your pieces in final copy quality.

       My pieces of evidence are:

3.   Preparing your cover letter. Your cover letter will be an essay about what you have learned this quarter. In your essay, describe what you know now that you didn't know before, what you can do now that you couldn't do before, or the ways your reading habits have changed. Be sure to explain what you mean. Be sure to use your evidence as supporting details for what you say. We will review the essay form in class. When you have finished your rough draft, read it to a partner for revision suggestions. Be sure to proofread your cover letter and final copy it. Put your cover letter on top of your evidence and staple or clip it all together.

Chapter 3

CREATING THE FINAL PORTFOLIO

Maria Fusco
Mechanicville Junior/Senior High School

I had hoped that, at some point during the portfolio project, someone would say to me, "O.K., you've had time to think about the program; you've experimented with your students; now these are our expectations of the portfolio program. This is your guide; go do it." I'm still waiting for a definitive answer or direction. Needless to say, my final year creating the writing portfolio was just as hectic, challenging, and experimental as my first year!

At the annual meeting of our project team, I marveled at my colleagues who excitedly spoke of their comfort with this year's program, the ease with which this year had progressed because of the previous year's experiences. Many of the teachers were able to reuse successful ideas and selections, thereby allowing the teachers a euphoric, organized state of mind and year, rather than the frenzied, experimental, tug-of-war state of mind I experienced in both of my years incorporating the writing portfolio into my curriculum.

In the spring of the 1993 school year, my school joined the portfolio project. After my initial meeting with the group, I went back to my school feeling like a young, exuberant new teacher, ready and willing to experiment with my ingenious ideas that would capture my students' attention and motivate them to my level of excitement. I did just that. The results were amazing! I couldn't believe my students' enthusiasm for the end-of-the-year project I had created for them. Mind you, I was starting this project in May and expected my students to be willing to work the last two months of the school year!

Aha! Instant success! Behavioral problems became my best workers. All but a few students shared all of our enthusiasm.

I peered through my crystal ball and projected a great 1993-1994 school year involving my students in the portfolio project. Over the summer, I devised quarterly assessment sheets, quarterly literature and writing assignments, collection portfolio ideas, and successful final portfolio projects, as well as plans for a *First Annual Portfolio Night* open to the public. Yes, a good deal of work on my part as well as on my students', but well worth the time and effort. Year one was a success!

If I had to base my next school year's projections on year one, I of course would experience a second fulfilling year incorporating the portfolio into my curriculum. I couldn't miss: I had labored to devise my first year's program—I could use the same questions with minor changes; the reading selections and writing activities I could basically reuse, again deleting and adding where I deemed necessary; the final portfolio project would also pose no problem. How could I miss?

Allow me to digress here and explain my lack of enthusiasm during the 1994-1995 school year. My first full year of including the portfolio in my eighth-grade curriculum was also a somewhat experimental year for the seventh-grade English class. At this time, I was sharing ideas I had learned from my project colleagues as well as my own activities with the seventh-grade English teacher. During my first year, the eighth graders had never before worked with the portfolio program; it was brand spanking new to them. I didn't have to worry about comments like, "We did this last year." During the 1993-1994 school year, however, the seventh graders were also being exposed to certain portfolio concepts.

I knew that my 1994-1995 eighth-grade students would now be familiar with the term *portfolio* and understand the concept. I assumed this would actually be easier for me and my students; after all, we both were familiar with the program. I was never more wrong! Immediately, on opening day, when I mentioned the word *portfolio*, I heard, "We did this last year!" "Are we doing this *again* this year?" "Why?" "Are we going to have that portfolio night where we have to stand around all night?" "We already did the autobiography." I graciously listened and accepted the throng of queries, but worried I wasn't—yet. I know junior-high students too well and I expected as much. I proceeded to explain my program, which appeased my students for the moment. I assured them the final portfolio project would be quite different, although at the time I had no clue! I was still enthusiastic.

This, however, definitely changed when I passed out the very first assessment page. To make a long story short, I discontinued the remaining assessment pages. I had to create a different form of assessment. Otherwise, I would be reading worthless responses. Needless to say, this school year had a disappointing beginning for me. So much for reusing the successful parts of my portfolio program.

I grudgingly accepted the fact that this year would, again, be a trial-and-error, experimental project! I trudged through the year with the reader response journal and old and new literature selections and writing activities. My students began compiling work into the *collection portfolio* folders that were accessible to them at any time. Included in this folder were unedited pieces, rough drafts, final copies, graded works, poetry, personal writings, artwork, and any other writing the student wished to house in this folder. Creating the final portfolio was the furthest concept from my mind at this time. I would definitely create a project, but not until February.

Still, there was the rest of September through January to experiment with and revamp the assessment portion of my program. I finally decided to use the reader response journal as my assessment tool. Before, during, and/or after reading a literature selection, I would be consistent in presenting a real-life question to the students as a way for them to evaluate their own values/morals/judgments without peer pressure. This I found to be more worthwhile than the dittoed question page. I would collect the journals, make comments, and, yes, give credit, but I never placed a grade in the journal. Each quarter, the students would have responded to anywhere from seven to eleven journal questions. I was honest in my assessment; after the first time, students took these responses seriously. The students seemed content with this. Most students were serious in their responses when they discovered the teacher actually read what was written and commented in a positive way despite the level of writing submitted. In a heterogeneous class, I would read elementary-to-high-school-level responses. But my goal was for my students to feel comfortable with me reading their opinions even though these opinions might be quite different from mine. I made every effort to be nonjudgmental in my responses. The only problem with the journals was returning them as quickly as the students desired them to be returned! Students would compare stickers, stamps, or comments I placed in the journals. The return of their journals became an event for the majority of the students.

Since this part of my program was successful, I knew I would incorporate at least one journal entry into the final portfolio. I did find a way, but I'll discuss this later in the writing portion of the final portfolio.

Before I knew it, the second semester had begun and pressure was mounting. I toyed with a few ideas for the final portfolio, but this was set aside when the art teacher approached me about entering an environmental project, *I*ma*GREEN*nation Celebration*, sponsored by the state in conjunction with Earth Day, 1995. She completed and submitted the paperwork and we were now involved in ecology! *Final portfolio* became the caboose, once again. From the ecology project, I was able to incorporate these writings into the final portfolio, although I wasn't aware of this at the time.

While the students began their art projects, I involved my English classes in library research: I presented a list of environmental problems, and the students, many of whom were already involved in ways to improve the environment in their own lives, chose a problem of concern or interest.

This was a perfect time to introduce note-taking skills, proper outline format, bibliography cards, title page, and works cited page, important skills the students would use in the future. Also, this was another opportunity for the students to use a typewriter, word processor, or computer for the final paper. The end result would become a required writing for the final portfolio as well as artwork the student would want to include.

Yet, again, where was I headed? After all, it was now the end of March. Time to concentrate on creating the final portfolio. I knew my problem would not be the writing selections. I wanted a project that would involve the students making choices and decisions and taking responsibility. After all, this is supposed to be one of the outcomes of the portfolio program, isn't it? I wanted each student to realize his or her potential—not just with the writings, but as a person. I wanted each student to realize that good work takes time and that the work reflects this.

Observing the students' excitement with their artwork for the environmental project, I realized this was my answer to creating the final portfolio: a visual arts presentation. What better way to illustrate and reflect one's personality than through art? And wouldn't the students realize how difficult it would be to throw just anything together the night before? The artwork would reflect the amount of time spent.

I immediately jotted down my own ideas but also consulted the expert: the art teacher. The environmental project lent itself to T-shirts, videos, and collages, but I wanted to expand the options. I was looking for unique methods of expression. Now my final portfolio was becoming an interdisciplinary project!

By April vacation, I presented my ideas to each of my classes. Since many students were traveling to warm destinations during spring break, I required my students only to choose one of the ideas for after vacation. I told them to be more observant in their travels; perhaps a spark would ignite a totally different idea from my suggested ones. And I *was* open to suggestions. My list of ideas was by no means the sole list!

After returning from spring break, it was now time to concentrate on creating the final portfolio. The eighth-grade portfolio would be twofold: first, a visual arts presentation; and second, a writing folder. Through perusing a student's reader response journal, I learned that she and her friend had gone beyond just the idea; they had already embarked on the art project—and were enjoying it! This, of course, lifted my spirits. Maybe I was actually fortunate to have to struggle again this year!

Class time was devoted to finalizing students' ideas for their artwork. In addition to the idea, I required a written document as to how the student would achieve this end result. I set deadlines for project ideas and written work. The visual arts choices were posted in the room as well as written in the students' journals. I spent time fielding questions and giving suggestions on how to accomplish the final product.

Following is the list of ideas I presented to the students:
- Cardboard figures
- Papier-mâché masks
- Dollhouses
- Trunk presentations
- Videos
- Pillows
- Shadow boxes
- T-shirts
- Humans (self-dressed in their future professions)
- Quilts
- Villages

When I saw the color drain from my students' faces, I knew I had a successful project: "No, a picture frame with photos (like last year) was not acceptable." "No, you couldn't use a scrapbook and photo album like last year." "No, posterboard with photos was not enough."

What, then, was I looking for in this visual arts presentation? I asked the students to imagine spending time at a museum. Many of the artists are deceased, and very rarely is the sculptor or artist present when I visit a museum. I asked them to think about this portion of the portfolio as artwork in a museum. What did the student intend the viewer to see? What will the museum-goer see? How will you, the artist, make the observer see what you intend? I wanted the student's work to be his or her résumé to the world. I wanted the artwork to scream, "Hey, look what I am capable of creating! Hey, don't look at that other art—look over here!" I told the students to "create a feast for the public's eyes!"

Of course, I anticipated certain individuals to wait until the last minute, like the night before, to piece together the art. This was confirmed for me when I read the assessment in the writing section of the portfolios. My English classroom was soon turning into a gallery. As students completed their artwork, they submitted it, if possible. This, in turn, helped the struggling artists who had yet to begin!

I was quite pleased at this portion of the portfolio. I had decided that the students need not present any writings on *Portfolio Night*, since my goal was to create a museum out of my students' artwork. Also, with over two hundred students participating, people would not bother to read. I wanted the student's individual pieces to *hit the viewer* on impact. If questioned, the artist would respond. I wanted to know the artist only by looking, not by striking up a conversation with the artist. Also, a title for each composition was necessary.

I feel it's important to briefly share with you the results of the artwork. Many of the suggested ideas were utilized, but with such ingenuity!

Cardboard figures: most were actual height and dressed in student's clothes; some sat at desks in the entrance to the cafeteria (location of displays); others sat or stood, gracing entrances.

Papier-mâché masks: I provided the materials and devoted after-school time with the art teacher; some were attached to cardboard figures; they were painted to reflect students' personalities; some were combined with hands; others were attached to pillows.

Replica dollhouse: complete with miniature furniture to reflect students' flair for interior decorating as well as their interests/hobbies.

Videos: reflected a typical day in the life of the student; included tour of interior of house, favorite room, hobbies, *jam* session.

Treasure chest: *Corey's Collectibles* (each student had to name his or her artwork); included various items important to student.

Villages: popsicle-stick constructions; student's dream place (what student envisioned for self); reflected likes, interests; for example, one boy's dream was to own a corvette and this was parked in the driveway of his home; another village reflected the two girls' ideals of the *seventies* attitude: love, peace, community spirit (a guitar case was dressed as a human—the mayor of this particular village).

T-shirts: professionally completed (first, student had to design shirt, which was then printed); puffy paint and photos were used, as well as decorative trim.

Humans: dressed in character; the following professions were represented: legal secretary (she had a desk at the entrance to the cafeteria, where she greeted the public and passed out the programs), mayor (dressed in suit and tie), lawyer (dressed in suit and tie), NBC news correspondent (who mingled throughout the crowd), army officer (female student dressed in her mother's actual fatigues; she also displayed her mother's photos from this time as well as her medals), golfer (complete with edible greens and photos).

Various other representations: felt flags; bulletin board representing Past, Present, and Future; a five-foot picture frame adorned with items important to the student.

I composed road signs and grouped the students by categories:

- Wearable Art
- Sportsology
- Future County (different villages)
- Real-life Classroom (cardboard figures)

The artwork was amazingly successful; I think each student not only impressed her/himself, but the public and each other!

As I mentioned previously, the final portfolio project was twofold: the visual arts presentation and the writing folder. Since the students had spent a great deal of time and money on the artwork, I gave each student a plain, manila folder to be used for the writings. There was only one requirement for the front cover: a yearbook sketch. Criteria included the student's name, nickname (if one), physical description, achievements (academic, sports, other), and motto (a quote that was a reflection of the student). For this sketch, I presented a sample, but I also suggested that students look at old yearbooks for an actual sketch; I gave the students no other specific instructions. The student decided on layout, grammar, style, etc. Again, the student's personality would be reflected in the sketch.

Next, each writing portfolio would include a table of contents, which, again, was decided upon by the student. I wanted a total of eleven writings included; the yearbook sketch and the table of contents accounted for two of these writings. The arrangement of the table of contents varied from simple to sophisticated. I presented samples for students to view. Each writing would have its own page number. In addition to the eleven writings, the student could include any other writing he or she felt was important to include, whether the writing was an English assignment or from another subject area or the student's own personal writing(s). There was an appendix devoted for these writings and/or other significant material/items.

The writing portion reflected the student's accomplishments. I intentionally chose writing selections completed by the student from the beginning of the year through the end of the year to illustrate the student's growth. I agree with Alan C. Purves, Joseph A. Quattrini, and Christine I. Sullivan, the authors of the instructor's manual for *Creating the Writing Portfolio*, that the portfolio "should show what they know, what they can do, and what they do on their own" (p. 1). This is exactly what both the visual arts presentation and the writing portfolio demonstrated.

Although I required specific writings, the writings were completed at different times during the school year, thus reflecting the student's accomplishment(s). Also, seven of the eleven writings were to be typed (on a typewriter, word processor, or computer), which in itself was an achievement for each student. Therefore, each student was successful despite his or her ability level.

Any arrangement of writings could be included depending on the activities completed during the year. Below is a list of the required writings as well as a brief explanation of each.

1. Yearbook sketch: This would decorate the outside cover of the writing folder. A picture and/or any other decoration(s) was (were) acceptable.

2. Table of contents and an appendix.

3. Parody: This activity was completed in September and was one of the first writing assignments. It was based on an actual fairy tale and was typed and illustrated, and it included a title page as well as a works cited page.

4. One narrative writing, and

5. One descriptive writing: Both the narrative writing and the descriptive writing were completed during both semesters; students had a choice, which gave them control over selections.

6. One journal entry: The students could choose any journal entry rewritten in another type of writing. For example, the student could rewrite the journal entry as a newspaper article, poem, essay, advertisement, composition, comic strip, etc. One student used her entry about the Oklahoma City bombings and rewrote this as a persuasive essay; another student, who kept a journal of day-to-day activities over spring break, created a comic strip of the seven days of his vacation.

7. Memoir poem: The initial assignment was quite structured, but reflected a part of the student's past. Topics included loved ones (living or deceased), important times in the student's life (divorce, sports achievement/other achievements), or a special object.

8. A graded writing: This writing did not have to have received the highest grade, but, according to the student, was exceptional for whatever reason. For example, maybe this was a work that was solely completed by the student from idea to editing to final copy. The graded piece and the rewritten piece were included.

9. Ecology outline project: This was rewritten if corrections were needed.

10. Two eco-poems: These were ecology poems written in conjunction with the environmental project and library research/outline.

11. A final assessment of the visual arts project: Again, this assignment was structured in that I wanted certain information includ-

ed. I expected the student to move from describing the point of conception of his or her idea, to devising a way to present the idea, to securing the needed materials, to the process involved in creating the artwork (e.g., steps taken, time it took and why, problems encountered, the completion of the final product), to his or her feelings about the outcome.

Perhaps the most significant part (to me) of this last piece, the final assessment of the visual arts project, was how the student felt about his or her work. This is what confirmed my assumptions about which projects were exceptional and which were mediocre. And, in a few cases, a project I thought was mediocre actually involved much more work than the finished product reflected. I never would have known this had I not included this information as part of the assessment.

Since one of the lessons to be learned from the portfolio is showing "the student as a responsible human being, capable of both working independently and being part of a group" (Purves et. al, p. 2), my goal of the two-part, final portfolio was achieved.

Students were honest about the final artwork. Student comments were as follows:

I should have started earlier had I known how difficult it would be.

I didn't realize how difficult it was to work with others (personality, schedule, idea conflicts).

I'm better off alone.

I can be creative when I'm serious.

I didn't stand with my project on portfolio night because I was embarrassed when I saw other projects.

This was too hard.

I needed to plan better and not put things off to the last minute.

I couldn't believe the time I spent on this but it was worth it!

The above student comments support Purves et al.'s contention that "a portfolio cannot be slapped together. . . . And a portfolio takes time; it is not the work of the night before" (p. 6).

The written portfolio seemed to involve more time and work, although I only required eleven pieces/sections. Much class time was spent on this portion of the portfolio as opposed to the artwork, for which students relied on themselves, family, peers, and friends. I did feel guilty about not allowing more class time for the artwork, but I wanted the students to learn to be independent of me. Even though the students might have had help at home, they had to dictate what they needed to complete their works. Although the art did not involve writing, I think it helped the students to think for themselves. As Purves et al. states: "We are seeking to help our students to become independent, responsible human beings who no longer need us" (p. 7).

As I sit back and reflect on another trial-and-error year, I appreciate the challenge now as opposed to before. There are parts of this year's program that I will continue to include in the English 8 curriculum. I realize that in most writers' eyes art does not count. However, if my experiences this year with incorporating the artwork into the final portfolio is any indication of importance of art in the English classroom, I'll continue with this approach. Just as a writer brainstorms an idea for a composition, the artist brainstorms ideas for the construction of an artwork. Unlike writers, who only need words to express themselves, artists not only need words to create the art project, but then they have to trust their artwork to express their words.

Whether it be a literary or art composition, there is still a thought process established. Creating the final portfolio by including a visual presentation with a writing portfolio made the portfolio take on a new dimension. Not only did I, the teacher, become the judge, but the public became the critic. And, the students? I hope that, from this project, they became somewhat more responsible, independent, and more confident human beings.

References

Purves, A. C., J. A. Quattrini, and C. I. Sullivan (1995). *Creating the writing portfolio*. Instructor's manual. Lincolnwood, IL: NTC.

Chapter 4

DESIGNING THE SHOWCASE PORTFOLIO

Rochelle L. Abelson
Mechanicville Junior/Senior High School

I

Tonight I celebrate victories. Although this may sound like hyperbole to some, to me this is not the case. I celebrate the presentation of thoughtful, hard work from my seventh-grade students at Mechanicville Middle School, students of varying ability—from the *poorest* reader, the *most limited* in writing ability; to the *accelerated*, the *talented*. But tonight these words are meaningless; such designations do not belong on Portfolio Night. They are judgmental and do not represent what this celebration is all about.

My students are here to present themselves through words and the visual arts, to offer their work to an audience: peers, parents, extended family, members of the board of education, and other community members. Somehow this presentation is connected to a sense of self, to whom these early adolescents are. It is indeed important stuff!

> *While you sometimes conceal yourself, a portfolio does the opposite, putting you on exhibit.*
>
> —Joseph

Many things have happened prior to this gathering. The creation of the final portfolio reflects planning and creating, writing and rewriting, self-reflection and shared thought, and new roles for student and teacher. In a larger sense, the portfolio and its formal presentation reveal the role of education: to produce learners who can live independently and function successfully within society.

But what is this entity called the *showcase portfolio*, and how did it evolve?

I begin with a brief history, for our showcase portfolio has a popular antecedent, one that requires explanation. For at least thirty years, seventh graders in our district have prepared an end-of-year collection of writing and art, a scrapbook/autobiography. Largely teacher-directed, it included assigned writings related to family, friends, vacations, sports, future plans, and accomplishments; it presented writing, but the work had little to do with the students' assessments of literature or of their own writing. Nor did they reflect on themselves as readers. A book report appeared, but students were not asked to become critics of their own or of classmates' work. In retrospect, it seems prescribed. It did not grant much choice to students or allow much critical thinking. Metacognitive pieces were definitely not a feature.

Although traditional writing remains part of the work now, the emphasis is different. The showcase portfolio reflects change in philosophy as well as format and presentation, and it relates to what I perceive should be the teacher-student relationship. It is more student-directed and a better assessment of student performance than its predecessor. It says, "What a minute! Consider who you are as a reader and a writer. Stop and think about what you are writing. Stop and think about what you have written."

> *This piece is like a piece of myself. You can tell what kind of person I am by reading it.*
>
> —Alissa

The portfolio allows the student to see himself or herself as a learner, and as a member of a larger community of learners. Respect for self grows with the work, and individual differences become apparent and are appreciated. It is an empowering experience, and both the daily work and the showcase presentation should show the community that a student has done his or her best. To this end, I encourage creativity and individuality within clearly established standards for good writing.

Both inscribing (issues of mechanics and grammar) and discourse (issues of ideas, style, and organization) are criteria in the showcase portfolio. Seventh graders typically think in terms of spelling, punctuation, and neatness; content and expression are secondary. They must consider new ways to look at their work as they work toward proficiency in basic skills.

II

At the start of the year, each student received a folder for the classroom file cabinet. This held objective quizzes and tests, not writing assignments. Pieces written with the portfolio in mind went into a *working portfolio*, color-coded for each of my four classes of twenty-five to thirty students each. The plastic cartons containing these materials remained accessible to students. The first writing was *Two Weeks in Grade Seven—I Made It!* I read it and commented, but did not assign any grade. Subsequent pieces were read by classmates and/or by me, sometimes using a form/content analysis sheet. At other times, students assigned their own grades based on established criteria. On rereading their work, I found that they are fair judges.

> *I love my portfolio. It has been the biggest project I have ever done. It is well-organized and well-prepared.*
>
> —Susan

I attempted to integrate areas of the curriculum by making use of the writing in a variety of ways. Emphasizing a specific skill area as the sole criterion for evaluating a piece of writing is often a good way to reinforce what has been taught. For example, correct comma usage might be the goal, or transitions. The portfolio is an excellent way to integrate all aspects of the traditional English curriculum.

The *official* portfolio contained ten pieces: a *story hill* book report identifying salient features, including conflict, climax, and resolution; a *viewer's response* to a play we attended; a holiday narrative; an essay based on a short story; a business letter based on a novel read in class; a poetry collection; an analytical self-assessment piece; a persuasive piece based on another novel read in class; and a *reader's response* to a short story. The final area—*free choice*—involved the students selecting existing pieces from their working portfolio, as well as new work.

At the beginning of the school year, each student purchased a composition book to use as a journal, and we housed reader response pieces here as well. Many free choice selections came from this resource. A few students chose to rework their entries for the final portfolio; they did not want others to read what they considered poor work. Some, though, did not want to expend more effort.

However, some sheepishly acknowledged that they had not worked well during the year, as they opened nearly empty folders and composition books with too many blank pages. Others required desk and floor to select, reject, and organize. This proved to be a moment of truth.

The ten-piece portfolio collection, the organization of which depended on the student author, was placed within the larger presentation, the actual organization of which was again at the discretion of the student. The decision of where to put things was left to the writer/artist. This definitely was a change from my first year in the portfolio project when, though I thought I had pulled away from the familiar teacher role to grant more autonomy, I had not granted enough freedom of choice. Students want independence, and they can assume a much greater role in their own learning, even at this grade level.

> *The writings that we had a choice to put in were better because they were more creative and represented us more.*
>
> —Carmine

Again, sharing and discussion ensued as parents joined in the decision-making process. Since many of the adults completed scrapbooks as seventh graders years ago, they often brought out their own work. Not only did they make suggestions to their children, but they shared themselves as writers and artists.

In addition to written work, all students prepared some type of artwork that would present themselves. I posed the following questions: What do you want people to know about you? How do you want to present yourself to them?

> *My portfolio was created to get across some feelings that I had about life at that time, and to get some feelings I had bottled up inside, out in some way. My writing was honest and from the heart.*
>
> —Sarah

Consistent with last year's visual presentation, this year's seventh graders used picture frames as their mode. Some purchased them, while the parents of others helped to build frames. A few checked garage sales for castoffs. Others used the actual covers of their scrapbooks; the more committed used molding to fashion a frame. A few used fabric to enclose the cover. Since our area is now home to many large arts and crafts stores, parents helped by transporting a number of students, some with specific items for purchase in mind; others wandered around and found items that would serve their purpose.

Four chose to create a videotape through which to present themselves. One collaborative effort taught an important lesson, for after sharing the work with the class, this twosome realized how sloppy they were in their work, how they needed to redo it. Another worked with his father in videotaping Portfolio Night; he told me he loved working with his dad. Since Dad had not been happy with much of this student's recent effort, or lack thereof, the video gave them an opportunity to share an experience and to take pride in a successful project. The third student, an equestrian, filled her video with too many walks around the training course, but she also included her family and created a worthy videoportrait. Another verbal, outgoing student offered her family secondary to her numerous pets; the viewer met each animal, with witty commentary accompanying the visual. Creative endeavors shone in this significant aspect of Portfolio Night, and much sharing of ideas and resources took place.

> *By doing this portfolio, I actually learned to do something without alot of help, but I admit I got some ideas from my friends. You can't always do a portfolio on your own. . . .*
>
> —Daniella

III

As I evaluate the second year of my work with the portfolio project, I think in terms of changes in future work. I am not satisfied with some aspects. For example, I would like more periodic assessment, for students to evaluate more frequently the changes in their writing. This requires time, but there's not much of it.

I still battle with myself about relinquishing some of my former program. Certain curricular areas cannot receive the same amount of time as they did pre-portfolio. It is frustrating to skip some literature. It's an old conflict, one that truly asks questions about the type of education afforded on behalf of our students. It encompasses age-old philosophical issues and healthy soul-searching.

> Knowledge emerges only through invention and re-invention, through the restless, impatient, continuing, hopeful inquiry men pursue in the world, with the world, and with each other.
> —Paulo Freire, *Pedagogy of the Oppressed*

The showcase portfolio serves many functions. It invites us to share work, and involves us to make choices. By its nature it encourages responsibility and functions as preparation for life. It also asks us, the professionals, to assess our own values. The night of celebration has implications for all who comprise this learning community.

References

Freire, P. (1970). *Pedagogy of the oppressed.* New York: Seabury.

Chapter 5

FINDING OUR WAY: AUTHENTICITY AND TRANSFORMATION IN THE USE OF PORTFOLIOS

Mary Sawyer

Suzanne Heyd

Approaching Portfolios as a Transformative Process

> The teacher who has come this far must now make a decision that demands professional courage—the decision to remediate himself, to become a student of new disciplines and of his students themselves in order to perceive both their difficulties and their incipient excellence.
> —Shaughnessy, 1976, p. 238

We all know the temptation as teachers to search for quick fixes and magic bullets—whether as a way to satisfy restless students, shake off an edgy administrator, or give ourselves peace of mind when planning for those vast expanses of curricular space. Yet if we want to make significant changes in our classrooms, we need to let go of that desire for the magical technique that suddenly makes teaching simple and always successful or learning straightforward and easily evident. Instead of approaching portfolios as new techniques, we can approach them as a transformative journey, a journey that can increase our understandings of ourselves, our students, and our schools.

> I just put in more effort and more interest in [the class]. I guess because you're using your creativity, your mind, and all of your feelings towards the work that you do. . . . It doesn't seem like an "A" is fair enough for what you do! It's the highest grade you'll get, but . . . I saw everybody's projects . . . and they were really, really good. And I thought, a grade isn't all that important anymore.
> —Rita, grade 9

Portfolios, in their simplest form, are collections of work and reflections that reveal our past intentions and our present understandings. They are a vehicle for reflecting on the significance of our learning. Many have said that portfolios are merely another educational fad—and, of course, they are just that for many people. It is not that portfolios themselves are a fad, for self-reflection as a means of learning is far from a new idea, but it is the way many educators approach portfolios that make them more a flash-in-the-pan than something meaningful and genuinely transformative. Those who *do* portfolios merely as a way to *shake out* a grade will invariably be disappointed in their efforts.

> *The portfolio . . . was a folder of memories, of the knowledge you knew back then, and what you know now.*
> —Arnold, grade 9

For many teachers, administrators, and politicians, portfolios are a means of reacting to the heated calls for increased accountability. Entire school districts and even states are implementing portfolios with the hopes of seeming to be up-to-date with the latest assessment trend and with the hope of then being credited by various constituents for being *accountable*. The danger, of course, is that portfolios are often implemented in such a way as to change nothing about the classroom relationships among teachers, students, and subject matter. Portfolios in these instances become, as one writer put it, "about change without difference" (Roemer, 1991, p. 447).

Portfolios are not a thing in themselves—they are our own creations. The satisfaction of exploring portfolios comes in allowing ourselves to be transformed in the process. There are as many variants of portfolios as there are teachers creating them. There is no singular, fail-safe portfolio recipe, for portfolios grow out of our particular values and our own development. This understanding of the very fluid and exploratory nature of developing a portfolio system is liberating, for there is no such thing as being wrong.

> *I like to see my work in the portfolio. Then I can see how I've improved.*
> —Alan, grade 9

Our explorations with portfolios can thus provide us with an opportunity to rededicate ourselves to our ideals and commitments. Less experienced teachers may find this approach to portfolios quite natural, as they are still in the process of forming their *teacher-identity*. Experienced teachers may find this approach difficult and burdensome, for it requires that they rethink those practices that they have valued, perfected, and identified with for a long period of time, as well as those practices that have formed as a response to making life livable within a certain institution and with particular colleagues and time constraints.

> *And I was thinking more about [the class]. Like the deer poem [I wrote], I was just thinking . . . could the audience picture it? I was just thinking about when I saw a deer, and what I did, and what it did.*
> —Jim, grade 9, discussing his learning and writing process

Portfolios are not a set of techniques, because that is not the nature of teaching and learning, which rest instead in developing and cultivating relationships. Just as we cannot have instant relationships, neither can we have instant portfolios, unless we are content to bypass deep learning for the sake of generating scores and decontextualized skills. Many prefabricated portfolios are used to train students rather than to educate them. When portfolios are used to train, students learn how to make acceptable responses in prescribed situations, but they have no deep understandings of our commitment to their work. Students learn how to light a fire but not how to collect the wood to keep it burning. Transformative portfolios work to deepen the classroom relationships that foster and incite learning (see Thelen, 1981).

> *Last year I used to go home and do my English homework first so I could finish it and then go to my more favorite subject. But now I always leave English for last, because it's nice. You have to think. I just sit down, relax, and write whatever I think, my responses to stories and stuff like that.*
> —Arnold, grade 9

The way portfolios are used in a classroom reflects our own stance. When we use portfolios to appear *accountable*, to teach predetermined skills and prove that a particular curriculum has been *covered*, our stance will be reflected in our students, who will then use portfolios to appear *learned*. When we use portfolios to attend more fully to our teaching and to our students' learning, our stance will be mirrored in the depth of commitment and attention evident in our students' work. We are mirrored in everything we do.

> *I absorbed the feelings of the characters. I tried to see the feelings that each character went through, not just Romeo and Juliet, but each individual character—what they felt.*
> —Rita, grade 9, discussing her learning of *Romeo and Juliet*

Creating a Responsive Curriculum Through Portfolios

> Improvement is not something we require of students so much as something that follows when we provide them with engaging tasks and a supportive environment.
> —Alfie Kohn, 1994, p. 40

When we begin a school year with the intention of working with portfolios, we realize that for the portfolio to be good, worthwhile, and worthy of student (and teacher) investment, we must provide our students with meaningful and appropriate learning activities in the context of an environment that encourages the realization of innate potential and fosters attention to personal growth. We must not become prisoners to a curriculum that we must then *cover*, for then we will not value, and in many instances we will not even hear or recognize our students' understandings. Instead, we will find ourselves trying to lead students down a line of argument or to a particular understanding.

> Instruction directed at achieving an authorized interpretation of a text may provide readers with literary knowledge in the sense that it offers them information on what constitutes a right reading, but insofar as it invalidates their own experience as readers, it disables their capacity to function as authentically literate persons. It will therefore be *false knowledge*, precisely as Milton used that term—knowledge that opens their eyes but closes their minds.
>
> —Blau, 1993, p. 12

This does not mean, however, that our standards are lowered or that our classroom becomes an anarchy of student whimsy. Instead, our focus is on involving students in the shaping of the course to meet their needs and goals. In this way, the concept of curriculum becomes that of a living entity, interpreted and reformulated around each student. Together, we work to develop a relationship between our students and the curriculum—we weave a web that will connect the two. We can do this through such activities as questionnaires, checklists, and goal setting. There are many ways to begin this process. The important element is that the curriculum is made visible, tangible, and flexible enough to allow for each student to be able to establish a meaningful relationship with it. These beginning goals and understandings can become artifacts within the portfolio to help students and teachers trace learning over time.

> *To the extent someone reads my portfolio, they would know almost everything about me.*
>
> —Arnold, grade 9

All too often, students are placed in a passive position in regard to the predetermined content and format of the curriculum; it is something that is done to them. In this context, students cannot make meaningful what happens in the classroom because it does not seem integrated with their understanding of themselves as learners. They may dismiss classroom activities as having little meaning for their own development as human beings. Academically strong students might see some value, especially those students who regularly motivate themselves by finding inherent value in academic tasks—but most students simply go through the motions, and many do not even bother to do that. Portfolios can support students' efforts to learn and grow from classroom activities, making them meaningful by providing students with opportunities to observe their own work, explore their own thinking, and reflect on their own progress in all aspects of the literary experience.

> *The first couple of times I [analyzed my writing process] I used to sit and say, "Oh my God! How did I get the idea?" It kind of blanked out on me. But now, whenever I write an essay . . . I just make a little note to myself of how I expanded [it]. . . . Because if I don't keep notes of what I'm doing,*

> *I could have straight A's in the class and have no idea what I'm doing. The*
> *[learning analysis] kind of gave me an advantage of, "If I did this one, I*
> *should be able to do that one."*
>
> —Arnold, grade 9

In preparation for their work with portfolios, students need to clarify, for themselves and for us, who they are as readers and writers; even on the first day of the school year, they arrive with a full spectrum of skills, abilities, fears, frustrations, insights, and questions pertaining to writing and literature. Based upon these literary histories, students can then begin to explore their relationship to literature and writing so that they can connect with new material that they will encounter as the school year gets underway. Once they understand that they have a preexisting relationship to the material, they can begin to build bridges, make connections, correct misunderstandings, and clarify ideas.

> *At first I didn't really want to do [poetry]. I didn't like it. But then when*
> *we got into it I learned about a whole bunch of different ways of writing*
> *poetry and that it didn't have to rhyme. . . . And then I got some ideas—*
> *it brought some ideas into my head. Because at one point we read about a*
> *guy who said, "Write poetry about what we know best" and so that's what*
> *I did. I wrote about friendship, girls, sports.*
>
> —Jim, grade 9

Goal setting in the portfolio-based classroom, therefore, must be a process of negotiation and reformulation of various (e.g., state, local, school, teacher, and student) curricular goals; student and teacher collaborate to develop goals that are meaningful, appropriate, and individualized, which can then be reflected and monitored within the portfolio. In empowering students to set goals and to monitor and evaluate their own progress and process, we take a risk: we are working to balance the nexus of power and control found in the traditional model of curriculum. If students find classroom materials and activities are not meeting their needs as readers and writers, then we all have a responsibility to help the student to individualize the curriculum in ways that will make it more appropriate. This is true accountability. Or better yet, this is responsibility (see Johnston, 1992, below). We are responding to our students in a way not permitted by a concept of curriculum that sets abstract objectives first, and then measures students' movements toward them. The responsive, and responsible, teacher recognizes the value of working with students to contextualize and individualize learning objectives.

> I use the term *responsible* as a contrast to the term *accountable*.
> Responsibility comes from the individual. A teacher or other learner
> is responsible, whereas he is held accountable. This distinction is critical in its implications. It requires that the individual (teacher or learner) become reflective about his own practice, and about students'
> learning. If he is not reflective, then someone else will be required to

hold him accountable. It is possible to be held accountable but at the
same time not to be responsible.

—Johnston, 1992, p. 6

Describing and Evaluating

Student Learning Through Portfolios

> In the absence of confidence in the authority of a writer, or just given
> the opportunity to claim authority to judge (as is typically the case
> when teachers read student writing), readers will tend without hesita-
> tion to cite any idiosyncrasy of form or technique, idea or style, any
> authorial choice that challenges their personal preferences, as an *error*.
> —Knoblauch and Brannon, 1984, p. 161

When we are successful in helping students connect their lives to the curriculum, we can no longer function as sole evaluators of their development. We
are challenged to listen, to understand, and to work with students. Assessment is
no longer relegated to determining if and where a student *measures up*.
Assessment cannot be the result of imposing our viewpoint on where particular
students are versus where they should be, thus focusing our attention on the cat-
egorization of the performance and not on the nature of the performance itself.
Our aim is to learn from the performance, not to judge or to categorize it.
Assessment becomes a heightened attention—an awareness—rather than a judgment.

> Perhaps assessment isn't about judgment, but about knowing our-
> selves intimately, about deepening in the kind of wisdom that only we
> can know: the wisdom of self-awareness.
> —Heyd, this volume, p. 229

Diaries and logbooks are common tools enabling teachers and students to
record and track descriptive, nonjudgmental observations. These observations
can be the fodder that feeds the more formal reflections contained in a final portfolio. While it is relatively simple to have students make observations of their
own and a few of their classmates' responses to literature (be it in classroom talk,
writing, drawing, or dramatic performance), it takes ingenuity for secondary
teachers to maintain observation logs on all of their students. Our high student
numbers make detailed and frequent observations extremely difficult and usually impossible. Our records, then, end up being less detailed and our observations
less frequent, unless we choose to focus on one or two *case* students. One way to
keep some sort of regular record is to set aside time at the end of every class for
teachers and students to record observations. These observations can be placed
in a matrix both to see which modes (e.g., talking/listening, writing, drawing,
acting) and contexts (e.g., whole class, small group, individual work) the course

might neglect and to more easily find patterns in students' strengths and weaknesses (for a sample matrix, see Barrs, 1989).

> Learning is not an open-and-shut business; at any one *stage* a child may have established some competences, and be consolidating others, while still others are becoming possible—with strong support.
> —Barrs, 1990, p. 251

Charting our students' literacy development is quite difficult. There has been very little research on the development of reading and writing in older students; thus, we do not have the already articulated language or concepts for describing what *literature learning* means—what lies beyond decoding and basic comprehension. This lack of articulation is partly a result of our past tendency to understand literacy learning by comparing one student to another or to an ideal, a standard, instead of analyzing the growth patterns of individual students. It is also the result of multiple and competing definitions of literature learning: *literature learning* for one teacher may mean their students' ability to analyze a text's structure and identify its figurative language elements; *literature learning* for another teacher may mean their students' ability to involve themselves in texts and to use them to rethink their lives and society. In using portfolios to track older students' literature learning, we are therefore charting new territory as well as defending and articulating our conceptions of literature learning.

What we do know of literacy development is that it is neither a neat linear progression nor is it evenly paced. In her intimate portrayal of teachers trying to help adolescents learn to read, Meek (1983) writes: "Readerly behavior is learned less by specific instruction than by personal discovery, and the process is neither clear nor straightforward" (p. 196). Meek's teacher-group found that these readers' progress could be documented, "but so minimally in terms that the outside world would understand. . . . Who else would recognize our fragile optimism and nourish these tender buds of new growth?" (p. 197).

> But the learner also has his private timetable and improves, often, in seeming indifference to outside schedules, lagging behind or lapping over the finishing lines of courses. Some lessons bear immediate fruit, some fall by the way, and others lie dormant until one day the student bursts out in an "I see!" or produces a piece of writing that moves him, seemingly overnight, to a new plane of competence.
> —Shaughnessy, 1977, p. 276

Because literacy learning is rooted in complex social and cultural practices that make progress developmental in nature rather than instantaneous, we might find ourselves tempted to teach mastery of superficial skills where progress can be quickly evident rather than accept the reality of uneven and often minimal progress. We may seek, through the invention of such skills as *the business letter* or *the five-paragraph essay*, to control and guarantee student progress rather "than accept the peripheral role of nurturing a competence that students already possess and will develop in their own idiosyncratic ways as well as on timetables of their own choosing" (Knoblauch and Brannon, 1984, p. 95). At some point we must acknowledge that we cannot control students' learning. What we can do is wholly attend to it and encourage our students to do the same. Portfolios can be the vehicle that helps both teachers and students reflect upon and celebrate classroom learning and accomplishments.

It is often argued that having one's performance judged by others is a *real-life* experience and therefore must be a part of the classroom experience. Most of us are required by our institutions to give students grades. If judgment is important, how do we then make it authentic and a tool for learning and transformation? One way is to share the responsibility of judgment with our students, requiring that student work be responded to by a team of students as well as by the teacher and the students themselves. We can also include a wider audience, such as parents, administrators, and students from other courses. Placing students in the role of judges is crucial if we want them to achieve the intellectual independence it takes to evaluate their own ideas, performance, and progress, as well as that of their peers. Assessment, when it takes into account multiple perspectives in this way, also provides students with valuable insights into the effect of their work and into the subjective and culture-specific nature of judgment.

> *When I write poetry, and I have other people read it, and they give me good feedback, it makes me feel like I'm doing good at something—that they like it. Fernanda always tells me, "You're doing so good, I like your poetry! Can you write me a poem?" And, it's just like, maybe I am good at it.*
> —Dana, grade 9

When we grade students, it is our responsibility to make sure that our judgments are informed by multiple perspectives, including those of the students themselves. A grade has little validity when a student does not, on some level, agree with a grade and understand the reasons for it. One way of formalizing the negotiated grading process is through *grade proposals*: students evaluate their classroom participation and learning and then document their evaluations with samples of their own work. These proposals are submitted to us for review. The proposed grade is either accepted or modified as need be.

> *We're earning a grade, she's not giving it to us. We're earning it.*
> —Jim, grade 9

Conclusion

> I now view teaching as an interpersonal relationship, more than a professional one. It is not fundamentally about skills and competence, but about integrity and openness. I have begun to measure success in terms of the quality of our interactions.
> —Newman, 1994, p. 52

When we teach, it is easy to lose sight of the fact that the teaching of literature and writing is not a simple act of helping students to acquire skills. Instead, we are working to develop students' existing sensibilities and to help them use reading and writing to find meaning in and take part in shaping this world and their own lives. To develop their sensibilities we must engender in students the desire to read and write and talk and listen. We do that by developing a classroom community that values students' thinking and places their understandings at the center of the curriculum. In a real sense, our students' understandings *are* the curriculum: Their interpretations of literature, and their understandings about their learning and about themselves as readers and writers, are all they *take* from the course.

We've described portfolios as a system of various tools that can be used to record, track, and validate students' developing understandings. We've discussed how they can be used to help students establish learning goals as well as to observe and to evaluate their creative processes and achievements. Thus, portfolios can be used to help students gain an intimacy with how their minds work and, in doing so, help them become independent readers and writers. Our students come to know what they know, and they know how to improve their work. By making visible students' intentions and understandings, portfolios also help us become more responsive teachers.

> *It's good for you to grade yourself. If you get a good grade, you know it's because you deserved it. And if you get a bad grade, it's because you know you deserved it. Maybe you didn't hand in everything that you were supposed to. So it's good for you to analyze yourself. That way, you won't blame too much on the teacher if you get a bad grade.*
> —Rita, grade 9

We have also discussed how when students' understandings are at the center of the curriculum, we can no longer be the sole evaluators of students' progress. We must become students of our students and learn to attend to their work in critical but nonjudgmental ways (Shaughnessy, 1976, p. 238, cited earlier). We must also provide students with opportunities to solicit multiple perspectives on their work, hence acknowledging the complex and multifaceted nature of literacy development and literacy evaluation. Responding to students' reading and writing is an act of interpretation; a single teacher's interpretation is rarely adequate. These perspectives on student texts can improve our teaching by opening our eyes to readings other than our own—they can help us to represent the text in other ways, and, in doing so, help us to reach out to students in ways that were not possible before (see Britton, 1970, cited below). A broad array of responses can also provide students with valuable feedback and prevent them from unthinkingly tailoring their work to please a single reader, usually the teacher. They force students to ponder revision alternatives and to take responsibility for their decisions.

> The world we respond to, in fact, the world towards which our behaviour is directed, is the world as we symbolize it, or represent it to ourselves. Changes in the actual world must be followed by changes in our representation of it if they are to affect our expectations and, hence, our subsequent behaviour.
>
> —Britton, 1970, p. 14

The philosophy informing our use of portfolios, our emphasis on non-judgmental observation and self-reflection, is nothing new. What is new is that portfolios and other reflective assessments are now more readily acceptable by schools, districts, and states as a valid—and often more desirable—way of assessing student progress. Others speak of holding students to high standards but say nothing about how to help students reach these standards or even how to go beyond them. Portfolios can be the vehicle that helps students internalize those standards. We are working to make this acceptance by educational authorities something positive—something that transforms teaching and learning—rather than something that simply bolsters status quo teaching. We invite you to join us in this effort.

References

Note: The students quoted in this chapter were from Suzanne Heyd's ninth-grade English course, 1992-93.

Barrs, M. (1990). "The primary language record: Reflection of issues in evaluation." *Language Arts, 67*, p. 244-53.

Blau, S. (1993). *Transactions between theory and practice in the teaching of literature* (Report Series 5.6). Albany, NY: National Research Center on Literature Teaching and Learning, University at Albany—SUNY.

Britton, J. (1970). *Language and learning: The importance of speech in children's development*. London: Penguin.

Johnston, P. H. (1992). *Constructive evaluation of literate activity*. New York, NY: Longman.

Knoblauch, C. H., and L. Brannon (1984). *Rhetorical traditions and the teaching of writing*. Upper Montclair, NJ: Boynton/Cook.

Kohn, A. (1994). "Grading: The issue is not how but why." *Educational Leadership, 52* (2), p. 38-41.

Meek, M. (1983). *Achieving literacy: Longitudinal studies of adolescents learning to read*. London: Routledge and Paul Kegan.

Newman, L. E. (1994, Fall). "Being myself, a teacher." *Liberal Education*, p. 52-55.

Roemer, M. G. (1991). "What we talk about when we talk about school reform." *Harvard Educational Review, 61*, p. 434-48.

Shaughnessy, M. P. (1976). "Diving in: An introduction to basic writing." *College Communication and Composition, 27*, p. 234-39.

Shaughnessy, M. P.. (1977). *Errors and expectations: A guide for the teacher of basic writing*. New York, NY: Oxford Press.

Thelen, H. A. (1981). *The classroom society: The construction of educational experience*. London: Croom Helm.

Chapter 6

CD PORTFOLIOS: A MULTIMEDIA APPROACH

Jeanne Stendardo
Shaker High School

Portfolios celebrate the accomplishments of our students as learners. Traditional portfolios are comprised of writings across a variety of genres, sprinkled with artwork and occasional photographs, bound in paper, fabric, or plastic by staples, thread, or clips. When I think about the learning that goes on in our classrooms, the creativity demonstrated by fifteen-foot time lines; intricate game boards; costumes crafted in everything from tin foil and brown grocery bags to fake fur; pencil sketches; and dramatic presentations of Shakespearean soliloquies, the traditional portfolio seems as outdated and confining as desks bolted to a classroom floor.

Creative projects showcase our students' depth as learners and critical thinkers in the English classroom, where they refine their skills in reading, speaking, and listening as well as writing, yet the traditional portfolio showcases only writing. Portfolios should, if they truly reflect authentic student learning, include the time lines, game boards, performances, and other means of creative expression.

Enter the multimedia compact disc (CD) portfolio. Imagine a classroom full of students excited about demonstrating their insights into the changing faces of Macbeth: Macbeth the valiant soldier; Macbeth the tempted; Macbeth the usurper and maniacal murderer; Macbeth the doomed. In an essay, a student details Macbeth's fall, step by step. As you read the text, three-dimensional images of masks—which the student has fashioned of clay and which depict Macbeth at various stages—appear on the screen. The graphics-enhanced time line that runs down the right margin on the screen attests to the swiftness of

Macbeth's decline and the escalation of his crimes. A glinting bloodied dagger floats before your eyes; thunder echoes and lightening flashes across the screen as roaring winds lash against crumbling chimneys; the clang of a crown hitting the castle floor is heard, and the crown rolls across the bottom of the screen, coming to rest after the paper's final period.

Along with the three-dimensional clay masks depicting the changing faces of Macbeth, within a multimedia CD portfolio you might find photographs of Macbeth's castle, maps of Scotland, and an animation of Birnam Wood coming to Dunsinane Hill. The essay's text is in front of you, as is a small inset of a video of the student orally presenting the text or elaborating on the architecture of the castle or the rationale for the changes the student perceives would have been evident in Macbeth's appearance. The possibilities are limitless; the students are excited, inquisitive, active, self-directed, and self-motivated; the teacher is a facilitator, excited and reinvigorated in a student-centered classroom; the curriculum becomes integrated as the students (and the teacher) expand their computer literacy and explore interdisciplinary connections; critical-thinking skills soar, along with creativity and problem-solving skills. Online services support student investigation and research as they begin to critically analyze literature, comprehend allusions, and prepare to make those interdisciplinary connections with reference materials available literally at their fingertips.

The technology needed to create the multimedia CD portfolio is available now and is in use in some school districts. Teacher input into the design of a custom computer network is essential and should be the result of extensive brainstorming and consultation with a network design expert who is current with the technology and understands the hardware and software that is necessary to generate the multimedia CD portfolio.

The greatest challenge in brainstorming and discussing plans for a multimedia CD portfolio lab is conquering the vocabulary and the alphabet soup that often accompany it. Perhaps the second most challenging aspect is getting comfortable with suggesting the *impossible*; it seems that computer technology is advancing at the speed of light, and what may not be possible or available when you begin to plan your lab could be in its second or third generation by the time the lab is up and running. What follows is a quick introduction to the multimedia CD portfolio lab. While it is certainly not the only possible configuration for a lab, it represents a good starting point for brainstorming a lab suitable for your own needs and those of your students. Along the way you will pick up a working knowledge of the vocabulary and the alphabet soup so that you'll be prepared to work with the pros in the initial design phase for your network.

What You Should Know Before You Start

Before we begin to explore what a lab should have, some terms need to be defined. First, you will have a *server*. This is the main computer that serves all the students. A server has lots of programs that all students can access, so it needs lots of *disk storage*, which is not the same as *memory*. Memory (also called random access memory, or RAM) is, in human terms, the equivalent of short-term memory. If a student is writing a paper, that paper, and the changes being made to it, are being stored in RAM. After the paper is saved, however, it is written onto the disk. When the computer is turned off, everything in RAM disappears, but everything that was saved (written onto the disk) stays and can be accessed later.

A server can be accessed by many students at once. Generally, students will work at stations that consist of a terminal and (sometimes) an individual computer. The station has access to the server through phone lines. These phone lines that connect the server, the stations, and other devices such as a scanner, a video camera, and other technological wonders create a *network*. The network is often referred to as a LAN, or local access network. This simply means that the network does not go beyond the building (or even the classroom, sometimes).

The Ideal Lab

The server for a multimedia CD portfolio lab of thirty individual student workstations (SWs) should have a minimum disk storage capacity of two gigabytes. One gigabyte is, in simplest terms, the capacity to hold one billion key strokes. While this may stagger the imagination, keep in mind that videos and other graphic images, when stored on disk, take up a significant amount of space. Try to picture yourself looking for storage space after collecting videos, scrapbooks, game boards, posters, masks, and dioramas from each of your students. They take up far more room than 130 research papers, which you can put in a large tote. The same is true when it comes to storing these different mediums on CDs.

In addition to looking at storage capacity, the speed with which information is saved and retrieved should also be considered. When there are many students simultaneously accessing programs, speed becomes an important factor. Each minute of the class period is precious, especially when other classes are waiting for their turn in the lab. Faster computers allow students to complete tasks more quickly and generate clearer graphic images. A computer's speed is measured in megahertz (Mhz); a very good rule of thumb is to get the most megahertz that you can at the time you purchase your equipment. You won't regret the expense (at the time this chapter was written, 150 Mhz was about as fast as computers could operate; however, this will undoubtedly change in the near future).

Because of cost considerations, this network design will employ a single compact-disc recorder (CDR) accessed through the server. A CDR is a CD-ROM drive that can both read and record (or *write to*) CDs. Individual student workstations will access the CDR through the server. Because of the cost of writable CDs, the server will store portfolios in progress on disk. The final portfolios will not be saved to the CDs until they are edited and prepared to be submitted. Traditional floppy disks do not have the memory capacity to hold the text and graphics that comprise the portfolio, making the CDR a necessity.

An optional but invariably useful lab component is an overhead projector designed to project the images that appear on the server's monitor. This provides an efficient method to instruct a large number of learners in the operation of the many programs they will be accessing as they develop their portfolios.

Network hardware will include thirty computers in addition to the server. Six of the computers will be *super* student workstations (SSWs). Each might operate at, for example, 100 Mhz and have a disk storage capacity of two gigabytes. These units are somewhat slower than the server, but will be able to input and output information adequately; they will also be considerably less expensive than the server, which might run, for example, at 120 Mhz. The SSWs will be used for final editing, including creating sound overlays for editing graphics and videos, animating, and accessing computer-aided design (CAD) programs and other special programs stored in the server.

Scanners will be attached to two of the SSWs. Students will be able to copy text or graphics from a source to the portfolio. For example, if a student wants to incorporate a pie chart from a periodical into a paper, the scanner will record the image. The student does not have to reproduce the chart using a desktop publishing program. Students creating a satire or farce can also scan a sketch and then distort or *morph* it for the desired effect. Students with limited artistic talents need no longer feel at a disadvantage.

Video cards can also be attached to the SSWs. Again, it is not necessary for each station to have a video card; two video cards would service a lab of this size well. A video card enables students to capture video and television, as well as view both from the source (e.g., videocassette player, cable television, etc.) on the monitor. Using a video card, students could demonstrate their speaking skills by including a dramatic presentation, or they could demonstrate both their critical thinking and listening skills by including a clip from a debate in which they participated. A video card also enables students to overlay text or graphics on a video presentation to be recorded on the CD.

Since students and teachers will require *hard copy* of certain documents, printers will be incorporated into the network. Eight to ten black-and-white laser printers would be augmented with two color inkjet printers. Dot-matrix and daisy wheel printers can be used, but the quality of print is inferior and these printers tend to be very slow, a consideration when thirty students are attempting to turn papers in on time.

The next step is to provide the remaining twenty-four SWs. They will be *smaller* than the SSWs, running at, for example, 75 Mhz and having a disk storage capacity of one gigabyte. Each will access word-processing or desktop-publishing programs and basic graphics programs through the server. Each SW should have a CD-ROM drive to enable the students to access research information while preparing initial drafts. This is where literature-based discovery learning originates in the lab. A mouse, speakers, and headsets complete the actual computer hardware package.

What about teacher workstations (TWs)? An SSW would certainly be nice, but in actuality, a SW as long as it is linked to the network. Teachers can edit and comment on student progress from their own desk, whether it is in the lab or a distant corner of the school. And remember that tote bag with 130 research papers? Obsolete! With a compatible home computer with a CD-ROM drive, the disks can be read at home; or, better yet, with a dedicated phone line, a modem, and a home computer, you'll never have to carry papers or CDs home. The server will allow you to access student work, including the entire contents of each portfolio, from your home.

Teacher and student workstations will require desks or tables and chairs, and the lab itself must be air-conditioned and vented to maintain a temperature in the range of 68°F to 72°F. In order to link the SSWs, SWs, TWs, printers, and other hardware to the server, a lot of wiring will be needed. Wiring a lab of this size could run in the area of several thousand dollars.

Security is another consideration. Programs are available to lock out unauthorized individuals. Password systems are commonplace, but with scanners, bar-coded student identification cards are an alternative. Theft of memory, hardware, software, and CDs is not uncommon, but with adequate security, the risk diminishes. In developing a security system, keep in mind that even the ball inside the mouse presents a temptation for some. Devices are available that lock hardware to the workstation. All labs should be connected to the school's alarm system to detect and prevent or discourage intruders.

In securing the software for computer labs, many schools and businesses purchase site licenses. A site license is an agreement that enables a server to allow a specified number of workstations to access a program through the server without purchasing multiple copies of the software. In purchasing a site license, it is generally a good practice to allow for a 10 to 15 percent growth in the number of workstations.

Computer software and hardware change rapidly. From the time you begin to brainstorm your wants and needs to the time you are ready to sign on the dotted line, items will become obsolete, but, with the guidance of a certified network engineer (CNE) or other computer professional, your lab will come to fruition. The CNE is the individual who you will look to as the *bugs* are being worked out of the system, and together with several neighboring districts, you may wish to retain a CNE to keep your lab in top operating form. The CNE will also be able to instruct students and teachers in the operation of various programs.

Like the hardware components of the lab, software is a matter of choice, and options will vary according to compatibility, needs, wants, and, of course, budget. The CD portfolio lab described here, with some leeway for additional or upgraded software, is estimated at about two hundred thousand dollars, exclusive of security measures. Given the funding cuts faced by many school districts, even a severe downscaling of this lab is a temptation, but it must be remembered that one gets what one pays for.

Funding a lab becomes an exercise in creativity, a search for grant money, and a partnership among industry, community, and school. The cost effectiveness to industry of a technologically-enhanced education is unquestionable. Students become more than marginally computer literate; they become proficient. Students who are critical thinkers and decision makers become inquisitive employees who exercise good judgment based on strong critical-thinking skills, and they become creative problem solvers. The contents of the multimedia CD portfolio renders college admissions applications and employment applications obsolete as the CD provides universities and industry with a means of authentic, multifaceted assessment.

Computer networks do not have to be purchased; they can be leased. Leasing is, in many cases, a better alternative because it insures, depending on your contract, a lab that is in top operating form daily. Troubleshooters are available to walk lab operators through difficulties at the touch of a phone. More stubborn difficulties are handled by the leasing company's technician. Upgrades are also available to the lessee as they come to the marketplace, thus avoiding the inevitable obsolescence of hardware and software.

My own drive for additional means of authentic, multifaceted assessment and teaching strategies resulted in the investigating of what I call the multimedia CD portfolio. It was fueled by my students and their creativity and excitement about using computer technology to create portfolios that were exceptional. Many of my students submitted exceptional writing portfolios this year, but they were frustrated by the limitations of the traditional writing portfolio. While I required a minimum of four selections, most students felt that they could not present themselves as learners and writers adequately within such a confined space. They also were concerned about presenting nothing more than words on a page. Visual images crowded their minds as they composed. Sounds, actions, smells, and music filled their heads when they wrote and rewrote; the words were too restless, too full of life to be relegated to paper and ink. The students wanted a broader canvas, a twenty-first-century canvas capable of sound and motion, and depth and space. My students wanted to breathe life into what they had created. I asked them to tell me more, as specifically as they could, about what they felt they needed to enhance their portfolios. This is when I became convinced that the multimedia CD portfolio was not only a vehicle through which students (and teachers) could find a new means of self-expression, but the single most comprehensive assessment tool for authentic student learning.

The Impact of a CD Portfolio on Student Work

Erika Mapes, a tenth-grade honor student, wrote *Jordan's Story*, an essay about her brother who underwent extensive, lifesaving surgery as a young child.

Erika recounts, "I remember being jolted awake by my brother's scream. . . . It was the second time that night that Jordan had cried out like that." Throughout her essay, Erika recaptures *frames* of the events that took place during the course of Jordan's illness: his hospitalization at Albany Medical Center, the ambulance trip to Boston Children's Hospital, and the "cheap motel" with the "two squeaky cots with thin blankets" where she and her other brother slept when they went to Boston to visit Jordan.

"I think we found the [hospital] room without too much trouble, but after I walked in, I ran back out. Cowering in the hall, I squeezed my eyes shut." Erika recalls the "seemingly lifeless form with tubes coming out from everywhere" and "telling myself that I had walked into the wrong room, that I had made a mistake" as she saw her three-year-old brother "lying in that bed with stuff hooked to him like there was no tomorrow. Like there was no tomorrow. Only, there really might have been no tomorrow for Jordan."

Erika's ability to recapture individual frames and to select and hold a single frame so successfully lends to both the pacing and vividness of her story. Had she had the opportunity to incorporate *special effects*, Erika says she would have videotaped the actual compilation of a scrapbook, photograph by photograph. She would have *framed* each event right through to Jordan's homecoming. Erika also suggested background music, but, because her voice is rhythmic and her reading is dramatic, I would have encouraged her to forego that in favor of using her own special talents with a voice overlay.

The multimedia CD portfolio would have created a most unusual difficulty for Erika's classmate Brian. Brian is a very talented writer across genres, and narrowing down his portfolio selections proved to be quite a challenge. Brian included a critical analysis of *Macbeth* in his portfolio. In it he discussed the changing faces of an evolving Macbeth: Macbeth the war hero and dutiful subject; the greedy Macbeth lusting for Duncan's crown; the insane and homicidal Macbeth. Brian would have included a series of masks of Macbeth, reflecting the character's metamorphosis from hero to villain.

I found that throughout my students' journeys toward their completed portfolios, there were many instances of academic metamorphosis. None was greater than Cindy's. Cindy is a wonderfully talented artist. She graced her ninth-grade classroom's walls with pencil sketches of Romeo and Juliet and stunningly beautiful chalks of mythological characters. Cindy is an articulate, creative, poised, and intelligent young woman who faced an incredible struggle with her writing.

In the introduction to her portfolio, Cindy writes, "My first piece is titled, 'A Fight to the Start.' I decided to open my portfolio with this personal narrative because it reflects my struggling years as a writer." Cindy believes that the portfolio presented her with the opportunity to "come face to face with [her] own unique writing," and I fully concur with her assessment.

In "A Fight to the Start," Cindy writes:

I felt I was struggling both mentally and physically. The endless ticking of the clock would constantly ring in my head. It's amazing how time flies when you are not having a good time. Sometimes, I felt I was trapped in a trance and found it impossible to get out. I knew this had to be something worse than a serious case of writer's block, but I didn't know what. Many times, my pen would suddenly stop in the middle of a thought which left me to sit in complete silence and under even greater pressure and tension. I found myself staring off into emptiness and darkness, desperately searching for at least one simple word or thought. This seemed to last for an eternity.

This kind of struggle was evident early in Cindy's writing. She was unable to follow a thought to its conclusion, and her writing was disjointed and confused.

Cindy's frustrations were evident at home and in school. When I returned papers, she sank in her seat. At home, Cindy writes,

My sister would say to me, "You're killing yourself by thinking too hard." I ignored her. . . . I thought to myself, "How would she possibly know what I'm going through." I knew I wasn't thinking hard enough because if I was, then I could have finished my paper two, three, four hours ago.

Cindy sat with me after school day after day and pulled apart sentences and put them back together. We talked about her topics, her ideas. "Tell me what you wanted to say here," I repeated over and over. And she did, but in half as many words and with directness and conviction. By the third or fourth paper, Cindy was critiquing her own work, not based on the complexity or length of her sentences, but based on the clarity of her presentation. Sentences became concise, and greater attention to word choice eliminated the tedious verbosity. She was on her way, and she knew it.

During that single moment as I sat face to face with my teacher and my papers, I felt I was once again at my Junior High graduation. As I walked up onto the stage to receive my diploma and shake a line of hands, a similar sense of accomplishment raced through me. I heard my heart knocking against my chest. . . . I felt the moistness of my palms sliding over the crisp, tightly rolled diploma.

Cindy has learned "that writing is a long and repetitive process." The portfolio and the importance that it engenders academically and personally to Cindy are evident. In her letter of metacognition, she writes, "I have struggled and fought with myself . . . every step of the way," and, in the end, the portfolio "gave me a new view of and attitude toward writing. I believe my portfolio signifies this new attempt for change and hope." Cindy titled her portfolio *Hope*.

Cindy's ability to convey her journey in words is matched by her creative response to my request that she couple *A Fight to the Start* with a different medium. Because she is such a talented artist, I had expected either the pencil sketches or chalk drawings for which she is so highly recognized. Cindy chose yet a different path. "I would guide you to my most cherished place, my secret hiding place in the woods behind my home. This is where my journal began to develop." Cindy would create a video journal of her struggle with writing at night alone in her room at her desk. She also believes that a set of dominoes, lined up, would represent a metaphor for her struggle and eventual success. "The effect that the dominoes create will signify my path for change. It will show that a helping hand is needed to effect change. Each domino will represent each step and each obstacle I had to overcome to meet the next challenge."

Lisa Burke, a classmate of Cindy's, creates a world as she tests her skill at writing a political farce. She beckons her reader to view *Our Political Circus*:

> *Come one, come all to the political circus. The show is a crazy, mixed up, and usually disappointing performance for the spectators. Every star in the circus is filled with hidden agendas and greed, whether it be for money, power, control, or just plain attention.*

Lisa's farce takes the reader on a journey through the side shows of the circus and the main tent. Political figures are satirized as "teetering on the hire wire" with "no net to catch" them. Elephants and donkeys "are hamming it up with their slapstick" act, while "numerous jugglers, clowns, and contortionists" try "relentlessly to bend the budget of the circus." Lisa's options for multimedia expansion are vast. She could create an animated cartoon using *morphed* snapshots and voice overlays of the political figures she satirizes. She could create a newspaper's special feature section advertising the circus and highlighting the various acts. Interviews of circus-goers could add yet a different angle to her farce.

While so many of the students merely scratched at the surface of the possibilities offered by the multimedia portfolio, one student actually began to take advantage of the technology, using her own home computer. Johanna, a sophomore, used a graphics package to create a background for her essay on Barbara Kingsolver's novel *The Bean Trees*. As a backdrop for her paper, Johanna created a desert canyon scene to highlight a quote from the novel, tying the graphic in with the content of her paper.

Johanna's letter of metacognition and her premier selection *Monstrous Remains*, which follows, offer still more fertile ground for a multimedia CD portfolio:

> *Dear Reader:*
>
> *This piece of writing which has become the premier piece in my portfolio is of great value to me. I enjoyed writing it very much, which is unusual for me for literature-based writing. Usually I only like writing creative things that I can set on other planets or have two-headed creatures in, or something else totally out of the ordinary. This was fun because of the unorthodox way I decided to do my premier piece. As far as I know, the narrated newspaper article format is unprecedented. I enjoy doing things that aren't like what anyone else does. It makes me a true individual and gives me my own personal style.*

I also liked writing it because I got to use my knowledge of genetic engineering. I plan to be a genetic engineer when I complete my education, and I took a genetic engineering course at SUNY Albany this summer, which is how I knew about DNA fingerprints and could draw one. I know what fingerprints look like because this summer I made four or five of them. I really enjoy showing off whenever I can without looking like a little bragger. I guess that's normal—who doesn't like to get compliments?

This piece went through many changes. As I wrote it, I constantly went back and proofread it, changing words to better convey my meaning, correcting spelling, and making it grammatically correct. Unfortunately, since I did all my writing and revising on the computer, I can't really cite specific examples [of edits] since that was written months ago and those kinds of changes don't tend to stick in my mind.

This portfolio is a good way to evaluate a student's performance through a school year and should be continued in years to come. In all honesty, I'm not sure which of two reasons dominates my suggestion to continue this project. It could be my sincere belief that this is worthwhile. It may also have to do with the fact that I want to see my brother, who is currently a freshman, go through this joy next year.

I hope you enjoy reading my premier piece as much as I enjoyed writing it.

—Johanna

Monstrous Remains

The things they find in the world today are beyond belief. I fail to see how people can think that some monstrous creature existed a long time ago. I suppose it was the offspring of Bigfoot and a little green Martian. The article I saw in the paper the other day said this thing was found in the mountains. It's absolutely absurd!

Monstrous Remains Found in Glacier   February 17, 1998

GENEVA—The remains of some creature of the past were found in an Alpine glacier yesterday. A Swiss Girl Scout troop who was taking a guided tour of a small glacier discovered the carcass. One girl, Bridgette Dunberg, noticed a "lump of something" in a crevasse. The remains were not immediately identified as anything recognizable. The tour guide, being educated about what to do in situations similar to this, called in Swiss authorities who removed the icy cadaver from the glacier. The remains were sent to leading anatomists for identification. First, a scientist quipped that it looked like Frankenstein's monster. After that, other literature parallels were explored. Ian Moore, an archaeologist who minored in medieval literature at Oxford University, hypothesized that it seemed that it could be the remains of Grendel in the tale of Beowulf, *if it had been a true story. When the text of* Beowulf *was reviewed, the sinewy appearance led scientists to share a shred of faith in the possibility that this once thought to be fictional tale may have a basis in truth. Testing is being planned currently to try to determine the origin or species of the carcass found in the crevasse.*

I said it was totally incredible! The things people will believe are amazing. I, on the other hand, am a complete realist, so I did not believe this stuff at all. I'd need some hard proof before I went around calling this new version of the mastodon or a Neanderthal man Grendel. *I thought, if this was a monster from a medieval piece of fiction, then O.J. Simpson did not kill Nicole Simpson and Ron Goldman. This was more like that criminal case than I thought.*

The field of genetic engineering has advanced by leaps and bounds, and, since the O.J. Simpson case, which was eventually dismissed due to long disputes over the validity of DNA tests carried out on Simpson's hair, DNA profiling, commonly called fingerprinting, has become accepted as court evidence. Techniques, similar to the fingerprinting *methods used in the O.J. Simpson case and many lawsuits since then, were used to attempt to identify the species of the remains. There were, of course, many articles in newspapers throughout the world, but this is the one from my local paper.*

Genetic Tests Performed on Alpine Carcass   February 19, 1998
GENEVA—Europe's top geneticists, paleontologists, and zoologists have been called together to identify the origin of the carcass discovered two days ago in a glacier near Geneva, just outside of a small town called Carouge, by a troop of Girl Scouts. The remains were rather well preserved, but nothing is yet known about the creature except that he was a large carnivore, about twelve feet tall, and it is believed that he did not freeze to death, but official cause of death has not been stated. This massive creature was first thought to be Frankenstein's monster. Latest theories include the possibility of this creature being Grendel *from the tale of* Beowulf. *Others believe it could be Bigfoot. The Bigfoot theory was dismissed because this being was not as hairy as a Sasquatch.*

The scientists are calling the creature Grendel *for lack of a better name. When the text of* Beowulf *was consulted, it was found that the description closely matched that of* Grendel. *The new* Grendel *has red eyes.*

Genetic tests are going to be carried out to compare the Grendel *DNA to other species. Also, molecular biologists are searching for cells preserved while dividing so that a chromosome number can be determined and that the species can possibly be identified. The chromosome number will only reveal information if the number is equal to that of a species similar to the new* Grendel. *When these tests are complete, we might end up with a key to the past or the most recent parallel to the Loch Ness Monster.*

Obviously, people were taking this thing very seriously, and I suppose it could have been a great advance in our knowledge of evolution if the results did not end up the way they did. The following Thursday, the testing came to an end.

Testing Complete: *Grendel* Not Identified   February 19, 1998
GENEVA—The final tests were completed on the glacier carcass Wednesday. The tests were inconclusive, and the mythological Grendel *is now born. The genetic tests revealed varied chromosome counts in different cells. Possibly this being had an irregular chromosomal configuration, or the cadaver was not as well preserved as first thought. The genetic profiles showed that the DNA had no similarities for it to qualify as that ani-*

mal. The DNA pattern on the left belongs to Grendel, *and the sequence on the right belongs to a gorilla. The pattern on the left in no way match-es the right, so the possibility of* Grendel *being a gorilla was dismissed. The same tests were done for numerous species, but none were any closer to a match. Thus we have the renaissance of the legend of* Beowulf.

So, the creature is now Grendel, *and the legend of* Beowulf *is believed to be writ-ten about the predecessor to the Loch Ness Monster, if that actually exists. Be on the lookout for the son of* Grendel, *lest ye be eaten and washed down with mead.*

Johanna's selection has enabled her to combine her interest in science fic-tion with her knowledge of literature, genetic engineering, and contemporary myth. Her creativity is evident both in her content and in her form. Her techni-cal expertise in using her computer program is also evident as she recreates the DNA fingerprints for her reader. Using the software and hardware that a multi-media CD portfolio lab would offer, Johanna could have sketched, morphed, and animated *Grendel*, incorporated a map of the site, filmed interviews with the Girl Scouts, shown the newspaper clips she actually created as clips torn from a local paper, and included copies of actual headlines from the O. J. Simpson trial in which DNA fingerprinting is alluded to. She could have created a color mag-azine cover with *Grendel* featured as the *person* of the week. Film footage that claims to have captured Bigfoot or the Loch Ness Monster on tape could be added. Johanna could even have created newspaper photographs of the remains taken at the cite. Other possibilities include an evening news segment where the public speculates on this find and, Johanna's favorite possibility, an animation of clay figures that she has created depicting *Grendel* on his daily rounds in his nat-ural habitat, which she has also crafted.

The excitement so evident in my students when we talk about the possibil-ities that a multimedia CD portfolio lab offers can only translate into learning. As teachers, we know that students become more aggressive learners when they feel that they are challenging themselves. The teacher becomes a facilitator for this type of discovery learning while students share with one another their enthu-siasm and their newfound knowledge. The multimedia CD portfolio enables stu-dents to proudly showcase a vast array of talents while exhibiting skills in read-ing, writing, listening, and speaking.

Chapter 7

The Reader Response Portfolio in the AP Literature Classroom: Creating an Autobiography of a Reader

Nancy Lester Elitzer
Shaker High School

I became a teacher eleven years ago because I love to read. I made my escape from the world of commercial banking to what I hoped would be a world of people who read and talked about books instead of balance sheets. I was, however, surprised to find that so many of my students were, by their own admission, not avid readers. Even in the honors-level classes, it was the rare student who had embraced reading as a value rather than something that was merely done as a school requirement. Why was this so?

I tried first to look inward, to find out why books are so important to me. I wasn't born an English major, but I was born into a family of readers. It was just something we did. Both my parents—my mother, a homemaker, and my father, a businessman—were always reading something. There was always a pile of books on my mother's night table and a list of book titles culled from book reviews or friends' suggestions in a small spiral notebook in her top night-table drawer. I remember these things vividly. Books were clearly important to them, and I got the hint. They also both read to my sisters and me, but it was my father—in his dark suit, exhausted after a long day at work and a long commute home, reading to us from *A Child's Garden of Verses* before we went to sleep—who seemed to personify the fact that there's always time to read if it's important enough to you.

When I talk to my students about their reading experiences and their families' reading habits, I see, not surprisingly, a correlation between the family's commitment to reading and the student's. Because the family environment is not usually producing readers, I have concluded that the school must establish reading as an important part of a fulfilling life. Therefore, I try to become a role model for my students, albeit a little late. If I can show them that reading is just one element of a multidimensional life and that books are a pleasure rather than a chore, I have a chance to impress some of my values on them and hope they stick. Before I could do this, however, I had to ascertain first why it was that I seemed to know who I was as a reader.

I have always liked having some tangible evidence of my intellectual achievements, if only as memory cues to compensate for my forgetfulness. The bookcases in my home are the most obvious evidence of most of my reading. Added to that would have to be local libraries and parts of my friends' houses, as well. If, in educational jargon, a portfolio is a sort of receptacle in which a student deposits materials to be used for future evaluation, aren't these bookshelves, in a way, my *portfolio*, my key to understanding myself as a reader?

The more I thought about my bookshelves, my metaphorical *portfolio*, the more I saw that the contents of my shelves are a visual, tangible reflection of the kind of reader I am. Even the way the books are arranged reflects the significance I give to them. The vast majority of my books are works of fiction. More than half are by women. They are split about equally between American and British authors, with a smattering of books in translation. Most of the hardcovers are by contemporary authors. There is an entire shelf of books by Victorian authors. I own everything that Jane Austen and Virginia Woolf ever wrote and most of what Edith Wharton, Jane Smiley, John Irving, Wallace Stegner, Anne Tyler, and Robertson Davies wrote. There are very few collections of short stories. My favorite books are the easiest to reach. What does this all say about me?

My goal became to take this unwieldy but very revealing *portfolio* and transfer it to my classroom. How could students discover the kinds of readers they are (or are becoming) the way I can by merely gazing at my bookshelves? The reader response notebook became the logical substitute, and herein lies my project. My students' reader response notebooks or reading portfolios had always been their tangible record of what they had read, but I had never examined the extent to which they could be used to chart a student's progress as a reader or trends in his or her reading.

The test group for my project is my twelfth-grade Advanced Placement (AP) English course. There are twenty-one students in my class, half of the students in the senior AP English program. These students are in this class for a variety of reasons, about which they were very forthcoming when I asked them at the beginning of the year why they wanted to take AP English. There certainly are the students who love books and language and who have always excelled at English. These students have kept journals on their own, love to write and have been writing poetry and stories for years, and are considering careers in which they can apply their love of language.

On the other side of the spectrum are the *math and science* people who have done well enough in English to qualify for the AP program, but who either don't

really like English or don't take it too seriously. One boy even admitted to sign-
ing up for the course because "one more AP course would look great" on his
high-school transcript, presumably increasing his chances of being accepted at
the most selective colleges. There is a sort of arrogance among these students
toward English classes. Because the work is not quantitative, they think it is less
important. These students are a tremendous challenge not only because their
math and science biases make them harder to reach, but because they are capable
of undermining the course by trivializing the subject matter. A flip comment
about a character in a novel, for example, can squelch another, more reticent student from participating in a discussion.

Somewhere in the middle of these two types of AP students is the student
for whom being admitted into the AP program is a personal coup, accomplished
after years of struggling for every A paper. Shaker High School's Advanced
Placement Preparatory Program begins in the ninth grade. Approximately half of
my students have been in the program since ninth grade, while the rest entered
later, with five entering as late as this year, on the basis of their performance in
their eleventh-grade honors classes, recommendations by former English teachers, and their personal reasons for wanting to be in senior AP English. These students typically are weak in one aspect of the course. They might not have read as
much for pleasure as other students in the class. They might not be accustomed
to writing critical papers as frequently. They might not have been expected to
participate in class discussions as extensively as the students with experience in
the AP program. For the most part, however, these students are a pleasure to
teach. They are hungry for knowledge, and they want to succeed. Not surprisingly, together we are often able to measure the biggest improvement in their
performance by the end of the year.

For the purposes of this project, I have decided to focus on three students
in this class. They represent a cross-section of the class inasmuch as individuals
can represent a whole. One falls into the first category I have delineated above—
Jennifer (all names are pseudonyms) has been in enriched or accelerated programs her whole life and is no stranger to the demands of an AP English course.
She comes from a home in which education is stressed and where reading is a
value. Evan falls into the second category. He is a star in math and science who
does not talk much in class. Carol is in the third category. She is in her second
year in the AP program and is noted in school for her excellence in athletics. She
plans to be a physical therapist.

Before I get to the case studies, I need to explain the evolution of what I
now call a *reading portfolio*.

I'm not entirely comfortable with the term *portfolio*. In many ways, it seems
to be a formalization of things I have always done in my classes. My students
have always kept writing portfolios that contain all the writing they've done over
the course of a year, from *creative* to formal, analytical writing. They use their
portfolios during the year to learn from their mistakes and assess their growth as

writers. I thought that the reader response notebook could be expanded and developed into a reading portfolio or, perhaps more appropriately, an *autobiography of a reader* for each student.

I decided to focus my research on the outside reading component of the course, because my students' response notebooks were used primarily to write about those books read outside of class. Initially, students did reader responses for books read in and out of class, but it became increasingly apparent quite early in the year that the responses they wrote on class material were more formal and stilted than the responses on outside reading. By limiting the writing in these notebooks to the outside reading, the notebooks became a place where students could write freely and uninhibitedly on books they had chosen themselves. Because I respond in depth but do not place a grade on their responses or correct their grammar and style, the notebooks, while still a required assignment, are not in the category of other class assignments. My comments focus more on what they have said, rather than on how they have said it, and I strive to be as nonjudgmental as possible. The purpose of the notebooks is to get my students to think and write about what they have read. There's nothing they can't write about. At the beginning of the year they are urged to write at least three times over the course of reading a book in order to trace their reactions at the beginning, the middle, and the end; but as the year progresses, they are encouraged to adapt the frequency and length of their entries to their own styles.

My hope is that each journal will give a vision of the student as a reader. By the end of the year, the journal should chronicle each student's choices, tastes, reactions, recommendations, and trends in his or her outside reading. It also, unwittingly, helps them in their more formal, critical writing because they are thinking, analyzing, and writing about literature in an informal, unthreatening context.

The first step in the outside reading component of the course is choosing a book. At the beginning of the school year, I passed out several book lists from which students could make their selections. During the year, I added titles and photocopied lists from newspapers and other places that I thought might interest them. They are encouraged to keep these book suggestions in their English folders. In their folders are lists of the Pulitzer Prize winners in fiction from 1918 to the present, the Booker Prize winners from 1969 to the present, a copy of a booklist from my Brown alumni monthly magazine entitled "A Multicultural Reading List," and a list of books that I compiled over one summer, which includes some of my favorite books and books that my students in the past have enjoyed (these lists are supplied in the Appendix). I always spend several days at the beginning of the year annotating these lists for them, because I think that handing a student a list of books is totally unproductive if something isn't said about the titles. Of course, I make it clear that my list represents my bias, that I haven't read all the books on the other lists, and that other books, not on the lists, are acceptable so long as they are not *schlock* (a wonderful, descriptive Yiddish word that defies concrete definition, but which anyone can understand in context).

The second step of an outside reading unit, as I have already discussed, is the reader response journal. I read these six times during the year, for each of the required outside reading selections. Many students opt to write on additional books they have read, and I try to comment on these as well. I collect the reader response notebooks on the day the book is due, and I usually get through them all within a week. I want the book they've read to be fresh in their minds when they reread their responses and my comments.

On the day the book is due, students do an in-class timed essay on a question of a kind they will likely find on an AP exam. I frequently give two or three choices from AP exams in years past, and I ask students to choose the question that best suits the book they have read. Most students appreciate this exercise. They usually do quite well on these graded papers, and they feel as if they are being directly prepared for the AP exam in May. It also gives them a chance to write formally on a subject about which they have been writing informally in their journals. I often see undeveloped ideas from their journals worked out articulately and coherently in their in-class essays.

On the day after the in-class essay, we start our book talks, which usually take about three class periods. Each person (including me) reports on his or her selection, giving a little background information, reading a favorite or representative passage, and then giving an evaluation or recommendation. We sit in a circle, as always, and there are sometimes conversations among people who have read the same books and among people who may disagree on a recommendation or condemnation of a particular book. The purpose of the book talks is for the students to illustrate orally what they have read and possibly to entice their classmates to follow their recommendations. I love it when they listen to each other, instead of depending on me for all their selections.

Many students begin the year reading books that I exclaim over, either because I love them myself or because they have been unequivocal hits with students in the past. John Irving's *The World According to Garp*, *Cider House Rules*, and *A Prayer for Owen Meany*; E. L. Doctorow's *Billy Bathgate*; Alice McDermott's *That Night*; Stephen McCauley's *The Object of My Affection*; Robertson Davies's' *Fifth Business*; and Jane Smiley's 1992 Pulitzer Prize-winning *A Thousand Acres* are examples of books that tend to make their way through the class by the end of the year based on student recommendations. If I get one student to read one of these, it's practically a guarantee that at least half the class will have read it by the end of the year. I am happiest when I hear my students telling each other which books they *have* to read. At the end of the course, we evaluate the reading list and try to figure out why people read certain books and not others.

Case Studies

Jennifer

Jennifer, as I mentioned earlier, is an excellent English student who loves to read and who comes from a home where reading is encouraged and valued. If anything, Jennifer is almost too prolific a reader; I think she sometimes races through books for the sake of finishing them and because she's been in a sort of competition with another student over who can read more books. I also think she wants to please me by reading many books, and after each long vacation, she proudly presents me with a list of all she has read. I'm thrilled that she loves to read, but I've tried to encourage her to take a little more time. She did, after all, read *All the President's Men* over a weekend, and, not surprisingly, could not really discuss it on any level beyond the details of the plot.

When Jennifer does focus on a book, however, her reactions and analyzes are wonderful. She embraces characters she admires, and they become alive in her writing. She understands characters in the contexts of their societies, while recognizing her late-twentieth-century perspective. She writes about *The Awakening* by Kate Chopin:

> *I enjoyed this book (except the ending) especially because Edna was a woman who challenged society's rules, was a strong character, and was not stereotypical of the women of her day. Also, she is an unusual woman by today's standards in terms of her thoughts.*
>
> *I do not condone her for her lack of maternal instinct and lack of true love for her children. Some women cannot be mothers or will not bind themselves to children and give up their freedom. There is nothing wrong with that. But women must decide whether to have children in the first place and how committed they will be to them. (Dan Quayle should read this book!)*

Jennifer's early entries were very long and often consisted of long quotations from the text and plot synopses. As the year progressed, she focused more on reacting and responding to the issues posed by the author. When she read *Cider House Rules* by John Irving, she tried very hard to see both sides of the abortion issue, even though she is decidedly pro-choice. She says of Dr. Larch, the doctor who "delivers orphans" and performs abortions:

> *It is okay to both deliver and abort babies as long as you know why you are doing it. If you believe strongly in your own cause and beliefs then no matter what society thinks, you have the right to act on it. However, there are rules for acceptable behavior. Thoughts and beliefs cannot be censored, but if your actions hurt others, then you cannot or should not have the right to act on them.*

Jennifer goes on to explore the controversy over a person's right to die and the variety of arguments for and against abortion, including the position of the Roman Catholic Church and the teachings of Judaism. She then takes these sometimes global, sometimes theoretical issues and applies them directly to Shaker High School:

> *Even at Shaker High, the number of teenage pregnancies has risen. When I was a freshman, it was a rare thing to hear of a senior who was preg-*

nant. Now, there are at least eight freshmen who are pregnant, or had babies, or had abortions. Also, there are so many risks involved because of all the sexually transmitted diseases out there and the HIV virus. Kids are sexually active at a younger age so choices are made earlier in life—regarding one's own body. It angers me that some organizations and administrations make decisions concerning teenagers, decisions which will have major impact on their lives. Why not let them make their own choices instead of imposing the morals of others on them? Democracy, as Dr. Larch says, is synonymous with individual freedom so if this country is democratic, then its leaders should allow the citizens the right to choose!

Jennifer's book choices for the remainder of the year focused primarily on books with historical or political themes. She is an avid student of history and began to read more books that dealt with events or time periods that had particularly interested her in her social studies classes. When she read *Gone With the Wind* by Margaret Mitchell, she was savvy enough not to be swept up by the romanticism of the book:

The high southern society in this book sees slavery as a benign institution. Slave owners thought that slaves were happy when in reality (look at Uncle Tom's Cabin*) they were miserable and uneducated. No brutality is shown or whip lashing. Mammy is depicted as a disciplinarian, a false portrayal of the position of the slave. . . . [T]he book lacks reality but it does show the view of the owners who saw slaves as happy and helpless. This type of attitude encouraged the spreading of slavery and probably prevented the South from changing its lifestyle sooner.*

Jennifer's journal entries synthesize her reading from in and out of class. Her closing comments on *Gone With the Wind* draw parallels to *The Age of Innocence* by Edith Wharton, which the class had just finished studying. She comments: "Both novels depict a type of materialistic society whose members hold fast to the status quo. Change comes and the societies must deal with the change or fade away into nonexistence."

It is with the next cluster of books that Jennifer read that I sensed an emerging Jewish consciousness that had not been evident in her earlier writings or in our conversations in and out of class. *The Winds of War* and *War and Remembrance* by Herman Wouk and *Exodus* by Leon Uris seemed to touch a nerve in this highly assimilated, secular, young Jewish woman. While she recognized that these books were not perhaps of the highest literary value, the issues and events in them captivated her. In her conclusion to her analysis of *The Winds of War*, Jennifer writes:

This book makes abundantly clear the injustices done to a group of people who differ only in their religion. They are singled out for extermination and even those supposedly humane like Franklin D. Roosevelt, aware of these crimes, do nothing to challenge the persecutors until it directly affects their own country. This fact made a powerful impression on me (as did

> *Elie Wiesel's* Night) *and left me with a deeper respect for my Jewish heritage and the heroic struggle of Jews to survive and preserve their culture. The killings that occurred in World War II must remain in the minds of today's teenagers so that there is never a recurrence. People must understand that each individual has the right to be different and worship in his/her own way. There will always be prejudice and violence, but reading books like this may serve to dismantle people's prejudices, or prevent wars, or educate the ignorant.*

On finishing *Exodus*, Jennifer writes:

> *My family visited Israel when I was nine and at the time all I could talk about was the sulphur infested water and the disgusting food. We visited the Wailing Wall, Masada, the Golan Heights, Haifa, Tel Aviv, and Jerusalem. As a little kid, I did not pay much attention to the historical places we saw. But now looking back, I wish that I had truly comprehended the sights I saw—created by the very men and women portrayed in* Exodus. *After reading* The Winds of War *and* Exodus, *I think that I have a greater understanding of my roots and the lure that a Jewish homeland has and had for so many children, and adults. No wonder survivors like Dou of the ghastly Auschwitz concentration camp wanted to go to Israel so badly. . . . I think that if I had the opportunity, I would visit Israel again.*

Since these journal entries, Jennifer and I have had numerous conversations about being Jewish in our society, the opening of the Holocaust Museum in Washington, the parallels to the genocide in Bosnia, and the recent conflict between black and Jewish students at Wellesley (where Jennifer will matriculate in September) over an allegedly anti-Semitic text used by an African American studies professor. I think Jennifer and I would have discussed some of these issues anyway; she is an articulate and loquacious person who is not shy with adults, but her reader response journal certainly provided a jumping-off point for our conversations and a perfect way to illustrate the relevance of literature to our lives.

Evan

Of all the journals I had to read during the year, I looked forward the most to reading Evan's journal. His writing—warm, sensitive, candid reactions to his reading—is in sharp contrast to his reluctant, monosyllabic comments in class discussions. He is one of the most reticent students I've ever had in an AP class. I'm still not sure I would recognize his voice if I heard it without seeing him first. I have tried every method I know to try to get him to talk in class, from prodding and cajoling to asking direct questions to *reminding* the class as a whole how important class participation is for their grade. Usually the last one work—these are very grade-conscious students—but not with Evan. After the first month of class, I even became a bit irritated with him. I saw his silence more as arrogance than shyness.

Then I read his journal. This practically nonverbal boy wrote the most wonderfully descriptive, conversational entries. I was surprised and delighted, and what ensued was a sort of pen-pal relationship with Evan that has lasted the entire year.

The only time Evan came to life in class was when he was talking about his outside reading. I thought, perhaps, that his talking so easily and confidently about these books would spill over into discussions on class texts, but it never did. After the first two rounds of book talks on outside reading, he even volunteered to go first, talking articulately about his book and reading competently from it.

The authors and characters of Evan's book selections come to life in his writing, and he lets them into his life by making connections from their stories to his own experiences. He writes about *An American Childhood* by Annie Dillard:

> *I really like the part where Annie talks about playing football with the boys on her street. (I know she's an author, but I feel comfortable calling her just plain Annie after reading this book because I feel like I know her). This is one of my favorite parts of the book, because I can completely picture the scene in my mind. It's strange, but the image of Annie playing football with a bunch of boys reminds me of my mother. When I was young, she would tell me how she was a tomboy. She has a scar on her forehead from falling off a desk. She was hopping from one desk to the other during a class, for one reason or the other, and she fell.*
>
> *The image of Annie Dillard playing football with the boys is one the best ways that one can understand her. There are no boundaries for her.*

Evan continues:

> *Early in her life, Annie awakens. It amazes me that such a young girl is very profound and thinks so extensively about life. When I was that age, I never thought about feeling alive or anything like that. It's only now when I think back on my childhood memories that I understand their significance. . . . For Annie, being awake meant feeling free, and realizing that the world around her is more than just a bunch of places you hear about in books or on the radio. I'm not sure what my awakened state is. Perhaps I am still asleep. Perhaps I'll never awaken. I don't think I'll ever understand my life as well as Annie Dillard understands hers.*

One of Evan's favorite books this year was *The Object of My Affection* by Stephen McCauley, a funny and poignant story of a young gay man, George, and his roommate, Nina, a young woman who, when she becomes pregnant by her longstanding boyfriend, wants George to help her raise her baby. Teenage boys are not usually the most enthusiastic audience for books about gay men (I'm not even going to offer my armchair psychoanalysis of this phenomenon), but Evan's enthusiasm about it helped make it one of the most read and well-received books in the class. He writes:

> *I seemed to really get to know George and Nina. George is funny and misunderstood. He kind of reminds me of my cousin Fred. Though Fred*

> *is not a homosexual, his outlook on life is quite similar to George's in that*
> *he is somewhat sarcastic but yet in awe of life. I like George because the*
> *reader really gets into his mind. I think if I saw George in a crowd, I*
> *could clearly recognize him. That's how well I think I know him.*

One of Evan's entries on *The Object of My Affection* was one of the most obvious illustrations of how ideas presented in a journal can later be developed and formalized into an analytical paper. One of the choices for the AP-style in-class essay that followed Evan's reading of this book dealt with setting. In his in-class essay, Evan shows how George and Nina's apartment is a metaphor for their lives; it is warm and comfortable, yet in a state of disarray. Evan very convincingly argues that the setting is essential to understanding the characters. I immediately recognized the roots of this analytical paper in his response journal. In his final entry, Evan writes:

> *Another thing that I enjoyed about this book was the Brooklyn apartment*
> *where the two lived. This is the center stage of the book. Come to think of*
> *it, I think this book could make a pretty good off-Broadway play. There*
> *aren't that many characters, and only a few major scene changes. And the*
> *story is very visual. The apartment is messy with food and papers scattered*
> *throughout the floor. There's an old record player with jazz albums scat-*
> *tered about, and an old, oversized air conditioner in the closet. It's the*
> *kind of apartment my mother dreads. Probably the kind of place that I'll*
> *be living in in a few years, considering the state of my room.*

I will certainly miss my correspondence with Evan.

Carol

Carol, our resident track star, impressed me initially with her confident, outspoken manner in class. An enthusiastic participant in class discussions in an unusually quiet class, Carol is a close, passionate reader who will defend a character she likes to the end.

Carol's selections for outside reading were often riskier and more experimental than most of her classmates. She prefers contemporary fiction and is not afraid of a writer whose style is somewhat experimental and who does not write in traditional narrative prose. She notices an author's style and often comments on it. Such analysis is surprising from a student whose critical writing early in the year was not always focused or well structured. About *July's People* by Nadine Gordimer, she writes:

> *Another example is the play for control and to be the* master. *At this point*
> *that seems to be Gordimer's main focus. This battle for power and sup-*
> *pressed feelings. A huge blowup between Maureen and July. You can total-*
> *ly see how ignorant of July's feelings Maureen was. July has a lot of resent-*
> *ment towards her. If he doesn't like her why did he take her into his home?*
> *This may be the most important part of the whole book and it amazes me*
> *how Gordimer included so much and got it to fit in so few pages. In about*

four pages she managed to convey the feelings that Maureen and July were feeling towards each other.

One of the most delightful aspects of Carol's entries is her commentary on the standards and morés of the societies in the books she has read. She writes about the southern society portrayed in *Cold Sassy Tree* by Olive Ann Burns:

> *Burns makes very clear that the whites in the south still had a superior attitude towards the blacks and that the Civil War hadn't changed their feelings on the subject at all. You can also see the attitude of the southern culture when it comes to social divisions. The fact that Will knew a girl from the Mill town was very disturbing to his parents because what if the community thought they were together? Not only is the southern culture divided between black and white but also by how much money they have. The saddest thing is society is still like that to a certain extent now.*

Carol goes on to analyze Penelope Lively's technique in *Moon Tiger*:

> *I like the way Lively casually has Claudia make really important statements: "Language tethers us to the world; without it we spin like atoms" (41). Claudia's view on religion is really true; all of us rely on God when we need something from him—we're willing to do anything for him if he'll just do that one thing and then later we forget what we promised.*

Carol elaborates:

> *It's hard to write my thoughts about this book because it seems like almost every sentence makes an impression on me—it is hard to choose what is important to write about and what is not. I like this book because like July's People it has really made me think and then reread them again before I can totally comprehend what is being said. "Giving presents is one of the most possessive things we do, did you realize that? It's the way we keep hold on other people. Plant ourselves in their lives" (110). It's totally true with guys. They love to give you things. I've just started dating someone and so far I've gotten a hat, a tape, and a pair of socks. It's just funny that I read this right now because I can totally relate to it. Right in the middle of all this deep psychological stuff that you have to reflect on is a simple statement like this one that just hits you because it is so true in your own life.*

Conclusion

At the beginning of the school year, I promised my students that they would read books in and out of class over the course of the year that would influence their lives, make them think, and get them excited about literature. I hope that I have kept my promise to them. These three case studies are the encouragement that I have.

At the end of the year, I asked my students to evaluate the outside reading component of the course—in particular their journals or reading portfolios or *autobiographies of readers* or whatever you care to call them. The mostly anonymous evaluations were overwhelmingly positive. Almost all of the students said they would continue to read for pleasure and that they expected reading to be part of their lives as adults. They found my annotated reading lists extremely helpful in deciding what to read. Most surprisingly, the majority of students actually enjoyed writing in their journals, and even the ones who did not were able to see the benefit of recording their thoughts.

It was interesting for me to see what they thought of themselves as readers. Some discovered certain genres they plan to continue reading, and others commented on how they had read books that they would never have read before this year. As one student said, "Now I may choose to read a John Irving book, for example, rather than another lame baseball biography."

A copy of my evaluation form is given in form 7.1. What follows is a verbatim transcription of Jennifer's, Evan's, and Carol's responses. I think they speak for themselves.

Form 7.1

OUTSIDE READING COMPONENT OF ENGLISH 12 AP: STUDENT EVALUATION

This evaluation may be done anonymously.

1. How did you decide what to read? Please comment on the usefulness (or uselessness) of the book lists I gave you, the book talks, and other sources of recommendations that led you to your choices.

2. Please describe your feelings toward the Reader Response notebook. What do you see as its function? Have your feelings toward it changed since the beginning of the year? What have you learned from it? What is your reaction to my comments? Should it be graded? The more detailed you are here, the better, since this is the focus of my research.

3. What did you think of the book talks? Did you enjoy them? Were they boring? Did you read a book because of someone else's book talk?

4. Please comment on the in-class AP-type essays that followed each outside reading unit. Did they help you prepare for the AP exam?

5. Please evaluate yourself as a reader. Have you changed since the beginning of the year? Did you read for pleasure before this year? Do you think pleasure reading will be a part of your life as an adult? Have you discovered particular authors or genres (types of books) that you will continue to read in the future?

6. What is your overall feeling about the outside reading component of the course? Did you enjoy it? Please make any additional comments, criticisms, or suggestions that may help me in the future.

Student Self-Assessments and Evaluations

Jennifer

1. *I decided what to read based on your book lists and your recommendations about books that I would enjoy. Also, our book talks gave me insight into books I would enjoy reading. The booklists also provided a wide variety of choices and genres so I was able to read a book with Native American culture (Animal Dreams), a multicultural book (I Know Why the Caged Bird Sings), and a book with a moral conscience (Cider House Rules). I also found friends' inputs to be helpful especially when their tastes coincided with mine. Thus, friends' enjoyment of books by John Irving and Leon Uris encouraged me to read (respectively)* Cider House Rules *and* Exodus.

2. *I found the Reader Response notebook to be very effective because it not only organized my thoughts coherently, but it provided me with a reference to look back on. I found that it was difficult to stop in the middle of reading a book and record my thoughts in the journal. Instead, I often wrote a synopsis, commentary, and specific passages I found important to my understanding of the book in my journal at the conclusion of my reading. But I did, however, write down page numbers of key passages I wanted to remember as I read. I think that the Reader Response notebook allowed me to examine in depth my own reactions to situations, characters, or themes in the book and relate it to my own life. The notebook for me was an avenue for self-examination and I experienced over the course of the year, a growing awareness of my own Jewish heritage and an understanding of different cultures and time periods. At first, I found writing in the notebook to be a chore but over the course of the year I have enjoyed writing in it. I think that grading the journals would be a big mistake because it would restrict the free expression of the reader and cause students to view it as an "assignment to be completed" rather than a means of creative writing. Your comments, including your suggestions for future reading, were very positive. I was surprised by the length of your comments considering all of the journals you had to read. But I always like exchanging opinions and ideas on books with someone else who has also read the same books so I liked your comments a great deal. Finally, I think that this type of response has enabled me to be more open in my writing and has helped me to analyze literature we have read in class.*

3. *This was the first time that I had been exposed to book talks, and it was definitely worthwhile. I enjoyed hearing how different individuals relate to the books—what they talked about and the quotations students chose also give a glimpse into their character. In some cases, too much plot summary tended to mix all the books together in my mind. A book stood out from the rest if the person describing it sounded enthusiastic. Quotations that are powerful also catch my*

interest. Although I did not choose a book because of someone else's book talk, now that APs are almost over I have more time to read. I would definitely like to read books by Tama Janowitz.

4. *I found the AP essays to be very helpful in preparation for the exam. I would suggest doing more in-class essays to resolve the time factor problem.*

5. *Recently, while studying for the AP, I reread my journal entries and found that my writing improved. For my first book, I found my chapter to chapter responses pretty boring although I would have a good commentary at the end. But with each book, my entries grew longer, not in plot summary, but in exploring topics covered in the novels. Now when I write an entry I have so much to say and examine about a book. My writing also evolved from a choppy stream of consciousness to a more coherent, linked series of ideas with more of my own experiences brought in. This has been the biggest year for me in terms of the number of pleasure books I've read because I have never had an English teacher who conducts book talks, reads voraciously, and loves books that a student my age can also read and enjoy. Usually, I read a great many books in the summer which are enjoyable but do not have that much depth in them in terms of themes. I have always loved books but this year, due to your lists, I have a whole new set of books and authors to delve into! I am glad that I have read historical fiction (my favorite genre) this year but I am equally happy that I had the courage (ha!) to try other genres like* Cider House Rules *and* Animal Dreams. *I will always read for pleasure because it is a stress reliever (mentally) for me and it allows my imagination to wander. I would like to read more books by Uris, Kingsolver, Angelou, Irving, and Doctorow in the future.*

6. *I feel very strongly that the outside reading component of the course is essential to the curriculum. It allows students to do more creative rather than analytical writing and encourages students to read more. I have never read so much for an English class or enjoyed reading so much for a class, and I hope my experience in reading will be even further heightened in college. I think that increasing the number of outside reading books in the future will cause students to read even more even though some may find that reading more is tedious and too demanding.*

7. *I think it is so unique and wonderful to have a teacher who reads so much herself for pleasure because it helps a student identify with the teacher and establish a good relationship. Many English teachers do not have the time or inclination to read for pleasure and also distance themselves from students because they believe in a firm wall of separation between a student and a teacher. This is not really bad but I think that the environment is not as conducive to learning and exchanging ideas.*

Evan

1. *I decided what to read primarily from that day when you first handed out the book list and gave a brief description of each novel. After that day, I already knew that I wanted to read* The Bonfire of the Vanities *and* The Object of My Affection *because what you said about them really appealed to me. For my other selections, I relied on the book talks. But I also tried to select books that not many people in the class had read, like* At Risk. *I stayed away from things like* Garp, *though I plan to read some of those over the summer.*

2. *As the year went on, I better understood the function of the Reader Response notebooks. In the beginning, I thought that we had to concentrate more on plot synopsis and that sort of thing. When I re-read my* Bonfire *entries, that was what I seemed to have done. But after reading your comments, I began to better understand how to approach the Reader Response notebooks and it became much easier to write entries. So I guess that as the year went by, I began to like the Reader Response notebooks more and more. The Reader Response notebooks made me think more about what I was reading a little more profoundly, but other than that, I really don't think that I can learn anything from them until a couple of years from now, when I can go back and re-read what I wrote. Then I can look at what I wrote and see what I thought back then, and see if I still feel the same way. Maybe it will even drive me to re-read the entire book over, just because of my curiosity. The reader response notebook should definitely not be graded because that would put some unneeded pressure on the student to try to write something that impresses the teacher, and it might not truly reflect that student's real feelings.*

3. *I enjoyed the book talks because it was fun to hear what the other students thought about certain books. Sometimes it was hard to listen to the passages people were reading because I didn't fully understand the context of the passage. Once I read a book because of someone else's book talk, and that was* The Male Cross-Dresser Support Group *(your book talk) because it sounded hilarious.*

4. *The AP-type essays that followed each outside reading unit were not bad at all. I found them to be straight forward and I could always find something to write about. They helped me prepare for the AP because they showed what kind of questions would be asked.*

5. *I don't think that I've changed as a reader that much. I have always read for pleasure, and I know that pleasure reading will continue to be a part of my adult life. The type of books that I have discovered I liked are ones about contemporary life, especially New York City life. That's why I read* Bonfire *and* The Object of My Affection *and others. Stephen McCauley is an author who I think I will read more of.*

6. The outside reading was a valuable part of the course. I like how it introduced me to a great number of great writers. I can't think of any criticisms about it. Reading and then periodically telling the class about it is a fine system.

Carol

1. I usually looked to the book lists that you gave us. At the beginning of the year I starred the names of the titles of the books from the list that I thought sounded interesting. Also, the brief descriptions were a big help because it gave me some idea of what the book was about. I tended not to read books that other people in the class talked about because I didn't want to give a talk on a book people had already heard about, but the book talks did give me some ideas for books that I can read during my free time in the summer. The only book I read from suggestions you wrote in my journal was A Thousand Acres. The way I chose books was probably pretty random—whatever sounded interesting at the time.

2. I have to admit that every time I went to write in my journal I resented having to do it because it reminded me of just another homework assignment. However, once I got started and was thinking about what I had just read I really got immersed in my thoughts and would end up writing a lot more than I originally intended to. I guess the function of my reader response was to serve as a means to rethink about what I had just read and see how it related or didn't relate to my own life. A lot of times while I was writing something would just click and I'd be writing about an aspect of the book that I hadn't even thought about previously. I guess now that it is over I appreciate the journal more because I honestly do go back and see what I had written about a book and it's interesting to see your own thoughts on paper. It kind of gives me an idea of how my mind works and how I relate things. It gave me a new perspective of myself and my thoughts on different issues that I wouldn't have had if I didn't write my thoughts on these books down on paper. I was always curious to see what you had to say at the end of my journal entries. It was interesting to see if you thought the same things I did or if you couldn't understand where I had gotten all of these ideas about the book. I was also usually relieved that for the most part you understood my views and I wasn't totally off-base and had misinterpreted everything. I guess your comments were reassuring. I liked the fact that the notebooks weren't graded because it gave me more freedom to express myself without the threat of a grade looming over my head. It's easier for me to write what I really feel when I know someone is not deciding the merit of my thoughts.

3. I enjoyed the book talks because it was interesting to hear other people's reactions to what they read. I did think it got a little boring

when people just went over the plot but never said why they liked the book or what it made them think about.

4.   *I thought the in-class essays were very helpful because they taught me how to think quickly. Since it was timed I didn't have the time to sit and worry about what I was going to say. The more of them I wrote the better I got at collecting my thoughts and expressing my views quickly and effectively. Also, I had to learn to find a way to make my book fit one of the questions even when I didn't think it really did. I think that by having experienced this already I was ready to handle the AP essay better and it seemed easier because I had more than one book to pick from. I'm glad the AP exam wasn't my first experience at having to write one of those essays under a time constraint.*

5.   *I've always liked to read and I have read for pleasure before this year. I think the biggest change that I've experienced as a reader is the degree of quality of what I read now and what I used to read. The books that I have read this year are of a better merit and now I think more about what I have read—maybe it's from doing all the journals. I know that now I can't just pick up a dime-store novel and enjoy it. I think now I'm a lot more critical in choosing what to read and maybe a more sophisticated reader. I found that I really enjoy books that deal with social issues and problems with society, when before I used to read a lot of cheesy romance novels. Now, I like books where I may get frustrated with the attitudes of some of the characters but like getting perspective on an issue, and I like trying to understand why a person would think the way they do.*

6.   *I really enjoyed the outside reading this year.*

Appendix

AP English Suggested Outside Reading

What follows is a list of some of my favorite books and books that my students in the past have enjoyed. They include long, classic, Victorian novels and short, fun, contemporary American books, fiction and nonfiction. This is by no means a definitive list! I will annotate this list for you in class, so that you will have an idea of what each book is about. Over the course of the year, I would like you to select books that represent different styles and themes by authors of varied backgrounds. If you would like to read a book that is not on this list, please see me first. I hope that by the end of the year, we will have added many new books that you will discover on your own.

Fiction

Author's Name	Title
Atwood, Margaret	*Cat's Eye*
Austen, Jane	*Emma*
Barker, Pat	*Regeneration*
Beattie, Ann	*Love Always*
Benedict, Elizabeth	*The Beginner's Book of Dreams*
Brontë, Charlotte	*Jane Eyre*
Brontë, Emily	*Wuthering Heights*
Burns, Olive Ann	*Cold Sassy Tree*
Cather, Willa	*My Antonia*
Collins, Wilkie	*The Moonstone*
	The Woman in White
Conroy, Pat	*Prince of Tides*
Davies, Robertson	*Fifth Business*
	What's Bred in the Bone
Dickens, Charles	*David Copperfield*
Doctorow, E. L.	*Billy Bathgate*
Dorris, Michael	*A Yellow Raft in Blue Water*
Drabble, Margaret	*The Ice Age*
Eliot, George	*The Mill on the Floss*
Erdrich, Louise	*Love Medicine*
Esquivel, Laura	*Like Water for Chocolate*
Faulkner, William	*As I Lay Dying*

Fitzgerald, F. Scott	*Tender is the Night*
Forster, E. M.	*A Passage to India*
	A Room With a View
	Howard's End
Fowles, John	*The French Lieutenant's Woman*
Garcia, Christina	*Dreaming in Cuban*
Gordimer, Nadine	*July's People*
Helprin, Mark	*Winter's Tale*
	A Soldier of the Great War
Hoffman, Alice	*Seventh Heaven*
	At Risk
Irving, John	*The World According to Garp*
	Cider House Rules
	A Prayer for Owen Meany
Ishiguro, Kazuo	*The Remains of the Day*
Janowitz, Tama	*Slaves of New York*
Kennedy, William	*Ironweed*
Kincaid, Jamaica	*Annie John*
Kingsolver, Barbara	*The Bean Trees*
	Animal Dreams
Lawrence, D. H.	*Women in Love*
	Sons and Lovers
Leavitt, David	*Family Dancing*
Lively, Penelope	*Moon Tiger*
Márquez, Gabriel García	*Love in the Time of Cholera*
Maupin, Armistead	*Tales of the City*
McCauley, Stephen	*The Object of My Affection*
McDermott, Alice	*That Night*
McFarland, Dennis	*The Music Room*
Mitchell, Margaret	*Gone With the Wind*
Morrison, Toni	*Song of Solomon*
	Beloved
Plath, Sylvia	*The Bell Jar*
Piercy, Marge	*Gone to Soldiers*
Quindlen, Anna	*Object Lessons*

Rand, Ayn	*The Fountainhead*
Roiphe, Anne	*Lovingkindness*
Shute, Nevil	*A Town Like Alice*
Simpson, Mona	*Anywhere But Here*
Smiley, Jane	*A Thousand Acres*
Stegner, Wallace	*Angle of Repose*
Steinbeck, John	*East of Eden*
Styron, William	*Sophie's Choice*
Tan, Amy	*The Joy Luck Club*
Tartt, Donna	*The Secret History*
Taylor, Peter	*A Summons to Memphis*
Tyler, Anne	*Dinner at the Homesick Restaurant*
	Saint Maybe
	Morgan's Passing
Updike, John	*Rabbit Run*
Uris, Leon	*Exodus*
	Trinity
Walker, Alice	*The Color Purple*
Warren, Robert Penn	*All the King's Men*
Waugh, Evelyn	*Brideshead Revisited*
Wharton, Edith	*Custom of the Country*
	The House of Mirth
Wolfe, Tom	*Bonfire of the Vanities*
Wouk, Herman	*Marjorie Morningstar*
	The Winds of War
Wright, Austin	*Tony and Susan*

Nonfiction

Baker, Russell	*Growing Up*
	The Good Times
Conway, Jill Ker	*The Road From Coorain*
Dillard, Annie	*Pilgrim at Tinker Creek*
Dinesen, Isak	*Out of Africa*
Markham, Beryl	*West with the Night*
Mayle, Peter	*A Year in Provence*

McPhee, John   *Coming into the Country*

Wolf, Tobias   *This Boy's Life*

Books I intend to read and books I haven't read or can't remember well enough to speak intelligently about that my former students have liked:

Capote, Truman   *Breakfast at Tiffany's*

Carroll, Lewis   *Alice in Wonderland*

Dillard, Annie   *An American Childhood*

Hesse, Herman   *Steppenwolf*

James, Henry   *The Turn of the Screw*

Kinsella, W. P.   *Shoeless Joe*

Paton, Alan   *Cry, The Beloved Country*

Vonnegut, Kurt   *Breakfast of Champions*

Chapter 8

TURNING PRO: STUDENTS AS COLLEAGUES

Melissa DiVisconti
Sarah Leonard
Joseph A. Quattrini
Austin Willoughby
Canajohairie High School

What Is a Portfolio?

What is a portfolio? First, what it *isn't*:

- a new name for what we've always done (it's not a new name, and we haven't always done it, not in language arts);

- the latest buzzword (*shared decision making* might qualify for a buzz word, but *portfolio* can refer to actual events);

- a glorified writing folder (a writing folder is a portable crypt, a holder of documents on temporary reprieve from the wastebasket, handed over annually, with great ceremony and no reading by anyone, to next year's teacher);

- a different angle on traditional instruction (collaborative learning might fit this category, especially when three people work together to memorize data no one really needs to commit to memory in the first place);

- a paradigm shift (reducing the number of strands in a curriculum model from five—reading, writing, speaking, listening, and literature—to three—reading, writing, and speaking/listening—is a paradigm shift).

None of these definitions wholly embraces what a portfolio can be, for a portfolio *can be* a wholly different circumstance:

- a philosophy of education whose focus is on learning and growth, rather than on teaching and testing;

- a methodology for learning that turns inside out, upside down, and out the door a good deal of traditional practice;

- a powerful generative context for working: the people, the activities, and the products of a discourse community; in this context—your classroom—you can abandon the attempt to apply authentic assessment to inauthentic assignments (*the* comparison-contrast theme, *the* persuasive speech, the research paper, etc.) and engage students in the activities of professionals in language arts.

What Does It Mean to Turn Pro?

During the portfolio project, I had the luxury and limitation of working alone at my research site, so I had to involve students as decision makers. To get outside the box, the typical contexts, I asked these students to turn professional in the game of language arts. To see what this means, consider what language arts professionals do. Professionals set their own standards, take responsibility for their work, communicate in insiders' language with others, have access to all the materials they need, plan their own work, assess their own performance, submit their work for peer review, read and write professionally, present at conferences and seminars, recommend works to their colleagues, conduct research, form and explore interesting questions, and make a thousand decisions every year about the nature and value of their work.

And consider what they *don't* do. They don't write many term papers or take many tests—not many book reports or worksheets, either. Professionals could go decades without taking a multiple-choice test. They don't have their work parceled out for them in one-day slices. Their work is used by themselves and by others, but their homework isn't collected. Teachers' guides and other resources are not denied them. Decisions are made by and about them, but they don't get grades every five weeks on report cards. Except for certain political circumstances, they spend their time thinking, not guessing what others are thinking.

There are some prerequisites for students turning professional in a secondary school context. For this to work, students, as members of a discourse community, need to understand and to be able to apply the metacognitive language of this community. Before they can do that, they need to know they're in one. Before they can do that, they need to *be* in one.

How Do We Know When Someone Is Ready to Turn Pro?

In professional sports, there's no problem telling. You get a tryout, and either you can play at that level or you can't. For high-school students, the language arts professional tryout should allow teacher and student to see who can play at this level, who can do what professionals do (that is, write, research, confer, collaborate, present, and manage their own learning).

Instead of endeavoring endlessly to articulate the *field*—which is only where the game is played—we should be attending to the *levels of play*.

What, Exactly, Is a Colleague?

Is a colleague anyone who has the same general job as I do—educator? Someone who works in the same field or discipline—language arts? Someone who has the same credentials—master's degree? Who works in the same school system—Canajoharie? In the same department at the same level—English, secondary?

Or are my colleagues the people I work with—in my classroom—five days a week for a school year, the people whose works and work I have come to know intimately, the people in my most immediate daily discourse community, the only people in the school system without whom I could not do my job, the people whose accomplishments are the best and most telling measure of my own?

There are some rules for honest dealings with colleagues. Here are some I try to follow (it is much easier for students to follow rules, since the system doesn't allow them to make many without my approval):

1. I don't withhold from them any resources at my disposal: answer keys, sidebar magic lore in teacher's manuals, methods of inquiry, evaluation criteria, models, rubrics, or anything else I need and use to do my work in language arts.

2. We engage in no activities in which the sole or main purpose is to produce a grade or to be able to say we have done it ("Okay, we've done the research paper").

3. We admit that, except for state-mandated Regents exams and exams such as the AP English exam, all activities, assignments, and assessments are subjective matters, matters of teacher and student judgment. (Commercially-made or teacher-made multiple-choice tests may seem to be objective, since even a machine can score them, but the decision to use them—indeed, the belief in their efficacy—is a subjective matter. A departmental exam is group or joint subjectivity.)

4. We need to negotiate almost everything, including what will be open to

negotiation. Our academic standards must be explicit agreements: everything from goals to activities to assessment criteria and methods.

5. As many revisions as wanted are allowed, until actual presentation or publication or contest deadlines arrive, or until a marking period ends. We have to be more concerned with revising ourselves as language users than with getting any one piece *right*.

6. Class time must be allocated for the individual activities they've planned to help them accomplish their language arts goals—as individuals, in portfolio groups, and as a whole class.

7. My goals must be in harmony with the *New York State Curriculum and Assessment Frameworks for English Language Arts*. Their goals must be in harmony with mine. We have to see the curriculum not as a box but as a group of vectors, all contingencies or possibilities.

8. We have to set a context for risk taking; I have to be as ready as they are to take them. Almost everything we'll want to do will involve breaking some rule or traditional practice.

9. Conversations about literature and writing and pedagogy—the ones I used to have in the faculty room and at conferences—I need to have in the class room.

10. We all need to be involved in real work, and I have to use their work fairly in ways that are aboveboard. Not sound bites or snippets I select, but copresentation and coauthorship, as in this piece. Rather than culling their portfolios for evidence to support my claims, I asked them to bring their voices to this conversation, to say what they have to say about turning professional in a high-school language arts classroom. Austin, Melissa, and Sarah accepted this challenge.

I asked them to work in three different ways. I asked Austin Willoughby, a senior, to expand on the ten *rules* and give his views on them. Melissa DiVisconti, a junior, was asked to focus on the effects of working for herself by setting goals and designing the activities to achieve them. I thought it would be interesting for Sarah Leonard, another senior, to make a chronology of her two years of professional activities. The views from these colleagues will reflect the kinds of collaboration made possible in a portfolio classroom.

First, Austin writes about these ten *rules* from his point of view, according to his two years of experience in a portfolio context. Next, Melissa speaks of the effects of setting her own goals and, as a result, working for herself. Finally, Sarah gives a two-year chronology of some of her collegial activities in and out of the classroom.

Austin Willoughby on Rules

1. *There are no resources that are withheld from us in the portfolio class.* In my traditional classes the teachers have always seemed to have the same general attitude—hide the answer key and hide it well. Those teachers kept the answers secret and the steps to achieving those answers secret purposely so they would be able to see how adept the student was at extracting the meaning as defined by the hidden answer key. In the portfolio class the teacher doesn't need to worry about leaving things hidden for the students to uncover on their own in order to test the students' abilities to fact find. The portfolio class doesn't test to see what facts the students can dig up and memorize to answer forty multiple-choice test questions. The material used for testing in the traditional class is transformed to serve a new purpose in the portfolio class—that purpose is to build a foundation for the students to expand on, forcing the students to look into the work more and to find the deeper meaning that the answer sheet does not contain. I found this type of reading more fulfilling because the class brought out many ideas and theories about the work that may not have been seen if the teacher only worried about reaching the answer key's surface value meaning. In the portfolio class the ideas were from the students, not the teacher-prompted answer key.

2. *We do no projects just to say that we have done them.* The research project isn't done just to do a research project, if it is done at all. If a research project is in fact done in the portfolio class, it is to help develop the goals of the student who does the project. No projects are done just to give the entire class an overall idea of how to do the project. Any project done is aimed at accomplishing the goals of the student who is completing the project. Students are thereby not tied down doing a research project with little significance in relation to their goals, but they are allowed to work on the goals they set. This year, in another course, I was involved in a research project that was intended to teach us the history of mathematics. This research project took up so much time that nothing else could be accomplished in the class. The subject of the project had little to do with the overall layout of the course, but still the project was required. The project was finished in about two weeks, leaving us behind in the coursework and with little idea as to the usefulness of the project.

3. *Instead of tests the portfolio class uses assessments and group ratings to determine progress.* The subjectivity of the course leaves much latitude for the students because they are not bound by the guidelines of a test as they are in a traditional class. In the portfolio class, a student might have the goal of writing for information and understanding. The progress of the student depends on whether he or she can show the goal was accomplished. If the

students, as I did, develop a way to keep notes in an organized and coherent manner, they could use this in their grade proposals by explaining that they developed a convention that facilitated the accomplishment of their goal. In the traditional class, this would not be a viable option because no test can measure the personal success of a student on his or her goals. Students are more free in the portfolio class to accomplish their individual goals, rather than worrying about the test coming on Friday.

4. *The first day of school we decided upon what we would allow to happen in the portfolio class.* It was in this negotiation of what the class would contain that we decided exactly what could be negotiated—the foremost product of that negotiation was the grade proposal. We decided there would be no individual grades, save one: a quarter grade proposed in the grade proposal and negotiated between the student and teacher on a basis of the work done throughout the quarter. The grade proposal uses *Toulmin Logic*—in the form of claim, warrant, and data—to present proof and justification for the grade proposed. This allows the students to express in words what they feel they deserve and then base this proposal on evidence pulled from the class.

5. *The multiple revisions that are allowed in the portfolio class give the students the opportunity to make their work the best that it can be.* We can make our writings as insightful and telling as possible because there are no limitations placed on us as writers. The revisions help make us better language users by allowing us to detect and correct our mistakes. They also make us better writers through improving our own works. I revised one poem several times—not until I received a high grade on the piece, but until I was satisfied with what the piece presented about me as an author. This poem became one of my favorite writings for two reasons: because it was a telling and compelling piece of my memory, and because I had worked on the piece for so long that there was a part of me on paper. This wasn't a poem written on a Thursday night to meet a Friday morning deadline.

6. *To increase student-to-student interaction and student-to-teacher interaction, time must be given in class for projects.* This time can be spent accomplishing goals through ten- or twelve-day plans that help the students to design methods for accomplishing their goals in class. This allows students to be in charge of their learning while giving them a schedule to work on and to facilitate the accomplishment of the goals in the areas in which the students feel they need more work. For instance, I wanted to focus on reading for information and understanding. On my twelve-day plan I worked with another student who took AP Biology with me later in the day. Together we went through parts of the text that were difficult for either of us and reviewed the parts until the text began to unravel and present itself to us.

7. *While we attempt to keep the class flexible for the student goals, which take on a wide range of different areas, the class must still remain in the realm of the New York State Curriculum and Assessment Frameworks for English Language Arts.* The curriculum, though, does not hold the students back or limit them; instead, the students work within it, and it gives them ways to accomplish their individual goals. The curriculum framework offers works and literary projects for the students to use toward accomplishing their goals throughout the year. The language standards offered by New York provide the students with the opportunity to work in areas where they need to progress. Because of its flexibility, the portfolio class is suited to this.

8. *In our attempts to break the confines of the traditional classroom, we break the rules and do some different things.* The traditional classroom is about the teacher leading the student and directing that student's learning throughout the year on a basis of what the entire class must accomplish. The portfolio class is about the student becoming more involved in his or her own learning. The students take the responsibility to understand what areas they need work in and how to accomplish the work needed to accomplish their goals. The portfolio class puts the student in the driver's seat of the classroom. In a way, the student leases the class from the teacher and is responsible for what happens and what is accomplished in the class. The teacher is like the landlord and only directs the class when new developments or repairs are necessary.

9. *Conversations usually held in the privacy of teacher conferences and faculty rooms are held within the classroom with the students.* It is important that the students are involved in conversations about the learning process, since they are the topic of the conversation. Students need to develop and help to formulate the process to suit themselves, making the class work for them. The portfolio class has given me the opportunity to attend many conferences and produce several writings for professional journals that were before closed to the very subjects they discussed—learners. I have written for the *Ohio Journal of English Language Arts* and for the New York State English Council (NYSEC) monograph series. I have also spoken at conferences for NYSEC and SUNY—Oneonta. These experiences were at one time regarded as teacher events to discuss how students learn; not until now could they be seen as learner-driven conferences to show teachers what helps students to learn.

10. *There should be no "busy work" in a classroom, and in the portfolio classroom this is true.* The class works at making students colleagues and co-teachers in the classroom. Students ought not to be separated from the learning process by the teaching process; they must be included in all decisions of the classroom. Everything is up for discussion and nothing is left totally in the hands of the teacher, because choices about learning decisions are mutual

and must be agreed upon by students and teachers alike. Students help decide which projects will be done and the ways in which those projects will be assessed.

Melissa DiVisconti on Setting Goals

My Goals

This past year has been my first in a portfolio classroom. However, it is already obvious to me that this program opens many more doors for me than any other class I have been a part of. In the past, my English classes could be described in one of two ways. First, there were the classes in which the only information I obtained was in the form of the rules of grammar, spelling, and vocabulary. My memorization, not my language skills, was tested on a weekly basis. The rest of my classes had a much lighter workload, but did not provide me with the challenges I was looking for. This year, however, I have been exposed to a completely new experience, one in which my work is significant and the assignments are designed by me in order to build on my strengths and work on my weaknesses. In this class I am treated as a colleague as well as a student.

In my opinion, all of us as human beings can know our own strengths and weaknesses. We can learn exactly what we need to do in order to eliminate those weaknesses. Keeping this in mind, it is apparent that, through setting our own goals and working toward them in our own ways, we as students can be more successful in achieving those goals. This idea is what makes a portfolio classroom so effective. For example, in the first week of school, I was asked to make a list of goals that I wanted to achieve in order to improve upon my language skills. I set four goals, one for each of the four standards of the *New York State Curriculum and Assessment Framework for Language Arts*. In the area of using language for personal expression, I wanted to expand my range. That is, I wanted to increase my writing's depth and breadth with respect to forms and subjects. In the area of using language for social interaction, I wanted to master the use of language conventions, such as the rules of language. For the standard for information and understanding, I wanted to gain flexibility and become more versatile with respect to purpose and audience. For critical analysis and interpretation, I decided to work on establishing connections and transferring learning from my experiences into my work. Finally, I wanted to use my work in all of these areas to become more independent in the development, planning, and evaluation of my own work. If a teacher had set these goals for me, I don't believe that I would have worked so hard to achieve them. On the other hand, because I knew that I was working for myself, I put all of my effort into my work.

My Activities

It hardly seems logical, after setting goals according to your own needs, to do only those assignments created by the teacher. This is the reason for projects such as the list of twelve activities that I had to construct. This list was a schedule for me to follow in order to achieve my goals. The activities were all selected by me, and some of theses activities were ones that I designed on my own. These activities included: writing a book review for the public library's newsletter, keeping a journal, writing a mystery, giving presentations in and out of class, and exploring new forms of poetry. All of these tied into my goals. I worked on these projects in class or on my own, but I finished the entire list before the end of the school year. In class, class projects on works such as *The Effect of Gamma Rays on Man-in-the-Moon Marigolds* and *The Adventures of Huckleberry Finn* could be used in order to create new activities or simply as a means for coming closer to achieving our goals. One especially important required class activity was to plan out a course of action for five days, the results including the completion of at least one of the twelve activities. I decided to write a poem and to begin a mystery short story. The first day of my plan was reserved for opening moves on my mystery and starting on my poem. The second was for the actual writing of the poem and possibly some revision. On the third day, I planned to work on the mystery. The fourth day was for revisions on the poem and for the completion of the final product. The final day of my plan was for the completion of an outline of my mystery's characters and possibly a draft of the beginning. I submitted my plan to the teacher for approval and set to work. At the end of five days, I had completed my poem and made a great deal of progress on my mystery. This project really gave me a chance to become a more independent writer.

Some New Challenges

One final way that we can achieve our goals is through extra activities. This is where I found the work the most challenging and also the most rewarding. These optional projects were always offered to the entire class, but only a few students would accept them. Through activities that I designed or decided upon, I was achieving my goals by completing my own assignments.

It was through these extra assignments that I was given numerous opportunities to *Go for Pro*. For example, my class wrote a series of letters and compositions for *Woman's Day* magazine about what children really want from their parents. This activity was something completely new to me and the idea of being published was so thrilling that I put extra effort into the writing. Likewise, I wrote a portion of a student-written article for the *English Journal*. I began to think of myself as a writer, instead of just as a student. I was also able to test my presenting skills when I volunteered to speak and lead a discussion group at a conference for English teachers sponsored by the Capital Area School Development Association. In my presentation, I described what it is like to learn in a portfolio classroom. This was an important project for me, because as with all of the other activities I took on, I was able to be a *professional* speaker and writer.

It's true that what you have just read is the work of a high-school junior with little formal training in writing. However, it is also the work of a colleague and professional writer, someone who uses her language skills to communicate with others for a purpose. Professional writers set goals for themselves, work toward them, accomplish them, and then set new ones. Professional writers do not have to be published or paid for their work. Being a professional writer is not a characteristic but an attitude, a way of looking at writing and at yourself on a more sophisticated level. This is why, with the proper guidance, even a student not yet out of high school—like me—can be a professional writer and a colleague.

Sarah Leonard's Chronology

The most important opportunity the portfolio classroom made available for me was the opportunity to create my own goals and work to achieve them. In this class I took risks—entering writing contests, writing for publication, and giving speaking presentations—risks that I otherwise would not have taken. The following chronology is, I hope, proof of both my own success and the success of the portfolio classroom as a context in which students can become colleagues.

October, 1993: Seminar Presentation

Each person in the class came up with a presentation on the book *Out of This Furnace*. The best presentation to the class would be chosen to be given at a seminar, which was funded by the National Endowment for the Humanities (NEH) and the New York State Council on the Arts.

I was extremely nervous about the class presentation. I did not feel that my speaking skills were good enough. After the presentations the class felt differently, and my presentation was chosen to be the final presentation at the seminar. This NEH seminar was the first step toward increasing my confidence in my abilities.

February, 1994: Journal article

Students from the senior and junior class each wrote a section of an article for the *Ohio Journal of the English Language Arts*, "A Wholly Different Circumstance," which focused on the portfolio classroom. The teacher wrote the introduction to the piece and to the other writers. The issue in which this article was printed was later picked up by the National Coalition of Teachers of English to be included in one of their publications on language arts portfolios.

I wrote the section of the article focusing on the problem of assessing portfolios. This was my first publication. I was surprised at how easy it was. I wrote my section, read editorial review comments, revised it, and I had something I had written published in an English journal. People were actually going to read what I wrote.

February, 1994: Interview

I was one of the students quoted, along with the teacher, in an article for *New Standards*, which focused on how we felt about our work in the New Standards Project for Portfolio Assessment in Language Arts. This was my second *publication.* I felt that I was becoming a colleague in my own education. I still was nervous about speaking, but the portfolio classroom was helping me improve my abilities. Being treated as an equal increased my motivation to improve my presentations. I felt that I was in control of my own growth as a speaker and a writer, and that I was doing real work.

March, 1994: Book Contribution

The book *Creating the Writing Portfolio* used students' opening moves, short stories, interpretations of books using a model, etc., as examples of the techniques the authors wished to encourage. Two of my opening moves and my sociological interpretation of *A Doll's House* were included in the book. The authors wanted real examples written by real students. This was my third publication.

April, 1994: Conference Presentation

At the Catskill Whole Language Conference, three students and two student teachers gave presentations and answered questions about the portfolio classroom. I was one of the students. This presentation, done without the teacher, was an important step in the process of becoming independent. We were on our own. This increased my confidence in myself. If the teacher thought I was capable, then I should believe in myself too.

October, 1994: Portfolio Project Presentation

My presentation to the Portfolio Project of the National Research Center for Literature Teaching and Learning at SUNY—Albany focused on the opportunities available to students in the portfolio classroom. I used the activities listed earlier as examples of these opportunities I had taken. We also had to answer questions about the portfolio classroom. We were introduced as colleagues and presented as such. This was my second presentation, one that finally proved to me that my speaking skills had improved and that I was capable of doing successful presentations.

November, 1994: Conference Presentation

Seven students and the teacher presented at the New York State English Council Conference, which focused on authentic assessment. My part of the presentation focused on the opportunities available in the portfolio classroom. We were introduced as colleagues and after the presentations we answered questions from teachers and professors. Our teacher allowed us to stand on our own. Presenting at this conference was an amazing opportunity for us because students, even AP students, did not even go to these conferences, let alone give presentations. We were the first. Hopefully now there will be more students with the ability to present there.

December, 1994: Article

A group of students worked on a monograph article asking for descriptions of teaching techniques and student motivators. The teacher helped with the audience and the revising.

We wrote about our experiences in the portfolio classroom from the point of view of the student. Using different voices in the piece, we each wrote our own section. My section focused on goals and grades in the classroom. Our whole point was that the teacher had become a guide to our learning. Students were capable of writing an article on their own. The teacher wasn't needed to tell other teachers what we were really trying to say.

December, 1994: Chapter Opener

The class and the teacher wrote a chapter opener for a book about teachers. The teacher wrote a paragraph of introduction to the piece, and we wrote the rest.

My section of the piece focused on the opportunity for students to be in charge of their own learning and education. Students had developed their own passion for writing and learning. The teacher didn't have to force learning on his students. He was free to learn with us.

December, 1994: School Literary Magazine

Students and the teacher started a school literary magazine. Students both edited and contributed to the magazine. Students from the whole school had the opportunity to contribute their writings and artwork. We published two separate issues of the magazine. Many of the pieces we included in the magazine went on to win contests. The magazine was a small opportunity for students in the high school to have something published. It may have given them the confidence to go on to submit their work to a contest. I was both an editor and a contributor to the magazine.

January, 1995: Article

A college student, seniors, juniors, and the teacher all contributed sections of an article for *The English Journal*. My section focused on the opportunities available to students and the risks necessary to achieve their goals. We worked on the article as equals. The teacher was the coordinator, but the students carried a share of the load. Students decided whether or not they wished to participate. (The same is true for all of these activities.)

February, 1995: Conference Presentation

At the Capital Area School Development Association Conference, junior and senior students and the teacher gave a presentation on how the portfolio context allows the *importing* and *exporting* of abilities and activities, both to and from other courses. I talked about the opportunities and accomplishments available to students by letting them take risks increasingly on their own. Most of my accomplishments wouldn't have occurred if I hadn't been in the portfolio classroom.

May, 1995: Presentation

I answered questions about our school program for the site visitor from the New York State English Council Program of Excellence Award. Students talked about their experiences with the visitor, who was here to gather evidence about our program. We were on our own—the teacher wasn't present. We gave our evaluations of the portfolio classroom and our entire language arts curriculum from the students' point of view.

The opportunities described above increased my confidence in my own abilities and motivated me to take control of my own learning. As I noted earlier, the most important opportunity the portfolio classroom made available to me was the opportunity to create my own goals and work to achieve them. These activities are, I hope, proof of my success. I took risks and entered writing contests, wrote for publication, and did speaking presentations. Before this class, I did not take any risks in my writing or speaking. The context created by the portfolio classroom allowed me to become a colleague, and I am proud of my achievements through this class.

A Final Note from Joe Quattrini

The briefest of final notes: It has been my pleasure to work with these colleagues, both students and adults, who have helped me to see how to make two important changes in my classroom. The first change is in *how learning takes place*. The second change, more sweeping and powerful, is in *what kinds of learning are even possible*.

Chapter 9

PORTFOLIOS AND STUDENT EMPOWERMENT

Marsha Casey
Nicole Elbert
Conard High School

When asked how he felt about reading and writing, Oliver, a student in a ninth-grade English class, wrote: "I hate English. I think its stupit and to hard. Im just gonna fale anyways." This answer was no surprise, as failure has been typical in Olivers academic career. The job of motivating students who see little or no value in English activities is difficult, albeit challenging.

When we started to do more research and looked carefully at portfolios and the reluctant learner, we found that many of the articles were directed toward motivated, college-bound, or honor-type students. We were interested in those students who were less able and more disinterested—specifically, those students who have had little success previously in their high-school careers. Some of their weaknesses come from lack of motivation or the reality of doing so little reading and writing over the course of their classes that their skill levels have fallen drastically, causing problems with speed, comprehension, and clarity. Many of these students are concrete thinkers and only see the literal. These are the students who ask, "What do I need this for?" and really mean it. After reading F. Leon Paulson and Pearl R. Paulsons contributions to portfolio studies, we realized that the most important portfolio concept is that of the *stakeholder*. With this in mind, we developed a rationale for the portfolio, identified specific goals, set standards, and selected content.

We teach ninth- and tenth-grade modified English and an eleventh- and twelfth-grade modified English elective at a high school with a diverse population of twelve hundred students. We wanted to incorporate portfolios in our own

English classes as a way to empower our students to have control over their academic destinies. For non-motivated students, the portfolio appeared to be an especially useful tool because these students rarely felt control over the final outcome of an assignment.

Using the Portfolio As a Transition

The student who enters these modified classrooms usually has poor self-esteem, weak academic skills, and behavioral concerns. Some of these are issues that can be addressed before the student gets into the classroom. In June, we requested that the students submit self-evaluated student portfolios (see forms 9.1 and 9.2). We read the students' writing and corresponded back to each student by postcard. Our rationale for doing this was to show students that their teachers were invested in them as individual learners. This also started a dialogue that would continue when the student entered class in September. This idea originated when a student had come to us after he had been accepted to Michigan State University. The university had asked each incoming freshman to submit a portfolio for placement purposes in English classes and so that English professors could establish a rapport with the new students. Our own idea was that, in addition to establishing that dialogue, it could also give our own students a sense of purpose for writing.

Giving Students a Sense of Relevance

The writing portfolio is a wonderful boon for students who love to write and perfect their writing performance. However, they are not seen in quite the same way by those high-school students who have lagged behind in reading and writing and that see creating a paper as a laborious, painstaking activity with very little relevance to real life. There are ways though, to create a portfolio experience that allows them to see relevancy and to create documents that show themselves as individuals who are more than just the poor grades on their transcripts.

By reflecting upon work he or she sent up from the previous grade, the student is able to establish new reading and writing goals for the new school year. This is especially useful with the transition from eighth to ninth grade because it provides an opportunity for students to reflect on where they have been academically and in what new directions they want to proceed. Students felt that they finally had a *voice* and could explain some of the obstacles that they had experienced in the past. As a result of our knowledge of those limitations, we could accommodate those goals realistically.

For the older students, the rationale was the same but the content selected was a little different. The first series of activities offered a round-robin experience where every student created a job/college exploration portfolio. In fact, these are the documents the students need in order to seek immediate employment or to

Form 9.1

THE PORTFOLIO

The time has arrived for you to reflect back on your year in English and evaluate yourself as a writer. Your portfolio will present your writing to the outside world, including your next English teacher. Your portfolio is also an opportunity to understand specifically what you have learned and the areas you would like to improve.

Part of your final grade will be based on your portfolio. It is perhaps one of the more difficult assignments because it is your responsibility to monitor your progress. Portfolios are to be handed in NO LATER than _____.

STEPS:

1.   Select three pieces of writing from this year.

2.   Revise your paper (ask a peer or an adult, other than your teacher, to read your paper and verbally respond to the areas that need revision).

3.   Fill in the self-reflection questions for each of the three pieces.

4.   Write a reflective essay in which you discuss the other three pieces separately. In the reflective piece, consider the following questions (use your self-reflection as a guide):

   •   How would you describe yourself as an (English) student?

   •   Why did you choose each piece for your portfolio?

   •   How did you feel when you completed each piece?

   •   In what ways or areas did you see yourself improving in over the year (make sure to include what your problems had been beforehand)? Be as honest as possible.

   •   What would you like to improve in your writing next year (where do you need improvement and what are your goals)?

5.   *All* of your work must be typed.

USE PEER EDITORS FOR ALL OF THESE PIECES.

Form 9.2

SELF-REFLECTION

Name of Writer: _____

Title of Writing: _____

FOCUS (clear purpose):

DEVELOPMENT (thoroughness):

ORGANIZATION (logical progression, clear transition):

STYLE (word choice, sentence variety):

MECHANICS (spelling, punctuation, agreement of subject and verb):

apply to college if they choose to do so anytime after high school. Each workshop lasted for two days and created a portfolio entry. Creating a usable résumé, developing interviewing skills, participating in personal growth exercises, building an essay for college or the workplace, and working on the computers in the Career Resource Center were the first five portfolio workshops juniors and seniors participated in. When the students were finished, they had a working portfolio that contained documents and a computer diskette. Students knew that these papers could be updated and taken to any job interview. Upon completion of the five workshops, students were asked to evaluate their experience. All students mentioned the feeling of a new sense of self-confidence and for the first time felt that they had some guided idea of what the future might hold for them. For those who had never contemplated going on to college, the realizations that the process for applying was manageable and that there were community schools or training schools that would see them as potential candidates were very exciting. Also, students felt that this was a school experience that had relevancy, and they all participated in each activity with motivation and interest.

Giving Students Choice

> Many students have been silenced or intimidated by the instructor's authority and the powerful curriculum that he or she represents. In this hierarchy many instructors have been telling students what topics to write about, what types of arguments to use, how to structure the essay, and what types of sentences to create—categorically controlling students' texts, suppressing their ideas, and silencing their voices. (Metzger and Bryant, 1993)

We also wanted to "break down the traditional hierarchy in order to enable students to become full participants in the educational process" (Metzger and Bryant, 1993). In theory, this idea was appealing; in practice, it was very hard to let go of control with a group of students who has marginal self-control. Therefore, we needed to establish a strong framework and very clear purposes. We first listed together various types of writing that could occur during the school year (personal narrative, critical analysis, etc.). We then formulated a list of discrete skills from which the students could formulate writing goals. Writing workshops consisted of designing work calendars, setting grading criteria (form 9.3), small-group discussions, peer-editing time (form 9.4), and teacher conference sessions. The purpose of the writing sessions was to allow students to use time in class to work on specific writing goals that they generated in an environment that supported and encouraged their ownership of the process. By doing this the students had a stake in *choosing* their writing projects and felt good about finally having a say in all aspects of the activity, and the teacher now played the role of facilitator as opposed to controller.

Form 9.3

WRITING ASSESSMENT OF THESIS PAPER

<u>Teacher</u> <u>Student</u>

INTRODUCTORY PARAGRAPH: (points out of ___)   _____ _____

   • thesis statement clearly indicates the direction of the paper, authors, titles

BODY PARAGRAPH ONE: (points out of ___)   _____ _____

   • well-organized, clear main ideas supported by details

   • focuses on the thesis

   • quotes used convincingly

   • [other criteria that are pertinent to the reading]

BODY PARAGRAPH TWO: (points out of ___)   _____ _____

   • well-organized, clear main ideas supported by details

   • focuses on the thesis

   • quotes used convincingly

   • [other criteria that are pertinent to the reading]

BODY PARAGRAPH THREE: (points out of ___)   _____ _____

   • well-organized, clear main ideas supported by details

   • focuses on the thesis

   • quotes used convincingly

   • [other criteria that are pertinent to the reading]

CONCLUDING PARAGRAPH: (points out of ___)   _____ _____

   • conclusion restates the main idea (thesis)

MECHANICS: (points out of ___)   _____ _____

   • paper has been edited for spelling, usage, and agreement

Form 9.4

PEER EVALUATION SHEET

Writer's Name: _____ Reader's Name: _____

Read through the paper once just to get a feel for it. Concentrate on the topic rather than the mechanics. Answer the following questions in detail. Your efforts will be reflected in your *use of class time* grade. Remember: Criticism may hurt, but it also helps, especially if it is constructive!

INTRODUCTORY PARAGRAPH:
1. Are both the title and the author of the work mentioned?
2. Is there a thesis statement? What is it? Is it clear?
3. Does the paragraph talk about the initiation process in general?
4. Is the information accurate?

FIRST SUPPORT PARAGRAPH:
5. Is there a topic sentence? What is it?
6. What is the first support paragraph about?
7. Does the topic sentence relate back to the thesis?
8. Are there specific examples (quotes) from the story?
9. Are the quotes appropriate? Do they fit in?
10. If not, can you suggest another example?
11. Is the paragraph convincing? Does it make its point? If not, why? What needs clarification?

SECOND SUPPORT PARAGRAPH:
12. Is there a topic sentence? What is it?
13. What is the second support paragraph about?
14. Does the topic sentence relate back to the thesis?
15. Are there specific examples (quotes) from the story?
16. Are the quotes appropriate? Do they fit in?
17. If not, can you suggest another example?
18. Is the paragraph convincing? Does it make its point? If not, why? What needs clarification?

THIRD SUPPORT PARAGRAPH:
19. Is there a topic sentence? What is it?
20. What is the third support paragraph about?
21. Does the topic sentence relate back to the thesis?
22. Are there specific examples (quotes) from the story?
23. Are the quotes appropriate? Do they fit in?
24. If not, can you suggest another example?
25. Is the paragraph convincing? Does it make its point? If not, why? What needs clarification?

CONCLUDING PARAGRAPH:
26. Is the thesis restated? Copy it down:
27. Does the paragraph move from specific to general by then summarizing the concepts covered in the body paragraph?

(continued on next page)

Form 9.4 Cont'd

Now, go back a second time and reread for mechanics.

Look for the following things:

> Spelling errors
>
> Correctly punctuated quotations
>
> - Is punctuation placed inside quotation marks?
> - Are author(s) and page number(s) parenthetically stated?
>
> Wordiness
>
> Redundancy (saying the same thing over and over again)
>
> Complete sentences—no run-ons/fragments
>
> Places where the writer could include more transitions-

- words or phrases to make ideas flow

> Clearly separated paragraphs

Giving Students Control over Their Grades

In the past we have always graded our students with traditional quizzes, tests, and writing assignments—all teacher-imposed. The portfolio has opened up new assessment arenas with which we continue to struggle. Ideally, the portfolio empowers students by allowing them to assess themselves by reflecting on the quality of the work and, more importantly, on their own development and progress (see form 9.2). Realistically, for a student who has severe skill weaknesses, this is a very difficult task. As a result, this has become our area of concern. We now understand that what we are trying to assess is really a process, not just a product. The process includes the student as an interested participant in a small group, as a competent peer editor, as a developing writer, as a realistic self-assessor, and as a maturing participant in the academic process. If we were to assign grades to the many subjective pieces of this process, it would be as if we were taking back the ultimate power that we have been working so hard to give the student. Perhaps there will come a time when a grade and a student's self-evaluation will be the report card of the future. Until then, we struggle with these dilemmas.

References

Metzger, E., and L. Bryant, (1993). "Portfolio assessment: Pedagogy, power, and the student." *Teaching English in the two year college*, (pp. 279-88).

Paulson, P. R., and F. L. Paulson, (1991). "Portfolios: Stories of Knowing." In P. H. Dreyer (Ed.), *Claremont reading conference 55th yearbook 1991. Knowing: The power of stories*, (pp. 294-303). Claremont, CA: Center for Developmental Studies of the Claremont Graduate School.

PART 2
PRACTICAL REFLECTIONS

Introduction

Portfolios change how teachers teach, and at some point this generally has an impact on how schools operate. Pamela Kiniry, who taught at three different schools in as many years, recounts her own experiences with portfolios in new environments. Her wish for heterogeneous classes to use with portfolios is echoed by John Hennelly, who also argues for creating and using portfolios in a heterogeneous class. An underlying assumption of Hennelly's essay is that the class will be structured by student-set goals and self-assessment, an assumption not apparent in the essays in the previous section.

John Hennelly is also the author, along with Marian Galbraith and Alan Purves, of the next chapter on negotiating a rhetorical community in the classroom, which offers a more formal evaluation of the changes that portfolios bring to classrooms and to teacher responsibilities. These changes affect a school system's policies, a point Charles Phelps ponders in his chapter. Phelps's colleague, Suzanne Heyd, ponders in the opposite direction—right into her own head, contemplating how teachers' perceptions of students can be rather limiting. In revising her perception of learners, she revises her own perception of herself as teacher.

Anne Kuthy describes how her department created a portfolio requirement. Carol Mohrmann, a middle-school teacher in a recently reconfigured school system, writes about the interdisciplinary portfolio, one that includes projects from math and science, and its effects on an eighth-grade teaching team. Gertrude Karabas concludes this section with the story of how one school made the shift toward portfolio assessment (and with the state's blessing).

Chapter 10

RAISING STANDARDS IN A VARIETY
OF MIDDLE-SCHOOL SETTINGS

Pamela Kiniry
McGee Middle School

Introduction

Reflections are always hard for me because I feel overwhelmed by the task of collecting treasures from so many different experiences. During the last three years of my career and the portfolio project, I have found many treasures in a variety of middle-school settings, and I have entered these treasures into the section of my being called *experiential background* for long-term reference and growth.

I began my teaching career at West Side Middle School in Groton, Connecticut, where I had the privilege of coteaching with Marian Galbraith in an eighth-grade developmental reading program. This experience proved to be one that changed the path of my career and helped me to become the teacher I am today. Through that assignment I became affiliated with the SUNY-Albany portfolio research project, from which I have learned the definition of commitment to education as I worked collaboratively on portfolio implementation in the classroom with Marian and two other teachers from West Side, Carole Mackin and Deane Beverly. Together we set out to find ways to capture those special moments of student learning in something called a *portfolio*.

My second year of the research project brought significant changes for me. Rather than picking up where we left off the year before, I found myself *out of the loop* in a new school, teaching a different subject and working with students who had not been exposed to portfolio work as I knew it. Little did I know at that time that each year would bring significant changes in the way I perceived portfolios in my classroom. I've learned that portfolios evolve as the year progresses and that they are indeed finely tuned to the particular needs of my students. What had changed during the second year is that I was on a solo mission. I had no one from the project in my building to share ideas with or to process difficulties with me. Consequently, I looked to one of my team members, Betsy Iiams, and bounced ideas back and forth with her. Again I was fortunate to have the expertise of an incredibly talented teacher at my side, and together we integrated our reading and writing workshops through projects with anticipated outcomes and explicit means of assessment for the students. We clearly had entered into a collaborative effort to turn our classrooms into student-driven environments where learning not only occurred but had connections, relevance, and alternate means of presentation. My students' portfolios began to take new shape as they expanded and included work from other classes as examples of their learning. I started to see portfolios in a different light, and I realized how limited my definition of the portfolio had been.

Just when I thought I had settled into a school where tenure was a possibility, I was faced with another major decision about my career. I had to make a decision to stay in a school system one hour and ten minutes from my home, a system that I had loved instantly because of its diversity and commitment to excellence, or to move to my home town, where a program similar to Groton's was going to be implemented that year. After much soul-searching and heart-wrenching thought, I made the decision to move to McGee Middle School in Berlin, Connecticut. Now, instead of a long drive to work, I have enormous phone bills as I continue to collaborate with my colleagues in the Groton system about the effects of portfolios on our classrooms.

My year at McGee has been a year full of changes and experiments. I now teach integrated language arts where the same students come to my classroom for two blocks of time each day. I continue to use the reading and writing workshop approach to instruction, but it is done thematically, drawing connections for students between reading, writing, and learning. I should also note at this time that while I had taught in a heterogeneous environment in Groton, I am now teaching in a homogeneous environment in Berlin. I currently have two sections of average integrated language arts classes and one remedial reading class. This change has required the most significant adjustment on my part. The good news is that we are moving to heterogeneity next year.

Since solo missions are not my style, I again recruited a talented colleague, Kathy Lotko, to collaborate with on both instructional techniques and portfolio implementation. This year she began using portfolios in her classes, and she has promised to *send them up* to me when the year ends. Finally a link is forming, and some of our students will be the benefactors of continuity and visual evidence of their learning in our middle school.

Getting Started

Moving a class toward portfolios is not always an easy task. Students who have never been exposed to portfolios first need a clear definition of the word and a simplified understanding of our use of portfolios in the classroom.

The first day of our portfolio instruction last year began with some brainstorming about who might use a portfolio. The students came up with a variety of examples of portfolios, including those used by athletes, models, actors, job applicants, college applicants, classroom students, etc. They described the kinds of things that might be found in a portfolio and why they would be included (that is, the purpose for displaying one's work). As more examples of portfolios surfaced and more reasons why articles might be included were uncovered, my students began to understand the need for maintaining a portfolio. We next discussed the kinds of portfolios they had used in other classrooms and what had been included in them. From this discussion I learned how much they knew about reflecting on their learning and whether they had ever had the opportunity to assess their work. Since most of them had very little experience with anything more than a working folder or a collection of their best work, I knew some strong groundwork had to be laid.

To further their understanding of the direction I wanted their portfolios to take, we talked about how portfolios might change over the course of a career and what a viewer would notice. Using the example of an athlete, we talked about what the early inclusions to the portfolio would demonstrate compared to the later entries of an athlete's career. As the picture became clearer, they were ready for the next task.

I needed a baseline of student self-assessment in order for them to watch their growth from quarter to quarter. Students needed to see where they were and where they were going. Growth needed to be visual and concrete if portfolios were going to have an immediate value in the students' minds at this level. Students followed the simple model of narrative reflection below:

> Describe how you see yourself as a reader, writer, and learner at
> this point in your life. Explain your response by identifying
> those factors that have contributed to your view of yourself.
> Your response should be no less than 250 words.

Initially, many students had difficulty with this task, so we discussed it in terms of making connections to their individual likes and dislikes about reading, writing, and learning. Soon after, they were able to settle into their first task of self-assessment.

The responses were open and honest. Many of my students had been forced to read books that they didn't like or to write about things in which they had no interest. A typical comment was, "I used to be forced to read books and I think that is why I didn't like to read so much. I used to skip pages and not really read, just look at the pages."

Many of their comments were related to grades they received for their efforts as with a student who replied:

> *In sixth grade we read a lot in class and accomplished quite a bit. I still didn't like to read and ended up with a C for a final grade.*
>
> *In seventh grade I tried to convince myself that reading was fun, but it didn't work. I think because of my age I finally tried to get my act together and read my first novel without skipping pages or chapters. The final result was a B+ which made my mom and me very happy.*
>
> *Now, in eighth grade, I'm enjoying the books I read. I like to be able to pick out the book I like to read. Reading still isn't one of my favorite activities, but nobody has to drag me into doing it any more.*

Similarly, students shared openly about their writing. Their biggest fears about writing were with regard to spelling and their inability to master the art of spelling. One student who was obsessed with spelling wrote:

> *I hate the way I write. Everything I write does not make sence or if it does make sence, everything else is spelled wrong. Sometimes people make fun of me becouse I can not spell as good as them. They think it is a big joke becouse I can not spell. I wish sometimes I could write a whole page of writing with out making one single spelling errar.*
>
> *I think my writing comes from my dad becouse he and I write the same, but he can spell everything right. If I could spell at least half of my words right, it would be like a dream come true. Then I would not have to wory about people making fun of me.*

This response, though full of spelling errors, contains good use of mechanics and, more importantly, is passionate and from the heart. This is the kind of response that has convinced me over the years of the value of content over spelling in drafting thoughts.

While this student was overcome with concern about his spelling, another student wrote:

> *One problem I have in my writing is spelling. I know this is something I can not improve on by trying to learn all the words in the English language. I am trying to improve on finding my mistakes afterwards in proof reading, rather than stop writing in my train of thought to look it up.*

For many students of reading and writing, learning was not even a consideration. Learning was something reflected in a grade as effort rather than knowledge carried through life. As I moved my students away from grades and into the art of self-reflection and self-assessment about their work as an example of learning and effort, learning began to have new meaning and value. In order to make the transition to this stage, we had to start setting goals for learning and growth. We were now ready for the next phase of portfolio construction—setting goals.

This proved to be a task of huge proportions, one that caused many students lots of anxiety.

Setting Goals

During the first year of the project, Marian and I had approached portfolios somewhat tentatively and experimentally as we tried to define their role in the reading classroom. We wanted the portfolio to be more than a working folder or a folder where all good work was saved for someone to grade. We wanted instead to invest our students in their work, to help them set goals for learning, to plan a method to achieve those goals, and to reflect on their efforts through some means of assessment. We had undertaken a task that also became a learning tool for us each time we entered a new phase of the process.

Last year, to begin this process, I asked my students to refer to their first portfolio entries, *How Do I See Myself As a Reader, Writer, and Learner?* and to the curriculum guide for the eighth grade, which I had rewritten for their understanding. After some discussion they were ready to begin setting goals for their first-quarter work. They began by reviewing both their assessment of themselves and the eighth-grade goals in order to determine their strengths and weaknesses before they selected an area of concentration for that quarter.

The guides, *Expanding Your Reading Experience* and *Expanding Your Writing Experience*, clearly outlined the areas of reading, writing, listening, and speaking from which they were to select a goal and work toward demonstrating knowledge of that goal through evidence submitted to their portfolios each quarter. I wanted my students to consider literature as models for their own writing, to view writing as readers while they also viewed reading as critical writers. They needed a clear understanding of the literary elements and the different genres in literature in order to do this, so many of them began setting goals from this angle.

Initially, when Marian and I first began using portfolios, each student had filled out a goal chart like the one we had used the previous year, but we soon discovered this procedure was not going to work because it did not allow enough space for discussion. As I noted earlier, I have often found myself fine-tuning my introduction to portfolios each year to meet the specific needs of my classroom. This demonstrates the need to modify and adapt portfolios in just that way. Consequently, students wrote out their goals in a few sentences and explained how they planned to achieve those goals in an accompanying paragraph.

This year I began goal-setting in the same way, but after realizing the value of goals in student work, I decided to incorporate them more often into their assignments. Rather than writing just quarterly goals, I asked my students to write a goal for each response they made to their reading. Since I have often felt the need to prepare my eighth-grade students for high school, I changed the way in which they responded to their reading at the end of the second quarter from four responses per book to one focused 250-word response per book. I asked students to set a goal for responding to their reading and to satisfy that goal through their writing using quotes from the text to support their ideas. The goals ranged in design from reading and identifying the characteristics of a genre different from what a student was used to reading to analyzing conflict and how it unfolds in a story or critically reviewing a nonfiction piece.

This task presented great difficulty for some of them, and I had to spend a lot of time working individually with these students when they were in both the goal-setting stage and the writing process. The goals were difficult because they had to think about their reading before setting their goals. They had to assess what they knew or recognized in a book in order to write a goal. Once we moved beyond goals like "to read a long book this quarter" to goals such as "to analyze a character's growth and the events that cause him or her to change," everything began to fall into place. My students wrote their goals at the top of their first drafts and referred to them often as they established their support. Their direction was always clear, though not always easy. For some students, this was too difficult a task, and I learned that I must individualize this process next year, moving students when they are developmentally ready to accept this challenge. Another concern about using this method was my fear that students would not respond to or state their own feelings about what they were reading. I didn't want these responses to their reading to be like analytical reports, so I had to carefully monitor and conference with my students to make sure we didn't lose their feelings in this new method of responding.

Students were asked to summarize the story in one paragraph and then satisfy their goals, at which time they were encouraged to include their own feelings in the discussion. The last paragraph was to include a personal response to the story with an explanation to support their feelings. Because so many students were quoting the text to support their statements, it also offered an opportunity for them to learn Modern Language Association (MLA) documentation style. Over and over again in assessment conferences, my students have stated the value of that knowledge to them in their research assignments.

Similarly, in writing class my students set quarterly goals for writing pieces, which they worked on during the quarter. For example, after reviewing the curriculum guidelines I gave them, they had to refer to their baseline assessments of themselves as writers. From there they set their goals for improvement. Many began with things like "to be a better speller" or "to learn how to punctuate," while others wrote goals that were more content-based: to "create strong characters" or to "write a lead that really draws a reader into my story." Students were encouraged to try to link their reading response goals to their writing goals. If they were analyzing themes in their reading, they should focus on developing them in their writing. In this way they were able to meet the curricular demands in both areas with evidence of that effort in their portfolios if they chose. Again, I wanted to carry over and connect the idea of reading like writers and writing like readers. Gradually they began to see the relationship between reading and writing—yet another positive by-product of portfolio use.

When students set their goals at the beginning of the quarter, they had to also jot one down at the top of a rough draft piece of writing. This helped not only the writer to stay focused, but it also helped a peer reader to respond to the focus of the writing. Goals were always present on student papers, and they slowly began to feel the direction that goal-setting gave them. It became their purpose for writing, reading, responding, and, in a sense, thinking about what they were doing. Eighth-grade students by nature lack focus, so this task helped to direct and guide them without nagging them after the fact. As they completed a piece of writing or submitted a book response, I gently pushed them to assess their work, always with their goals in mind. Occasionally a student had written a goal that was never once satisfied in his or her writing. During the assessment of that work, it was clear to the student that the writing had moved in a different direction than had originally been intended. Sometimes, in such cases, students changed their goals to meet the standard of the finished product. Usually, however, they went back and rewrote their work to satisfy their goals. Whichever route they chose to follow, it was clear that goals were a clarifying factor in thinking, reading, writing, and consequently in learning. Assessment, on the other hand, confused and rattled even the best students in the beginning.

Assessment

Since my students over the years have been so programmed to use grades as tools for assessment, this road has been a difficult one to reroute. The most familiar questions in my classroom at the beginning of each year were: "Did you correct our papers? What grade did I get? Is this any good?" I knew I had to rethink assessment and tailor it to my anticipated outcomes for specific lessons. Through portfolios, I gradually saw the power of student assessment, peer assessment, and teacher assessment and their effects in the classroom. At the onset I, too, thought primarily in terms of grades. Slowly my responses to those questions changed: "I didn't correct your papers; I read them, though. You didn't get a grade, but I did comment and respond to your work." By turning questions back to them I was also able to begin to move them toward self-assessment: "Did you follow the focus of the writing piece? Did you satisfy your goal? Have you had a peer respond to your work? Have you thought it through carefully, revised, edited, and proofread it? Are you satisfied with your effort? If so, I'll be glad to read your work and respond to it."

These were big philosophical changes for me, and they have raised my method of instruction to higher levels. Through the use of portfolios, my emphasis on a grading structure has changed dramatically. I had often wondered why everything had to have a grade attached to it before it had value, and the more involved with portfolios I became, the more I realized how little grades actually have to do with long-term learning. One thing I knew was that I wanted my students to learn and to realize that they had learned by assessing their own work and by choosing new ways to demonstrate their knowledge. My students do not take tests; rather, they assess their progress daily through their performance on either a written piece for writing workshop, in a response to their reading, or on a project in which they may be involved in to demonstrate knowledge of a curricular goal. Additionally, my evidence requirements are varied and include such things as artwork, music, drama, dance, research papers, and many other forms that they submit for assessment of their learning. Learning is fun, creative, and student-driven. Students take responsibility for what they are doing as well as for what they haven't done, though this practice takes nurturing and requires a trusting relationship between not just the student and the teacher but also between the student and his or her peers. Assessment has become a cornerstone of my classroom. This year I have branched out and worked enthusiastically on assessment, trying new methods and using a system based on comments rather than grades.

For example, in our writing workshop environment, students are required to write about any topic they choose, but they are given a focus. That focus may include anything from clear, organized, and sequenced paragraphs to developing a character, conflict, or theme in a particular genre. Whatever the focus, students are responsible for assessing their performance on that piece. Throughout their writing, they maintain a log of their effort and accomplishments each day. They are to write a brief paragraph stating what they did, why they did it, and how it went. When they have finished their first draft, they are to seek an *RPQS* from a peer. Simply stated, an RPQS is a peer-assessment form on which the student *responds* to the writing, *points* out something positive about it, *questions* what is not understood, and makes *suggestions* to the writer. The writer always has the option to refuse these suggestions, but must document on the form his or her reasons for doing so.

One of my students this year felt very strongly about his writing and refused a student's suggestion on a characterization paper he had written. The peer reader wrote:

> *I liked your description and the variety of your word choices. This was a funny story and I enjoyed reading it. I especially liked how you made up the name,* Charlie Lutz *because it gave me insight about how the character behaves. The dialogue was another strong point when you said things like "Lutz the Klutz once more comes through." Question: What is Charlie serving for breakfast, hot soup? Suggestion: I think you should describe the mess he made a little more. It will make it funnier.*

In turn, the writer acknowledged the RPQS and responded to it, stating how it affected his revision and why:

> *I added some more description to the mess as Ryan said, but I didn't want to make too many changes because this is based on someone I know well, me! I wanted the reader to see a klutz, not just a mess. I also used the camp that I go to in the summer as the setting. I sat in a quiet place and visu-*

alized every detail I could remember. Then I started creating. If I made
too many changes, it wouldn't be real any more.

The RPQS gave my students the freedom and time to rethink their writing
and to assess what they had done and why. It also gave them the opportunity to
defend their pieces, which helped build confidence in their ability to create.
Halfway through the year I offered them an opportunity to move away from the
form for the RPQS and simply to write an assessment paragraph to the writer
including the same information. They preferred this approach because they felt
stifled by the format of the RPQS. Now that they understand the requirements
of this kind of assessment, they are frequently asked to carry it over to other
assignments, such as responding to news articles or observations of human
behavior. The latter was used when we studied the way people exhibited acts of
intolerance. My students, in order to understand the behaviors, had to respond
to the act, point out whatever they didn't like, question where it may have originated, and offer any suggestions for correcting the offensive behavior. Again,
they were reflecting, assessing, and evaluating.

Another form of assessment I used last year and will use again this year is a
daily performance questionnaire for long-term projects and group work. Last
year during our playwriting unit, the students were grouped and one person was
the group leader. Leaders were responsible for initiating discussion and docu-
menting the information about how the day went. They were to summarize their
groups' accomplishments for that day, discuss any problems they may have had,
and discuss what they liked best about their writing. Again, this became a means
for self-reflection as well as a checkpoint for me regarding their work.

Similarly, all writing assignments that were ready to go to final copy were
submitted to me with a form that included simple narrative responses to
self-assessment questions. These were questions regarding the writer's effort on a
piece of writing, the problems the writer encountered, the strengths and weaknesses of the piece, the areas the writer would like me to look at, what he or she
had learned from writing that paper, and how he or she had improved over earlier papers. This assessment gave me an idea of how my students viewed their
papers both in effort and quality, and it offered me an opportunity to comment
and direct their thinking with additional questions about their writing.

Assessment took many other forms in our classroom. Students performed
speeches for our schoolwide *Declamation Contest*, for which we devised a rubric
to assess each other so that the class could select two candidates to represent them
in the contest. My students also studied the diversity of our classroom as each
student researched one of the nationalities from his or her family history. Because
the classes worked independently for a period of three weeks, they were again
required to maintain a daily assessment form of their efforts and learning. The
culminating activity was for each student to prepare a scrapbook about his or her
nationality that compared how the culture presents itself in the United States to

the way it appears in its native country or territory. Again, the class created a grading rubric to assess the projects, which were also presented orally to the class. Many students learned words from foreign languages, created music from their cultures, learned dances of their countries, wrote poems of tribute to their ancestors, and brought in numerous artifacts to help their classmates understand the cultures from which they came. All of these forms of assessment became the foundation for our biweekly visits to the portfolio.

Every other week my students pulled out their folders and began the search for new material for their portfolios. Initial responses to this task were often in the form of groans and complaints similar to those heard in your house when you ask your teenager to take the garbage out. This task required real effort—thinking. Eighth-grade students don't like to think unless they are forced to, so I forced them. There are not many things I force them to do, but thinking is a requirement in my classroom. Thus, making decisions about what to include was often painstaking.

We began each visit to the portfolio with questions like "What have I done that shows growth in my reading/writing/learning ability?" or "What goals have I met in my reading responses or in my daily writing? Do I have evidence to support this?" Some students were unable to find anything new or unusual to submit, while others often went back to their earlier work and looked for things with possibilities for improvement that might satisfy a goal. By the end of the first quarter, some students were beginning to use their portfolios independently. When work was returned to them, they reviewed the comments and made needed adjustments to their pieces to submit to their portfolios. In order to place a work in the portfolio, students had to justify its inclusion by writing a paragraph stating what that submission showed about their learning. One student wrote:

> I have entered this piece because it shows what I have learned about my heritage, who I am. I spent many hours on my Tapestry project. Of all the things I have done in this class, I think I have learned the most about myself and my heritage from this unit. It took a lot of research, time, and a bunch of effort, but I accomplished it. I wrote in lots of different ways and I was able to speak some Gaelic words to my classmates. Learning the beginner's jig and dancing for everyone was also a big accomplishment. Since I can't put Irish Soda Bread in my portfolio, I will just warn you to buy some in Ireland. Mine was pathetic.
>
> After I was finished with this project I felt that I was full of knowledge about my heritage; I was complete. Entries such as this one to the portfolio which result in the assessment of not only work but also of self-value, are catalysts for my future lessons. They direct and guide my thinking toward more creative and challenging ideas for my students. What better way to learn than through self-discovery.

At the end of each quarter, I set aside a week during which students engage in independent reading and writing while I conference with each one of them about their work for that quarter. Before they come to the conference table, they are to make sure the work in their portfolio is in final copy form, is complete with a prewritten goal, has a justification paragraph for submission to the portfolio, and that another attached paragraph is included stating what the grade should be and why. I am responsible for providing each student with a rubric of the required work for the quarter and a checklist of what was completed. Since part of their grade is based on participation and cooperation, I do provide a percentile based on my daily records of their efforts. Finally, each piece of work, when returned to the student, has my comments about the effort and product, which I have written on the rubric. It also has comments for improvement should the student wish to rework it. From these comments I have a general idea of what grade I would attribute to that work, and I mark a coded representation in my grade book. For example, an A would be an S++, a B would be an S+, a C would be an S, etc. This affords me the time to really listen to the student's negotiations and to make sure we are in agreement about his or her report-card grade. Because I feel so strongly about the need to say something about my students' work to their parents in a narrative form rather than through a letter grade, I also include an individualized note, which is sent with the computerized report card and which our school secretaries so graciously put in the envelopes for me.

This method of nongrading has caused some problems, however. Because the emphasis on grades is lessened in the classroom, I have a greater difficulty answering the administrative demands for student updates in the form of a grade. I can state emphatically whether a student is performing well or poorly, and that he or she is completing all of his or her work. In fact, I know my students' work so well as a result of frequent conferences and constant demands for assessment that I can talk about their progress easily without having to refer to my grade book for verification. I can also provide a general range in a typical grade form as to where the student will land, but I cannot and will not affix a grade to a student's performance without first conferencing and negotiating that grade.

Though this is the first year I have negotiated grades with students and abandoned grading all of their work, I have found that this method of assessment has revolutionized my classroom both from an instructional perspective as well as from the students' assessment of themselves.

Giving up what has always been the standard form of assessment, a teacher-graded piece of work, has not been an easy task for my students or for me; however, as comfort levels have increased, learning has moved in a new and exciting direction. The grade is no longer the single motivational tool for performance. At long last my students are vested in their learning; they are moving from what they know to what they need to know to meet their goals. Now we are all at crossroads in our learning, and I am committed to this new path because the possibilities along it are endless and fruitful.

The most important thing I have learned over the last three years is the power of the portfolio to bring learning and teaching to new levels. Yes, the portfolio is a place to demonstrate what a student knows, but it is far more than that. It is a tool for directing teaching in a way that helps students learn; it helps them to take responsibility for their learning by continuously assessing their efforts and results and raising them to new heights. As one student summed up her year in the closing statements of her portfolio:

> *This year I questioned more and thought more critically, more than any other year at McGee. I wish the years before this had the same challenges that this year gave me. I hope the years to come will provide me with both the challenges and the opportunity for success that I found in this year.*

For this student and many others, the portfolio has given them another way of thinking about themselves, another way of showcasing who they are. I hope that they always think of themselves as capable of setting goals, establishing a plan, assessing their efforts, and moving forward to success.

Chapter 11

BALANCE IS EVERYTHING: PORTFOLIOS IN NON-TRACKED ENGLISH CLASS

John Hennelly
Conard High School

Recently, one of our district's high-school principals asked me why West Hartford doesn't provide honors-level English classes for juniors. Other departments do, and several parents had expressed concern at the absence of such courses in English. I suggested that the elective offerings offer a range of challenge implicit in their names. For instance, by glancing at course descriptions most students can deduce that British Literature may be more academically challenging than Issue-Centered English. Still, relatively few students take either of those courses. Instead, most opt for courses like Modern American Literature, Humanities, World Literature. These courses, as well as our semester writing courses, draw a wide range of students, a characteristic that appeals to me and that makes these courses a natural setting for using portfolios—the topic of this chapter. And though neither the principal nor the concerned parents have inquired about portfolios, I'm confident that if either were to look at the work produced by almost all of the students in my classes, the question about honors classes would become "Why aren't all West Hartford students preparing portfolios?"

Portfolios lend themselves to learning in any kind of class, but they're especially well-suited to student-centered, heterogeneous classes. But before discussing the hows and whys of using portfolios in such classes, let me share a few thoughts and biases about skill grouping, at least as it manifests itself in high schools.

In any English class a range of skill, talent, and motivation exists; however, more often than not, the motivation is the most salient variable. In honors-level classes students are motivated or driven; in modified classes, few students feel compelled to achieve. In many classes, the environment contributes to a self-ful-filling prophecy. Students rise or fall according to expectation. And the great mass in the middle—our college-bound band—moves along, a few excelling, a few failing. And what the three groups share is a false sense of placement. They exist in the objective case, and we—the instructors—function in the nominative case. For the most part students haven't elected their skill group (perhaps their parents have, but that's another issue). Instead, they've been placed. And being placed, especially being placed in the cellar, doesn't promote a great sense of well-being.

I realize there are exceptions: many honors-level students feel pretty good about their placement. And some are modest, self-effacing, cooperative, and sup-portive of each other's efforts. But then there are others who may feel competi-tive, academically or intellectually superior, or just a little bit . . . different from the others. Occasionally, even their teachers feel this way. Students in modified classes generally don't behave in these ways.

Then there's the issue of student-centered versus teacher-centered classes. Everyone knows that the former are preferable, but most of us still keep the spot-light on ourselves. It's hard not to. And it's even more difficult to create an envi-ronment where group work is really collaborative and productive, where students push themselves to achieve. Possibly, this is related to their inability or unwilling-ness to find meaning and purpose in what we ask them to do. However, the fact remains that until they see some personal value in developing literacy, chances are slim that they'll engage fully in either teacher- or student-centered activities.

If our sense of effectiveness and well-being as teachers depends largely on our students' achievement—in the broadest sense of the word—I'm convinced that seeing ourselves as professionals working with clients or mentors working with apprentices are more rewarding and productive relationships than some of the teacher-student power struggles or passive-aggressive patterns that I've seen consume so much energy in classrooms. The student-centered portfolio practices outlined in this article help develop the former.

I'm not being naïve and idealistic when I say untracked classes are prefer-able for students and staff alike. From a practical point of view, both short and long term, mixed classes work by openly acknowledging the range of talent, skill, and interest, and allowing students and teachers to work with each other more comfortably and honestly. And with the tacit understanding that a range of skill exists, a kind of intramural ethos evolves, one that discourages meanspiritedness, criticism, and elitism. There are no special interests, no severely gifted students, no exceptionally limited students. Not unlike the English department, or the custodial crew, or the congregation, or the adult education class—if they're work-ing effectively. And as for being forced to teach to the middle—the only option available to those overburdened souls stuck with a mixed group that won't sit quietly for lectures and Socratic gamesmanship—I've never met an instructor who either knew what that meant or who was that accurate. Effective teachers work with students, monitoring and adjusting constantly, based on what their students request, need, or demonstrate.

And there are other reasons I chose to use portfolios in nonleveled or mixed classes. For instance, I was curious. Most of my project colleagues who were working with high-school students had honors classes. To some extent this may have been happenstance; to some extent I believe it was deliberate. After all, when exploring new territory, everyone hopes to be successful, and given the experimental nature of portfolios, some colleagues' skepticism, and the problems with Vermont's implementation of portfolios, it makes sense to work with students who already have a strong interest in literacy and academic achievement. That's not a criticism. It's simply an observation. For instance, one of my first portfolio classes was a senior honors class from which I drew much of the material for my first article on portfolios. This class also provided me with the incentive to expand my understanding of and approaches to portfolios.

However, while working with honors classes I also worked with academic, modified, or mixed classes, and I learned that what attracts honors-level students to the portfolio also attracts other students. And that's chiefly what I'll discuss in here: the activities and dynamics that make the portfolio attractive to most students . . . and quite a few teachers.

Finally, here are just a few more practical reasons for my using and discussing portfolios in mixed classes:

1. Since changing jobs two years ago, I have worked almost exclusively with mixed classes.

2. As a department chairman whose colleagues have shown a willingness to explore portfolios with their students, I want them to see how well it works with a range of students, not just the honors students.

3. As a member of the portfolio project, I promised to write this chapter.

In a dirigible-sized nutshell then, these are the reasons why I ask my students to prepare portfolios three to four times yearly and why I believe this activity is especially well-suited to mixed-ability and mixed-motivated classes. Without chronicling every step and procedure, let me highlight the ones that have worked for my students.

Getting Underway

The note I shared with students the first day of class is reproduced in form 11.1. It sets the tone, suggests a design and purpose, and, I hope, begins to convince my students that I'm here to work with them. There's a lot to be said for putting it in writing, whether it's the course syllabus, the weekly overview, the response to the portfolio, or the writing workshop plan. It provides a sense— granted, sometimes only an illusion—of structure. Still, that can be helpful.

Form 11.1

To: Modern American Literature

From: Dr. Hennelly

Re: Hopes and expectations

Date: 8/30/94

Before beginning our first unit (American Adolescence), I want to highlight some of my expectations and beliefs about how we might best work together toward making this course as educational and enjoyable as possible.

You can expect me to:

- treat you with courtesy and respect
- be available before, after, and oftentimes during school
- help you achieve course objectives along with any language arts goals that you choose for yourself
- be well-prepared for class
- vary class activities
- have high expectations of both you and myself
- return your work in a timely manner
- show a sense of humor
- assess your work and effort in as thorough and constructive a manner as possible
- be receptive to your suggestions and assessments about the course and my efforts

I would like you to:

- treat me and classmates with courtesy and respect
- work constructively and comfortably with members of your group and this class
- drop by my office or the *Pow Wow* [school newspaper] office to let me know how things are going
- work toward achieving course objectives along with any that you choose for yourself
- be well-prepared for class
- participate in class activities
- complete assignments
- have high expectations of both you and me
- submit work in a timely manner
- show a sense of humor
- assess your own work and effort thoughtfully and honestly
- be receptive to my suggestions and assessments of your efforts

Form 11.1 cont'd

Course activities

The Portfolio Project: As part of the course, I would like you to participate in a study about how we come to understand and appreciate literature. This will involve a fair amount of writing, goal-setting, and self-assessment. What you'll need is a writing folder, a reading response notebook, and an open mind. I'll tell you more about this.

Writing workshop: I would also like to devote one period every six classes to writing. You may use these to work on pieces that you have selected and planned (e.g., a literary analysis, personal narrative, newspaper article, poem, one-act play). I will ask that you not use this time to complete written work for other classes.

Scholastic Aptitude Test preparation: Based on my assessment of interests and needs, we may spend some time working on SAT preparation.

Homework

I will never ask you to *think about* something for homework. I may ask you to read, write, practice, record—anything that you can demonstrate having done. I will not assign busy-work, nor will I assign work that requires more time or skill than is reasonable. My purpose in assigning homework is to reinforce or sharpen course-related skills and understandings. Generally, homework will be directly connected to the next day's class work. It is essential, therefore, that you complete assignments and complete them on time. Homework loses much of its meaning and value when it is completed and submitted late.

Oftentimes, others will be dependent upon your having done your work. If a question arises about homework but you are unable to see me after school, please feel free to call me at home (555-1234). This is especially important if you or your group plans to present the next day.

Grades

You will receive a letter grade at the end of each quarter. The grade will reflect your performance in these areas:

- writing and writing portfolio*   50%
- unit and objective tests and quizzes   20-25%
- homework and participation   25-30%

I expect all of you to do well, earning grades of B or better.

*Note: Your self-assessment based on the goals you set at the beginning of each quarter will be included in this grade.

Form 11.1 cont'd

I would appreciate your sharing this note with a parent or guardian—that's a request, not a requirement—and returning it to me tomorrow, with any comments. Thanks.

I look forward to working with you.

Please complete, detach, and submit the portion below this line.

- -

Parent or guardian comments:

Student name:

Telephone number:

Address:

Please circle the days and periods (first semester) when you're available (study halls):

M	1	2	3	4	5	6	7	8
T	1	2	3	4	5	6	7	8
W	1	2	3	4	5	6	7	8
R	1	2	3	4	5	6	7	8
F	1	2	3	4	5	6	7	8

Extracurricular activities:

Work (type, place, hours):

Comments and questions:

Form 11.2

WRITING WORKSHOP: PLANNING FORM (SAMPLE)

1. What kinds of writing do you plan to do during this term's five or six workshops? Specifically, what pieces would you like to have completed by the beginning of November?

   - a sonnet for my wife

   - an article on portfolio assessment for English journal

   - a humorous piece on trying to handle all the junk my family and I accumulate

2. For each of these pieces, please indicate the information, models, techniques, etc. necessary to develop it.

   - Shakespeare, E. B. White. Need to know the sonnet form, concentrate on imagery, avoid being crippled by meter and rhyme.

   - My notes from the past three years, a sense of humor. Need to avoid preaching to colleagues. Use lots of anecdotes and illustrations. Provide some forms—materials teachers can use.

   - Time. Again, lots of illustrations. Can't be too serious, but need to be concrete. Approach it from fall vs. spring cleaning. Garage, basement—in our case living and dining rooms. Eight years to empty the basement? An archaeological dig.

3. What kinds of reading—or which writers—might be helpful to you in developing these pieces?

   - Again, E. B. White. Maybe Hopkins, too. Has Stafford written any? Need to run the lines through on morning drives.

   - The LitNet group. I should review the materials from last year. Joe's stuff was especially persuasive and solid. Invite students to participate. November assessment should help.

   - Just the regulars: McEnroe, Barry. Simply need to write. Probably on timed blocks. Saturday mornings.

4. Besides me, whom will you ask to read your work? What makes this person—or persons—a good reviewer?

   - Jan [my wife], without question.

   - She's candid and takes the time to read carefully.

Writing Workshop

The perennial portfolio test for me has been holding to the writing workshop schedule: once every six classes. I'm still not satisfied with it, but the workshops did work better this year than they had previously, for at least one reason: I held *myself* to the schedule. In past years, I would delay or cancel a workshop, either because I wanted to complete something I felt was more important or because I thought that the students weren't taking it seriously—and some of them weren't. Keep in mind that portfolio preparation and writing workshop take a relatively small portion of class time. Therefore, it's important to emphasize their relevance to what we do daily and to give them their due. To do this I have asked students to submit quarterly writing workshop plans with time lines. A model I used last year with one class is given in form 11.2.

I also suggested they plan to use the last workshop to do some portfolio preparation. Still, time lines proved stressful. The difference was this: students had set their own time lines; if they were frustrated, they didn't take it out on me. I had my own time lines to be frustrated by.

During the first term I also ask my students to complete *Two-Minute Assessments*. The form is simple, asking students to identify what they set out to do, assess whether they did it, and ask any questions they'd like me to respond to. I don't respond unless I'm asked. The questions range from "What do you think?" (not my favorite) to "Is this a good ending?" to "How can I make this character sound real?" (this, I like). The range of writing is every bit as wide as you'd expect: newspaper articles, journal entries, poems, personal narratives, horror stories, scripts, interviews, and a good number of false starts. Having only forty minutes every six classes clearly isn't enough to accomplish much writing, but at least it's a reminder. My being the school newspaper advisor has also helped. Students know I'm always looking for articles. And they're willing to oblige me, especially when it comes to portfolio crunch time. But that's about as coercive as it gets.

Before leaving writing workshop, let me share a story about Kyle,[1] an accomplished athlete who was less than enthusiastic about writing workshop or English in general. At the beginning of the year Kyle told me he neither read nor wrote—but had a supportive network that helped him squeeze by. He announced—as opposed to confessed—this in response to being asked to complete a writing workshop plan. I had shared my model and suggested different types of writings, but none of these appealed to Kyle. I figured I'd get him where he lived:

"Well, I know you're into body-building. How about a feature story on that?" I asked.

"Nah."

This was not going to be easy. "Well, kiddo, you need to come up with a plan. I'll be back." Ten minutes later Kyle wondered aloud, "I don't suppose I could write letters?"

"Why not?"

He proposed writing letters to his sister, a college sophomore, and sharing these with me. I told him that would be fine, but I didn't want to cramp his style. No problem. I wasn't about to cramp his style. In the writing workshop section of his first quarter portfolio, Kyle included half a dozen letters he'd sent to his sister. I learned about his injuries, his preferences in girlfriends, his thoughts about being the solo child at home, and his efforts to do well in school. I liked this kid. I also learned that he had completed reading *Catcher in the Rye* and two of the four assigned stories from *Nine Stories*, the first readings he had completed in four years. I was pleased. His other portfolio selections, submitted late and under duress, were poor: a halfhearted attempt at imitating Salinger and a comparative essay. Still, things were looking pretty good. And they got better. By year's end, with a video rendition of what really occurred between Daisy and Jay Gatsby while Nick excused himself, some mezza mezza literary responses, a decent research paper on addictive personalities in *Who's Afraid of Virginia Woolf* and *A Streetcar Named Desire*, here's what Kyle had to say:

> *My dad read one of my papers and was shocked by the improvement I had made in my writing skills. Scary thinking of what they used to be. Anyway, in your class I have made the biggest strides I have ever made in an English class. I like doing the portfolio. That's one of the things I like best about the class.*

And some excerpts from his last portfolio:

> *My second entry from the first semester is the letters I wrote to my sister. . . . I do not write often so this helped. . . . It was somewhat of a learning tool for me and I think it helped my writing. A stepping stone . . . .*
>
> *My first piece from the second half of the year is a paper I spent hours stressing over, organizing, and watching a movie within an inch of the video's life, and typing and then re-typing. Of course I'm talking about the Big Daddy of them all, the research paper. I'm including this in the portfolio because I gave it a real honest effort and I am proud of it just for that reason. I feel it is not the best of my work but it symbolizes to me I can get through and hang in there. . . .*
>
> *My final entry is the poem. I wrote this because you had asked us to try it out and tell what we thought of it. . . . I found it interesting, I actually enjoyed it. . . . [We published it in the school paper.]*
>
> *How I handled the course expectations? Poorly, for the average person but for me not bad. I could have done better, but if I look at the bright side instead of the lazy side, I did begin to read this year. I improved my writing in a big way and my vocab. I don't have the grade so far to show it but I know it. . . .*

For Kyle, the flexible but structured quality of the writing workshops and the portfolio made a difference.

First-quarter Portfolios

The guidelines for this past year's first portfolio submission are given in form 11.3. This form closely resembles the one I used toward the end of the previous year. Obviously, there's some structure and clear attention to weight. Still it differs from earlier forms in that it is less restrictive than those in which I asked for four pieces, three of which I determined. By year's end, I required no specific pieces; students were free to choose among their best written work. My sense is that as my students and I became more comfortable with portfolio practices, the need for an explicitly structured and weighted framework diminished.

Here are a few sample assessments from students' initial portfolios:

Prejudice in Brewster Place—literary analysis

My focus is well-defined in this piece. It is about the prejudice that some characters can or can't handle. This was a very developed piece. I used quotations and organized it well. There aren't many mechanical problems at all because I revised it. I find that when I use quotations I have a stronger paper. I'll remember that in the future.

—Cindy

Applying yourself ain't easy—news article

Not only my first opinion piece but also my first attempt at humor. Attention-grabbing lead followed by effective parallel structure. Well developed with good description. Topic that students are interested in. A little rough around the edges. Ends abruptly (cheesy ending). Catchy headline, did I write that? Once again, it's a topic I enjoy, which always makes it a better piece.

—Jessica

Summary and Assessment—exercise

Writing this assessment told me one thing, I have bad usage. It's not that bad, but it could be better. My solution: administer Writers, Inc. *to everyone. Specifically, to teachers and students, and have them go over it. This is probably the best English book I've ever received. Those dinky vocab. books were no good and neither were the spelling books in elementary school. This book has everything, even good illustrations [Jeff drew cartoons]. Don't think I'm getting off track by giving a review of* Writers, Inc. *I'm only assessing how to solve what I believe is a bad grammar problem. . . .*

—Jeff

These responses reflect different interests, proficiencies, and personalities. They also show students' willingness to look at themselves and their writing.

My Response to Portfolios

I write back to students. It's time consuming, but it's generally pleasurable. Thus far, I've tried several formats:

Form 11.3

MODERN AMERICAN LITERATURE

First-Quarter Portfolio

In choosing and discussing the selections for your first-quarter portfolio, please keep these goals and considerations in mind:

- your portfolio should reflect your best efforts at reading and writing
- it should reveal your recent growth and focus as a reader and writer
- it should demonstrate your ability to discuss your reading and writing
- it should reveal those skills, beliefs, and understandings that you consider are essential to being an effective reader and writer
- besides you and me, at least one other person whom you choose will read and comment on your portfolio

Procedures: Your selections and commentary should be word-processed.

1. Write a short introductory note, briefly noting the highlights of your portfolio. (10%)

2. Next, select and discuss several pieces of your work. These should include a minimum of three works. Included among these should be your writing workshop and one piece from this class. With one of these selections be sure to submit notes and drafts that show how you developed and revised it. Briefly discuss your writing process. Be candid, but give it careful consideration. (60%)

3. Include another reader's discussion or assessment of your portfolio. Remember: *you* select the reader, and *you* select the criteria that person uses in discussing your portfolio. This portion of your portfolio does not have to be typed or word-processed. (10%)

4. Answer the following questions:

    a. How well have you kept up with the reading assignments, notetaking, and extended responses this term? How often do you contribute to class discussions?

    b. Within and beyond class, how well have you used writing workshop?

    c. What were your writing goals for this term? How successfully did you achieve these? What helped or hindered your achieving these? (E.g., did you use the writing resource room or confer with me or others about your writing?) Along these lines, what can you now see in your or others' writing that you didn't see before?

    d. To what extent do you feel capable of assessing and directing your growth as a reader and writer? (10%)

5. Conclude by assigning a grade to this portfolio, based on its overall quality (A = superior, excellent; B = good, solid; C = OK, but less than what it could be; D = poor, last minute, hardly worth the effort). Then discuss the kinds of reading and writing you would like to focus on during the second quarter. Be specific and honest, keeping in mind that this will be the plan you will work on during the second quarter. (10%)

- using the guidelines as a format and just typing in comments
- word-processing letters, memo style
- recording responses on my drive to and from work, which I then type or (when I'm lucky enough) have a secretary type

For me, a twenty-five inaccurate-words-a-minute-double-digit typist, the memo-style letter is the most flexible and efficient format. Since I have already read and responded to most of the work that appears in the quarterly portfolios, I can generally write two to three responses hourly. This year I worked with forty students. I've used portfolios with as many as seventy. I would be hard-pressed to respond to 100 or 140 students each quarter. I might choose to do so twice yearly. My colleagues are now asking students to submit portfolios once or perhaps twice yearly. I think they'll soon find that once is not enough. That's like having students give one speech or presentation yearly. What if they blow it? They have to wait until the next year to get another crack at it? Recently, a colleague, a superior teacher very interested in portfolios and committed to working with low-achieving and oftentimes unmotivated students, asked, "How do you get your kids to write so much about their portfolios?" For a moment it felt like a TV commercial. "Here, look at this," she showed me a sheet of responses that one of her better students had submitted. I read them; they looked good to me. Concise, but candid. I said as much. "But this is the exception. Most of the kids give me one sentence—or one word—responses." I suggested that her students might have more to say the second or third time around. These were their initial, year-end responses. Again . . . once is not enough.

Despite what writing researchers suggested back in the seventies and eighties—that students pay no attention to our comments—I know that students appreciate my notes. And that's because the purpose of the note is as much instructive and supportive as it is evaluative. Consider these comments:

> *The biggest positive factor in the portfolio that separates your portfolios from others in the past is your extensive letter to us in response to the portfolio. . . . Your letter to us is another thing altogether. It really isn't a grade that we're looking for (even though we may think it is) it is the positive comment that supports us when we try something new, like poetry. In comparison to the moral support that a full response to our portfolios gives us, the grade is immaterial.*

> *It takes a dedicated teacher to type up responses on our portfolios and be candid, and honest about our work.*

They may be pressing the right buttons, but it still feels pretty good. It also occurs to me that those of you reading this probably need little convincing about the value of writing to students. Writing conferences are fine, but having it in writing is better. It's especially important to write to students who haven't been successful in English because chances are much of the commentary they've

---

Form 11.4

To: Dave

From: John Hennelly

Re: Fourth-quarter portfolio

Date: 6/10/95

For at least two reasons, my comments on this quarter's portfolio will be briefer than usual: (1) this portfolio is largely directed to your next year's English teacher; and (2) at this point, what you have to say about your reading and writing is more important than anything I might have to say.

- *Your introductory note:* A good, clear overview.

- *Discussion of selections, your growth as a reader and writer, what you're pleased with, plans:* Dave, you did a nice job discussing your selections. Where do I order my Mclaren F1? The social studies paper seemed a little unclear in focus. Your English research paper still looks pretty good. Good use of sources.

- *Course expectations, deadlines, work with others, and skills work:* You discuss this aspect of your work clearly and honestly. You might think of modifying your approach to notetaking—don't always think of them as dialectical notes: just jot down thoughts and questions as you read.

- *Your grade recommendation:* I think a B is right on the money. You've done some good work.

Dave, I've enjoyed working with you this year. Have a good summer, keep your skates sharp, and take care.

To: Deb

From: John Hennelly

Re: Fourth-quarter portfolio

Date: 6/10/95

- *Your introductory note:* Clear and to the point.

- *Discussion of selections, your growth as a reader and writer, what you're pleased with, plans:* I'd like to see your *Stress Factor* paper reworked for a *Pow Wow* feature. You could use all the secondary material you've included, but enrich it with anecdotes from friends and personal observations. *Letting Go* still comes across as your most successful and ambitious piece, although I like the wrap on *Love and Lies*. Thanks for the draft on your recent odyssey. It's getting there. I'd include more dialogue and maintain that attention to description and setting that you begin so well with.

- *Course expectations, deadlines, work with others, and skills work:* Again, your discussion is right on target. Group work is something to think about for next year.

- *Your grade recommendation:* Sounds reasonable to me, Deb. Were you expecting something different?

Deb, it has been a pleasure working with you this year. Have a good summer, get some rest, and take care.

received thus far has been critical and impersonal. A letter conveys the subtle message that writing is enjoyable. (A few notes from the last batch are given in form 11.4. Although they're shorter than some of the earlier notes, they still convey a message: I'm familiar with the writer's work and interests.)

Before moving on to other communication-building practices, I'll briefly discuss another course activity, probably well known to most of us, that has figured prominently in students' willingness and ability to handle a variety of texts and genres: dialectical notetaking.

For the past three years I have asked students to keep a reading notebook in which they cite passages from their reading. I explain that they may select passages for any reason: they like it, it confuses them, it seems significant. Beyond recording the passage, they must also make a comment. Form 11.5, based on samples gleaned from students' initial notetaking, was the model I used last year to get them started. I couldn't resist adding my two cents (*Ed. note*). We were reading *Nine Stories*.

The best thing about dialectical notetaking is that it allows students to jump in wherever they're comfortable, an important consideration in a mixed class. But it does require jumping in. Other considerations that make this a practical if not a desirable practice include these:

- As part of our state's academic performance test (CAPT) in English, students are asked to discuss significant passages from a reading.

- Notetaking promotes more active reading.

- Students are more likely to have something to say, even if it's "I didn't understand this passage. That's why I wrote it down."

Still, I was a little surprised this year at the many students who discussed dialectical notetaking in their portfolios and course assessments. Here are two representative observations:

> *As a reader, through the use of dialectical notes I've delved deeper into the books we've read and have understood them better.*
> *I have read more books this year than I have in prior years. I used to read and take in the main idea of the story and some details, but I would not analyze. Now when I read, I have an analytical approach to it. This is due in part to dialectical notes. They have helped me.*

Communication and Quality Control

At points in the year I ask students for their suggestions about the course. They have an opportunity to do this with each portfolio submission, but occasionally, I ask them for their suggestions at a time and in a manner that encourage them to be candid. Here's one of those requests:

Form 11.5

Passage:

"Can I have this?" Ramona said, taking a burned match out of the ashtray.

"*May* I have this. Yes. Stay out of the street, please." (Salinger, 27)

Response:

Is the match supposed to be some sort of toy for this child? I mean look, her only friend is make-believe, and there are no children in the neighborhood. There is no mention of toys around the house or in her room. She is forced to make her own toys, and apparently to her, a match would be one of them.

Passage:

Mary Jane let go of the curtain and wandered back to the blue chair, passing two heavily stocked bookcases without glancing at the titles. (Salinger, 31)

Response:

The fact that there are bookcases in this place is ironic. These people seem to party their lives away. The books are probably just for show, which would most likely place them in the upper class.

Passage:

"She's sitting on her big black butt, reading *The Robe*." (Salinger, 22)

Response:

My first reaction to this statement is that Eloise is prejudiced and somewhat cruel because her statement is unkind. I interpreted from the statement that Grace was sort of a servant.

[*Ed. note*: Also consider the possibility that Eloise resents Grace because Grace actually reads books.]

Modern American Literature: Some thoughts and questions

April 17, 1995

Now that you've submitted your third-quarter portfolio and received some response, how would you assess this procedure and the course itself? I'll be more specific. In planning Modern American Literature, I made a few assumptions about what might best help you grow as writers, readers, and learners. For instance, I assumed that given a chance to select your own goals you would work toward achieving them more willingly, perhaps more energetically. At the same time, however, knowing that few of you have had much experience directing and assessing your own reading and writing, I wanted to provide some structure that would help you to develop the language and skill to do this. Hence, I give you the writing workshop plan, the dialectical notetaking, the literacy charts, and the lean writing exercises.

*And there was the larger consideration that modern American literature, being the chief focus, would require a good deal of time and attention. Again, I've tried to organize the readings around topics that I felt were of interest: identity (Salinger and Dorris), personal relationships (Kingsolver, Albee, and Williams), self-expression (poetry), and, most recently, race, roles, and economics (*The Women of Brewster Place *and* The Great Gatsby*). Obviously, there's some overlap, and that's intentional. All of these topics and authors' views contribute to a modern, diverse, and contemporary American literary experience. And my asking you to explore a literature-based research question was an attempt to have you achieve two goals: (1) distill and connect some of this literature to real life, and (2) exercise and strengthen your research skills.*

The usage and vocabulary exercises are nothing more or less than grim reminders that mechanics count.

I would like you to assess the course thus far: specifically, the activities and design just outlined along with anything else that you believe is pertinent. Have these exercises helped you become a better reader and writer? Does preparing a portfolio help or hinder your progress? You might also review the attached charts.

I appreciate your giving this some time and thought. Thanks.

And here are a few of their responses. I've excerpted only the passages about portfolios:

The idea of giving us a chance to select our own goals so that we could achieve them more willingly was a good idea. It made us be more responsible and aware that we are adults and have to use our time wisely.

—Jesse

I believe that the way the class is set up presently is ideal. You have made it clear that you as the instructor do not take this course lightly or consider it an elective. You also have made us aware that we should consider this an academic course and work to our potential so making our own plans, coming up with our own work schedules, and assessing our work at the end of the term shouldn't be too much to ask. Personally I enjoy not having to do your assignments all the time. It allows me to pursue ideas and projects that I come up with on my own. The portfolio was something new to me. I hadn't ever been required to assess anything I'd write. In other classes we had done peer evaluations, but I have never critiqued my own work. It is very helpful to be able to step away from a piece of writing and attempt to look at it objectively—especially if it has personal themes in it.

—John

I think that being able to decide what I write about is good because it gives me a chance to do different types of writing. Also it's easier to write about something I want to write about rather than a topic that a teacher has assigned me. I feel it is good that I can set my own goals and work at my own pace. It helps when I know what I want to do and what goals I want to achieve. Doing the portfolio is a very time-consuming project. I feel it does help me in that I get to put it all together and reflect on what I did. It's nice to be able to see what I have accomplished in a quarter. Overall, I think this course is a good one. I have learned to assess my work and how to set goals for myself, and how to go about reaching them.

—Phil

As for the portfolio, I like having to go and organize my writings and write about them also. It has the ability to help you but also hurt you, so you basically make that decision when you choose to do your work (or not do it).

—Jane

Thus far I have truthfully found this course to be quite enjoyable. It may be hard to believe that a student would enjoy anything related to school work, but I did. The one thing that I found most rewarding was the fact that this course, unlike any other, was planned to give the student a lot of freedom. . . . This course also gave us freedom to decide what pieces we thought reflected our best ability. This really worked to our advantage because even though all papers were graded, we reflected our best work in portfolios. I believe that the writing workshops are very helpful, because even though it may have seemed like a lot of us weren't working, it helped a great deal. Specifically it gave me a chance to run a few ideas by on my classmates, which really helped me out. The one problem I have always had with my writing is that I can relate to it well, but it's kind of confusing for others. But when I was able to ask my friends in class and get their opinions, it helped me develop my work into stronger pieces. On a happier note, portfolios are a great idea because of the ability the student develops to assess and recognize the good and bad in their own work. As I explained before, it gives students the chance to put their best work forward, no matter if it's from Biology, or American Government. Portfolios are a reflection of the student's true abilities. I really enjoyed doing them.

—Sandra

After putting together my portfolio and writing an assessment on it, I feel better about the course. I enjoy writing once I've found a topic or subject that I'm comfortable with and can really enjoy writing. I was overwhelmed with the work load in the beginning, but that was for a couple of reasons. First of all, I expected a lot from myself as far as the reading and writing plan went. Second, I didn't budget my time as carefully as I should have so I found myself writing a lot in a short period of time. I think I have some pieces planned for this quarter that will get me motivated to write and budget my time more carefully.

—Emily

The portfolio is not the most enjoyable assignment in the world, but it does give us a chance to assess our own writing. It forces us to put our best work together and take a good look at our accomplishments for the term.

—Pete

I believe this is a very beneficial course. It requires a lot of independence, and self-motivation, which are qualities that should be developed by junior and senior year. Unfortunately not everybody has them and these are the people that have trouble. . . . The portfolio procedure is very tedious during the first term. Due to the lack of experience it takes more thought, and time. The later in the year, however, the easier. The portfolio is not as hard to produce at the end of the year. No matter how hard it is to produce, it is always valuable. It allows me to slow down and think about my accomplishments. Portfolios are extremely valuable.

—Barbara

Had they been skill-leveled, these students would represent all three levels. What their comments reveal is their appreciation at having been invited to direct some of their learning. And that, I believe, is one of the best reasons for asking students to prepare portfolios and participate in writing workshops. Another equally compelling reason for asking students to work with us in directing their learning is that so few students have a vested interest in literacy, and fewer still see themselves making much headway. For instance, last month, much to my colleagues' credit, we surveyed most of our sophomores (218 completed from a 260 population). The results were disturbing, especially in light of our view of this community's being educationally supportive and culturally rich. Consider these two findings:

- Only 14% of our sophomores indicated that reading and writing were valued in their homes.

- Only 8% felt that their reading and writing skills had improved this year.

Whether we attribute it to their age, passive-aggression, or early June impatience, this is disturbing news. I'm confident my juniors would respond more positively.

Lest any reader mistake my Modern American Literature for Metacognition 101, let me share a few other surveys that also serve for technical and interpretive writing exercises. Several times a year, I ask my students to complete surveys about the course, views on marriage, school issues, etc. I then tabulate the data and share it with the students. I ask them to summarize and assess the data, a writing activity I recommend for three reasons: (1) it causes students to think critically; (2) it causes them to reflect on their own views, comparing these with others'; (3) it creates a more meaningful context within which they develop some practical, technical writing skill. Here's a preliminary (prewriting) model I shared with my students based on their responses to Rotter's I-E inventory (internal and external locus of control):

Summary Notes:

- Hennelly's MAL students' scores on the Rotter I-E test suggest that the class as a whole has a fairly strong internal locus of control (i.e., they feel they have considerable control and responsibility for the quality of their lives).
- This class also completed a related survey on factors over which they felt they had little to a lot of control.
- Class members felt they had at least some influence over all of these social and psychological factors.
- The two factors over which they had the least—but still some—influence were family ties and financial success.
- Class members believe that they have considerable control over their appearance, making friends, and happiness.

Assessment Notes:

- Students in this class reflect the values and beliefs of their environment: a comfortable, middle-class community in which people believe they can succeed.
- These students will probably assume greater responsibility for themselves.
- Interestingly, they feel less responsible for and secure about family relationships and financial success.

Nuts and Bolts

Perhaps in no other area is difference in proficiency more obvious—though arguably less significant—than writing mechanics. And this is an area that more than any other requires treading carefully. But, given teacher-student ratios, that's next to impossible. What I stumbled upon this year was a student-managed activity that bears further investigation. By request, I had built some pre- and postin-structional skills inventories and a diagnostic profile form for use with our fresh-men. As English teachers, we identified those skills (homophones and various agreement) we believed freshmen should know. The students' performance as a whole was lower than we expected. I knew that my juniors would not take offense at being asked to complete this fifteen-minute skills test. It didn't say *Grade 9*, and I assured them that it would serve simply as the basis for some skills work.

The important part of this exercise was "skills needing most attention," which was derived from the scoring. After students had listed the skills they felt needed attention, I simply asked them to submit evidence, on a biweekly basis, that they were attending to these skills. To help them in this pursuit, I issued each a copy of a 1958 grammar book, three hundred of which I discovered in a clos-et. When I gave a post-test eleven weeks later, the average gain was fifteen points. It required little time—less than a class—and a number of students felt it was worthwhile.

Parting Thoughts

After six years of teaching through portfolios, I realize there are no tricks. It's a matter of balance and establishing honest working relationships with the students. That's not to suggest it's easy. But it is clear. It's also a lot of fun. Five of my students have joined me at various presentations this year to share their work and views about portfolios. They were the ones who were convincing. They convinced me. During this past year I've read the two best personal narratives that I've had the pleasure to read in my teaching career.

It seems appropriate to close with a letter written by Scott McNamara, a young man whom I worked with two years ago and who emphatically attests to the importance of good working relationships and some self-direction. A portfolio pro-ject colleague had proposed to the *English Journal* that it publish some student work. There was no shortage of that, but *EJ* evidently chose not to publish the let-ters from students. So here's the better part of Scott's unpublished letter to *EJ*:

> *I would first like to thank Joe Quattrini for his persistence in open-ing the* EJ *forum to students. I thought I would never hear a teacher utter the words "professional apartheid," but here we are, in a culture where stu-dents can speak without being spoken to. I intend to take advantage of this rare opportunity, after having been told what to write and think for twelve years, to tell the teachers what to do. I expect them to listen. . . .*
>
> *I trudged through two years of the Conard High School English department not knowing where I was going with my writing and feeling as though I could write nothing above a satisfactory level. My confidence as a writer had been broken. Meaningless assignments and tedious thesis papers were shuttled across the teacher's desk and, when they finally land-ed back in my hands covered in red ink, they usually found their way to the garbage can. . . .*

What works? It's hard to say. Perhaps the enthusiasm of the teacher. . . . The second piece of writing. . . was an imitative piece, using J. D. Salinger's style in The Catcher in the Rye. *I let go on this piece and just allowed my feelings to come out in Salinger's words. On top of that I was asked to read it in class, which was the single most powerful way to boost my confidence.*

I continued with this confidence through the rest of the year, writing papers that actually meant something to me, not ones that simply gave Hennelly what he was looking for. I got to the point where I wouldn't hand in anything but my best effort, out of respect for him. How did he gain my respect? He asked my opinion. My thoughts on something I had written actually mattered. I was not only asked what I thought about a piece, but also where I thought my writing was headed.

The vehicle used to promote such confidence and personality in my writing was something he refers to simply as the portfolio. *We submitted a portfolio every quarter, and it enabled me to take off with my writing. This selection was not one of your normal run-of-the-mill folders that one leaves in the file cabinet to forget and collect dust. This was a submission of approximately three works that you were particularly proud of and which you felt best represented your ability as a writer. You were also asked to discuss each piece, noting its positive and negative aspects, along with a general discussion about how you felt you could grow as a writer. I use the word* discuss *here because it was just that. I wrote down my questions and comments, and, in turn, received answers along with a commentary.*

. . . I realized that this was what the portfolio was truly about. The development of your writing through the use of your own personal beliefs was how to gain confidence as a writer. Writing for myself and actually being able to freely incorporate my emotions into a literary analysis were the steps I needed to take to bring my writing to a new level. Even today as a senior I am able to churn out those thesis papers, but now they are full of me, the one element that was missing before. What brought about this strange turn of events? I attribute my growth to the use of the portfolio in a comprehensive yet very personal manner.

—Scott McNamara

And for balance, a few comments from students who cut to the chase:

This year was a lot different. I enjoyed doing the different things we did. . . . You listen to our opinions and usually agree with us on our assessments. . . . I enjoyed assessing my work. I had never done that in the past. Assessing really makes you analyze the quality of the work being handed in.

—Kim

Lastly, I think the portfolio and writing workshop are good ideas. They give me a chance to write some stuff that I want and even submit the pieces for a grade. Keep them.

—Chad

I like that suggestion.

Endnotes

1. I have received verbal permission to use all the student materials in this article; however, until I receive written permission I've changed some names.

Chapter 12

Using Portfolios to Negotiate a Rhetorical Community

Marian Galbraith
John Hennelly
Alan C. Purves

Based on our reading of various articles and books on portfolios and on the discussion among a larger group of twelve teachers at seven schools, we agreed early in our project that portfolios are not just nice but necessary to the teaching of English. We came up with a set of principles to guide our work, which are outlined in the introduction to this volume. It is the fourth principle—a portfolio should be the responsibility of the student—that will be elaborated in this chapter, but it must be seen in the context of the other five, namely, that the portfolio is a product created and arranged by the student to represent the individual accomplishments of that student to the outside world. Thus, the portfolio is more than a folder or a collection of writings; it has a rhetorical purpose; it is a complex argument concerning that student as reader and writer; it should be comprehensive; and it should be assembled over a period of time, with the assistance of the teacher who acts as a coach until the point at which the student says, "I'm ready to be judged."

A portfolio should be created by the students. It may have guidelines from the school or teacher about the kinds of things that might be included (or must be included), such as a number of different kinds of writing, a self-evaluation, a list of books read, or a number of original compositions or performances (film, music, writing). (We do not see English language arts or writing as limited to traditional text production.) But the decision as to what specific pieces are to be included and how they are to be arranged should remain the students'. They must also work out how best to put group work into the portfolio. If it is a project that involves the building of a model, they might have to use photographs. If there is a dramatization, there might be an audio- or videotape. If there is a really good discussion, the students should figure out how to put that into the portfolio, how to show why it is good, and what part they took in it. The students are laying themselves on the line—before the whole school perhaps, or before a jury of teachers. It is their choice as to whether they should be seen as uncaring or prideful. Teachers cannot do this for them. By taking responsibility for what they show of themselves to the world, students have a new power that they don't have when they are simply handing things in and getting grades. It takes time for them to realize that they are not helpless—that they earn the grade or the rating, a teacher does not give it to them.

This chapter is based upon the narratives of Marian Galbraith and John Hennelly; Marian was working with an eighth-grade reading workshop, and John was working with a twelfth-grade honors course. The format of the chapter will be to rearrange Marian's and John's narratives into a topical framework and to intersperse segments of their narratives with comments by Alan Purves.

Getting the Students Started through Negotiation

If these are the general outlines and goals of portfolios, how does one proceed to get students to shift to this new view of themselves? The solution we see is to practice the delicate art of negotiation. The teachers and the institution have a set of standards experienced in a curriculum. The students have a set of aims for survival in the system. Rather than simply present the curriculum and say "do it," the negotiating teacher seeks to lead or nudge the students toward the social goals and also to encourage the students to form their own views of those goals and thus begin to see how the institution and the individual can become a viable community in which group and individuals are each represented. The first step appears to be that of dealing clearly and honestly with the students concerning goals. As Marian writes:

> My first tentative moves toward negotiation took place over goal setting. Teachers have always known the goals. Whether they are the formal goals of our system curricula or the informal goals that develop throughout our school year, it is imperative that we reveal those goals to our students. We reveal them not to inform them of the goals to which we will herd them, but so they can determine, within certain parameters, the pathways they will travel with their own learning. These goals become the foundation upon which students build their portfolios.
>
> When I instituted the use of portfolios as part of the middle school reading program, my students and I began by negotiating the responsibility for setting goals. My first offer to students was an outline of the curricular goals rewritten to be comprehensible to students. I asked them to choose the curricular areas toward which they were ready to

move. In addition, I asked them to consider personal goals—ones that I may not have considered—and to set goals for themselves. What I discovered was that students had long ago given up on understanding my motives and were more than willing to submit themselves to my will. The goals they developed, more often than not, consisted of *getting better grades, writing better responses,* or *getting work done on time*—all goals designed to return the control to the teacher. This student presents an example of such a goal:

> *Some of my goals as an eighth grader is [sic] to get better grades than I did in seventh grade. The reason why I think this is an important goal is because it will help me later on during high school or even college. Not only that, but most importantly, I want to do it for myself. When I get good grades on my report cards, I feel real good about myself. Another thing I want to do as an eighth grader is to write better entries. Often I find myself writing too much detail and I would like to stop that and write more response and explanation.*

Since this type of goal was far too common, my next proposal was that goals be more closely tied to curricular goals. I made out of the system's curricular goals a Reader's Profile. This was a list of indicators that might serve as evidence of what eighth-grade students should know or be able to do. These indicators were grouped into five goal areas: Stretching Your Reading Experience, Responding to Books, Understanding How Books Work, Understanding How an Author Writes, and Gathering Information. Within each of these goal areas were curriculum objectives that students could use as indicators of their strengths or weaknesses within a given goal area.

For instance, for the goal area Responding to Books, students used the reader's profile to consider whether the following were ways they responded to books:

- used their own experiences to understand characters and situations in books
- connected the issues in a book to the lives of others or the world around them
- compared different books or genres
- used their own experiences, knowledge of other books, or details in the book to make and revise predictions about the plot, characters, or theme
- used art, music, graphs, drama, or discussion to respond to books
- wrote about their struggles—what was confusing or hard to understand

Students were able to review the list and determine whether these were things they did rarely, sometimes, or usually. Although most students were familiar with these strategies for responding to books, others often found themselves literally unable to think of anything to say about a book. They lacked ways of thinking about or responding to books. By completing their own Reader's Profile, students could see which goal areas might be most accessible and could explore ways to reach those goals. In this way, we reached a point of compromise in our negotiations. As their teacher I was satisfied that the goals fell within the curricular parameters, but the students determined which of those goals were important to and necessary for them. They had taken a giant step toward taking responsibility for learning by committing themselves to specific achievable goals. Instead of the vague goals chosen earlier, students were more likely to choose goals like this one:

> *My goal for this quarter is to work on making and revising predictions as I read, because I haven't been doing that a lot. Usually I just read faster to find out what happens and end up missing a lot of things that may be important to a story. This way I'll be able to read slower so I won't miss out on anything.*
>
> *My plan to prove that I'm meeting this goal is to write the predictions in my journal entries.*

The point that can be gleaned from Marian's narrative is that the teacher sets forth and clarifies the goals of the curriculum, but the students need to personalize those goals to put them in their own language or put their own *twist* on them so as to make them meaningful. In doing so they may also see the level at which they can best operate (to make the predictions at all before making more detailed ones). Some students may be new to English and to the American culture, some may have been writing on their own for quite some time. Their goals need to be set within a level or band of expectation and operation (using words like *better* or *more*), rather than to a single, unyielding criterion (Purves, 1993).

Another aspect of the clarification of goals deals with the initial negotiation of criteria. A goal may be specified, but unless there is also clarity as to how one knows when it will be reached, it remains somewhat inert in the students' minds. In writing, particularly, we have found that the use of a detailed scoring rubric has a pedagogical advantage in that it enables the teacher to specify what is being looked at by judges of writing (Purves and Hawisher, 1990). By giving a clear and specific rubric at the beginning of instruction, a teacher is able to share concepts and language to talk about students' writing with them and to have them talk with each other about writing. John describes it this way:

> During my first few years' teaching, I responded enthusiastically to students' writing, pointing to its merits, downplaying its flaws. If writing was their task, grinning and bearing it was mine. Even in my mid-seventies peer-evaluative classes we rarely moved beyond the *what I like, what I'd like to know more about* rubric. Students still knew that I was

the only one who would or could provide the straight dope. In short, they did not direct their own writing development. Here is what I was not doing often or effectively enough:

- encouraging students to identify specifically some elements of good writing
- helping students set specific writing goals based on those elements
- providing them with instruction and models specific to achieving those goals
- expecting students to participate in assessing their success in meeting those writing goals

I may have overlooked these procedures due to inexperience. Perhaps such considerations as development, explication, style, and organization were just becoming clearer to me; perhaps I was unable able to convey these to my students effectively; perhaps, like many of my colleagues, I believed the ability to write was as much talent as it was learned behavior; perhaps I believed that covering the content of a literature- and mechanics-driven program left little room for negotiating the writing curriculum.

Since then I have reconsidered and revised my writing pedagogy, adapting and developing techniques to help students improve their writing. I have come to believe that young and inexperienced writers can improve by identifying what they wish to achieve in their work. This realization evolved through trial and error, lots of writing and talking to students about their writing, experimenting with models and forms, having students assess my courses and methods, and, most important, using writing folders and writing portfolios.

The chief focus of my instruction has been challenging students to assume greater control of and responsibility for their learning. And in the past few years that challenge has become increasingly a process of negotiation—negotiation among student, teacher, and curriculum.

As have many teachers of English, I have often asked students to describe their growth as writers, the changes they have observed in their written work. Generally, their responses have been disappointing.

At the middle school:

I use more description. I know how to use commas, and I can write longer stories.

At the high school:

I use more description. My grammar has improved. I know how to organize.

Obviously, there is little qualitative or quantitative difference between many thirteen- and eighteen-year-olds' commentaries. Does this explain the high-school student's frustration at writing? It's difficult to feel good about something you've failed to improve at during the past four years. If teachers have difficulty seeing proof of progress in their students' writing—instructors trained to discern shifts in anything from homophones to t-units—imagine how much more discouraging it is for the learner.

It seemed to me that helping students use language effectively to describe or direct their writing could give them greater control and understanding of the process and craft. But developing this lexicon required more than mere naming of parts. And it involved more than clearly-presented teacher models and frequent student and teacher practice. It required students' using and owning this language to describe and improve their own and others' writing. It required fuller student engagement and a different kind of teacher engagement. If students and

---

Form 12.1

SENIOR LITERARY ANALYSIS SCORING SHEET

Name: _____   Date: _____

1.   Reasoning and Development: __/50
     • How clearly has the writer established purpose and focus?
     • Has the writer maintained this focus and thoroughly explored theme or question?
     • Has the writer focused on theme and interpretation rather than on story?

2.   Organization: __/20
     • Within paragraphs, has the writer clearly organized information?
     • Has the writer clearly connected paragraphs, being especially careful in making transitions from one work to the next?
     • Is the overall design of this essay clear and logical?

3.   Style: __/15
     • Has the writer varied sentence beginnings and sentence lengths?
     • Has the writer chosen appropriate language (phrasing and diction)?
     • Has the writer maintained consistent tone?

4.   Mechanics: __/15
     • Has the writer avoided usage errors?
     • Has the writer used the correct APA citation format?
     • Punctuation?
     • Spelling?

teacher were to succeed, they needed to become vested members in a larger writing and learning community.

Several years ago, I began exploring portfolio applications in the hopes of vitalizing what was for my students, my colleagues, and myself a very passive and inconsequential writing folder procedure. To encourage students to look more closely at their work, I initially developed and used assessment forms like the one in form 12.1. While models like this offered a comprehensive assessment guide, the criteria were still largely teacher-determined, and little if any negotiation was involved. I was simply trying to find descriptive language and illustrate qualities I hoped students would bring to their writing. Consequently, although they were willing to apply the criteria, they may have been discouraged for several reasons:

- the 15- to 50-point scales were unmanageable
- the number of criteria was overwhelming
- students were at different developmental stages

Though designed by me for my students, the form was nondiscriminating.

In retrospect, I may have overcompensated for my students' inability or reluctance to look at their work critically. Like many teachers, I wanted my students to understand and apply a common language (development, organization, style, and mechanics); however, in my effort to explicate these four descriptors, I'm afraid I left some students in the dust.

My challenge then was to help students identify qualities they felt were important to effective writing and to apply these as they saw fit. Recently, I asked two groups of students to review their second portfolio submissions and identify the elements or criteria that they valued in good writing. One group compiled this list:

- be flexible
- imagination
- developing ideas/organization (clearly)
- correct, constant mechanics
- focus/purpose
- attractive to reader (can relate)
- flows well
- detail
- self-satisfaction
- use of quotes
- dialogue

- paint a picture
- imagery
- strong opening/closing
- less is more (essay writing)
- good use of humor
- don't write about something you know nothing about
- don't leave reader hanging
- transitions
- balance
- tone—be consistent
- word choice/don't repeat
- stay on task
- be personal
- underlying message
- be passionate/convincing/inspired

What this list reflects, as does that submitted by the other group, is an understanding and appreciation of writing. It reveals attention to those qualities outlined in my literary analysis form; however, it gives greater attention to affective concerns and to the writer's relationship to the reader. It also represents students' heightened awareness of what makes writing effective.

Having identified these qualities, students then discussed their own work, using these descriptors, caveats, and guidelines. Not surprisingly, their written assessments were more thorough, reflecting attention to qualities they hadn't previously considered. Granted, students chose different descriptors and the exercise didn't lend itself to a linear, quantitative assessment, but this follow-up exercise suggested that students could write within a larger, richer frame of reference.

I believe these two exercises were critical in helping students and me begin to negotiate our roles and responsibilities in portfolio presentation and assessment. And although the quarterly portfolio design initially remained teacher-directed, with students selecting from a limited collection of pieces (literature-related and writing workshop-related), I found myself asking for more written feedback about my service as a reader and facilitator and their progress with long- and short-range reading and writing goals. And even that quarterly design has changed, a process I'll discuss later.

What my students and I achieved was a redefinition of our roles as writers and readers. And again, although I was initially responsible for priming the pump with models and forms, the process gradually became a negotiated one through which students extended their understanding

and use of descriptive language to direct and assess their and others'
writing.

Viewed over the course of time, John's approach is a classic example of negotiation, one that is clearly taken from the model for negotiation used by professional writers, publishers, and labor-management experts. The first step in the
process of negotiation is one of realizing the otherness of others and then moving
to sharing, both the sharing of goals and objectives and the sharing of criteria or
standards (Purves, 1993). For John, it involves a set of steps: first being specific
about one's own judgments that may have seemed almost automatic and then recognizing that these need to be placed in relationship to the goals and understandings of the students. This step requires respecting the students. The goals
may be general and focused on process or more specifically centered on product.
The spirit, however, is the same. In both goals and criteria, the teacher is a representative of a broader society, the literate culture of which the teacher is a representative and into which the students are passing (Kádár-Fülop, 1988; Purves,
1991), but at the same time the teacher sees the individual as worthy of sharing.
The portfolio idea helps make that act of sharing and including apparent to all.
The criteria and goals are used not as a barrier, but as a gateway. As in any negotiation, the positions and assumptions of the negotiations must be open and
above-board.

Developing a Monitoring Strategy

The setting and clarifying of goals is not accomplished overnight; rather, it
is the first stage of a procedure that is carried on and modified throughout the
period of instruction. The clarification and elaboration of these goals takes shape
in the work of the course, while the students are gathering the evidence that will
eventually appear in their portfolios and monitoring their progress. Marian elaborates the working out of these steps in her class:

Gathering Evidence

Once the students have set their goals, the portfolio became the
record of goal attainment. Within it students compiled the evidence
they needed to measure their progress. It would have been naïve to
assume that, having set goals, students would take on the initiative to
move unerringly toward them. The negotiation of responsibility continued as teacher and class experimented with ways to help them move
toward their goals.

If students were ever to accept the responsibility for realizing their
goals and building a portfolio, they had to understand two things. First,
they had to realize that the portfolio belonged to them. They might show
it to others, but it was their record of learning. I could not and would not

presume to fill their portfolios. Each student had to make his or her own choices about what would be included.

Second, they had to learn how to make those choices. They had to begin to think of their own work as evidence of learning. Students needed to see that what they produced was tangible evidence of the ways they thought about books and their ability to express those thoughts. It was evidence of the ways they were learning to think about literature and writing. The process of assembling a portfolio required them to accumulate evidence and to make conscious decisions about the evidence they were collecting. A portfolio could no longer be simply a storage place. A piece would be selected for the portfolio based on its ability to provide evidence of learning. For most students this was new and difficult. They did not think that way about work.

Up until this point, students had been asked to evaluate their work based on certain criteria. As part of the reading program, students wrote journal entries and created various artifacts in response to their reading. In the past they were accustomed to looking at their work and determining whether it met previously disclosed criteria. Had they responded to the piece rather than simply summarized? Had they explained their response? And had they provided enough details to anchor it in the text? They were able to recognize the difference between response and summary, between a reasoned response and a general, nonspecific response, but they were unable to examine the nature of that response. They did not, for instance, notice when they had made the move from writing about their responses to the book to recognizing how the author had used language, events, or characters to evoke a response. They were unaccustomed to looking at their writing as tangible evidence of what they knew and could do in response to literature. It was only the teacher who had the power to see growth in the students' work. It was the responsibility of the teacher to recognize growth, to record that growth (usually by assigning grades), and to point it out to students.

The first attempt to move students toward assuming that responsibility was to ask students to identify their best works—the literary log entries or projects that were evidence of their attempts to meet their goals. Students were asked to reflect on those works and what they revealed about themselves in those works as responders or learners. First responses, once again, were grounded in how an entry measured up to teacher expectations. Students were able to look at themselves as students but not as learners. One student responded, "I worked really hard on my board game [a book project], and it shows I can meet deadlines"; another wrote, "I write a lot in my entries and I always answer any questions you ask about what I say"; yet another might say, "This is a good entry because it's all reaction and it's longer than I usually write."

Needless to say, we had not reached a settlement. As we continued to negotiate responsibility for the portfolio, two main strategies helped students think about their work as evidence. One of them was modeling. As their teacher, one of my responsibilities was to respond to the students' literary log entries in writing or in conference. Just as I was asking students to think about what their entries revealed about them as readers and writers, I modeled the same behaviors in myself. Student entries have always revealed a great deal to me about the kinds of readers who are in my classes. Now, in addition to responding to the issues they raised in their entries or asking questions to direct their attention to specific aspects of the text, I made explicit the ways I think about them as a result of their work. I peppered my responses and conferences with observations such as the pat on the back:

> *I love the way you talked about the author's word choice in his book. You're very aware of the way the author chooses words to help you see the setting.*

or the nudge:

> *Your last few entries demonstrate that you understand the things that are happening in the story. You've retold a lot of it. Are there other goals you are trying to work toward with your reading and writing?*

Gradually, students started to assume some of the same types of thinking. One student chose this *best entry* and wrote this reflection, showing a move beyond retelling and writing that focuses on comparison:

From *Treasure of Acapulco*
The main character is Tony and now his parents want to move away from Acapulco. Tony doesn't want to. I don't think I'd want to either because it's a nice place because it's right on the water. Tony decides to go diving with a friend. They both go out from the beach with their scuba equipment on. I would love to go diving because it would be so exciting seeing the underneath world. When Tony was underneath the water he met up with a 6 ft hammerhead shark. I would have been scared to death if I was in the water with a shark. I really like this book a lot. I hope to finish the book soon because of how interesting it is.

Reflection
I think this is my best literary log entry of all the books I've read so far because I explained everything including the way I thought on different things. I even explained it from my point of view if I was in that situation. I think it shows about me as a reader because the person reading my entries can tell that I experience a lot of things in the book. I can relate what I would do and how I would feel about it. This quarter I've learned it's not that important to just tell about the book. It's much more important to explain and respond to what you read.

Peer response is the second strategy in negotiating student responsibility for gathering evidence. Students soon learn to ask their classmates the same types of questions we ask them. If during a discussion one student offers the observation that a given book has two characters who are veterans of different wars and who have very dissimilar reactions to war, another student will ask why the reader thinks the author wrote the book that way. A third student will offer a guess as to what the meaning might be, and the discussion unfolds. In this way students model the types of dialogues that should take place in literary logs and in conferences.

By asking students to read the entries of others and notice what those reveal about their peers as readers, students begin to practice the type of reflection we want them to apply to their own work. "Dear _____," one student wrote to another, "Your goal says that you are going to learn more about how authors create characters and how they change, but all you wrote about is what was happening in the story." That nudge helped the writer to use his next entry to focus on his goal.

Time

The most important part of these negotiations lay in making explicit to my students the connection between their writing and their goals, helping them to see their work as evidence of their learning. For this I had to put my best offer on the table—time. If I was going to ask students to take on the gathering of evidence, I had to provide them with time to reflect. At frequent and regular times throughout our months, marking periods, or year, I had to set aside the time for students to review once again their goals and assess their progress. They needed to get into the habit of taking out their portfolios, rereading their goals, and instead of mentally guessing at whether or not they'd progressed with them, finding the tangible evidence of progress, neglect, or accomplishment. Based on these periodic checks, goals were reestablished or modified.

This was a time-consuming process. It meant carving time out of what already seemed to be an impossibly short teaching year. This was especially difficult in a workshop where students work according to their own time schedules. It required my near-constant creation and revision of tools that would help students to become independent in their use of the portfolio. The Reader's Profile mentioned earlier was kept in the portfolio so students could easily refer to the curricular goals. Through trial and error I developed forms intended to help students record progress and goal attainment in a simple way.

I finally settled on a Goals Chart. As students finished reading and responding to each of their books, they measured their responses against the goal, reinforcing the connection between the literary response and the personal goals. They looked for evidence to support their work toward the goal. As students become more independent in gathering evidence, the portfolio fit more easily into the flexible schedule of a workshop. Form 12.2 represents one student's use of a Goals Chart as close to a reading log. This same student used his Goals Chart to write:

> *My goal for this quarter was thinking about how leads affect the story as it went on. To keep up with this goal I have paid close attention to the leads because in the beginning of stories you get the first descriptions about the character. So you can compare yourself to most of the characters by their first descriptions. But if I don't find anything there I read on to find more about the plot and other characters having to do with the story. And also leads can tell you how the book will be through out the rest of the book. Or give a summary of past events if it is a sequel. I think the lead and the ending are the most important parts of a story if you don't want to be confused about the middle.*
>
> *I think that my goals were met for this quarter because I always would read through my entries when I finished to remember each of the ways I showed improvement on each of the goals, but also I don't think I showed my goals in any other ways than by entries. Maybe I could . . . have drawn a picture to represent the comparison.*

Form 12.2

GOAL CHART

Name: _____

Goal: Understanding what a lead means in the book

Date	Progress	What needs to be done	Evidence
4/19	When I pay attention to the lead I better understand how the lead affected the story.	at end tell how the story is going to be	entry 3/31
5/1	The setting and the intro. to the characters are in the lead so I know more about them.	tell in the entry the final description of the setting	entry 4/20
5/11	The lead in the book got me into it. It made me notice the book.	decide in the lead if I will like the book or not	entry 5/3
5/19	I have learned that a good lead doesn't mean the book will be good.	same thing as last time	entry 5/11
6/2	That a lead in a sequel will remind you of all that happened in the last book.	use more than entry to prove progress	entry 5/18

But no matter how independent students became, I was not able to avoid the fact that the use of portfolios meant taking time from some aspect of the reading program. In my case, I decided that I could afford to ask students to respond to literature a little less so that they could respond more to themselves as learners. Underlying this decision was the belief that the portfolio is not simply another grading system, but a process that will help students to see themselves as learners, readers, and writers. Step by step, students came to understand the purpose of the work they did. They were able to take pride in their own growth because they could see it. And in successively greater ways they came to understand the nature of interpretation. Said one student whose goal had been to move away from her previous diet of formula mysteries,

> *It isn't enough for me to read mysteries anymore, I need something to think about. I didn't like books with description before, but now I like description because it helps me to understand the places and the people.*

Teachers often lament not being able to see the results of their work. Gathering evidence can change that—for teachers and students. Both parties can win at the bargaining table.

Marian's point about time is, perhaps, one of the more crucial points to make. We think of time in school as being *instructional* time, a term that implies that we as teachers use the time to divulge our lore or to engage in the kinds of seminars and conversations that we enjoy. The term makes it *our* time. In the reconstruction of the classroom betokened by portfolios, the time is *practice* time for the students—*learning* time, not instructional time. Many teachers at first find they are losing the comfort of the familiar routine and they worry about the portfolio as taking away from the class time that they had been used to seeing in their portfolios. Time becomes student time.

Marian, however, points out that the time spent in gathering and assembling evidence is a time spent in the workshop seemingly self-managed by the students. The classroom becomes indeed a workshop, an atelier of people developing and practicing their craft. The classroom does not look familiar to some teachers and observers, because things don't seem to be going on. Anyone who has worked with an art class or in some sports, however, knows that much intense work is going on there. The students are all engaged in the activity of writing whatever it is they are writing, and the teacher becomes much more of a resource than a traditional pedagogue.

The Results of Negotiation: Assembling the Portfolio

While engaged in gathering the evidence, the students have an eye toward the day when the evidence will be put together into a portfolio. The students have an eye to the product. In the case of John Hennelly's classroom, the assembly takes place quarterly, with a chance on each occasion for change and reorganization to form a cumulative annual portfolio:

> Striking a balance between curricular expectations and student preferences is the key to assembling the portfolio. The first quarterly assessment form, one that I have since revised but that remains more teacher-directed and course-dependent, specifies those criteria I want students to consider. Again, while subsequent forms have become more student-directed, students' inexperience with self-directed writing and portfolio preparation argues against my making the first quarter's structure more open-ended. Form 12.3 represents my initial effort at striking this balance.

During my first few years of exploring portfolio preparation and assessment, I asked students to submit three or four pieces each quarter. For the first term I might ask for two pieces related to course readings (e.g., a literary analysis and an imitative piece) and a writing workshop piece of the student's choosing. The second term's portfolio might include a college application essay, a three-way literary analysis, and a self-selected piece. I also asked seniors to submit newspaper articles, at least two yearly. They elected the type and the time.

I liked and to some extent still use this approach to portfolio assessment for these reasons:

- It offers evidence—to any and all concerned—that students have achieved course objectives.

- It implies that breadth and versatility in writing are important.

- The criteria include the essentials of effective writing: development, organization, style, and mechanics.

- It provides students with opportunities to revise or polish work a second or third time.

- It invites students to discuss their work objectively.

- It gives students and me opportunities for planning and goal setting.

The process, as reflected in the forms, evolves during the course of the year—and over recent years—to reflect a greater degree of student direction and control. Consider, for instance, form 12.4, a fourth-quarter form recently developed and used with a heterogeneously mixed class of high-school juniors.

Some teachers may find these forms restrictive. I find them helpful, as I believe my students do. They provide us with an opportunity to assess and refine our efforts. And to the extent that I have invited students to adapt the assessment to their tastes and needs, more students

Form 12.3

ENGLISH IV
First Portfolio

Name: _____

I would like you to submit three pieces of this term's writing. One should be a writing workshop submission. Please submit a variety of work, as well as your writing workshop plan, along with earlier assessment forms and comments.

- Summer Book Review:

    Lead:

    Development:

    Organization:

    Style:

    Mechanics:

- Comparison and Contrast Essay:

    Effective use of format:

    Citations from text:

    Development:

    Style:

    Mechanics:

- Survey Write-up:

    Umbrella:

    Three significant findings:

    Wrap-up/extension:

    Mechanics:

- Literary or Character Analysis:

    Development:

    Organization:

    Citations:

    Style:

    Mechanics:

Notes:

- All finished pieces should be word-processed or typed.

- Please attach the completed writing workshop plan and writing work shop evaluation sheet with the first term's submissions.

- Your writing portfolio and summary and assessment pieces constitute 50% of your first-term grade.

Form 12.4

MODERN AMERICAN LITERATURE
Fourth Quarter Portfolio
June, 1994

In choosing and discussing the selections for your fourth-quarter portfolio, please keep these goals and considerations in mind:

- Your portfolio should reflect your best efforts at reading and writing.
- It should demonstrate the range of your reading and writing interests and achievements; therefore, it may include selections from classes other than this one.
- It should reveal your growth as a reader and writer this year.
- It should demonstrate your ability to discuss your reading and writing.
- It should reveal those skills, beliefs, and understandings that you consider are essential to being an effective reader and writer.

This portfolio differs from previous portfolios in at least two ways:

- Your next year's English teacher will be reading it, possibly over the summer.
- Besides you and me, at least one other person whom you choose will read and comment on it.

Procedures:

1. Write a short introductory note, briefly noting the highlights of your portfolio. (10%)

2. Next, select and discuss the range and variety of your written work. Your selections may include—but are not limited to—the following: research papers, persuasive essays, literary analyzes, imitative pieces, poetry, comparative essays, summaries and assessments (technical writing), expository essays, newspaper articles, short stories, personal narratives, reviews, and reader responses. For each piece selected, please discuss in detail what it reflects about your writing and reading skills, habits, development, and interests. If you prefer to use those criteria specified on previous portfolio guidelines (focus, development, organization, style, and mechanics), please do; however, keep in mind that this is *your* portfolio and should be discussed as such. (60%)

3. With one of these selections be sure to submit notes and drafts that show how you developed and revised it. Briefly discuss your writing process. Be candid, but give it careful consideration. (10%)

4. Include another reader's discussion or assessment of your portfolio. Remember: you select the reader, and you select the criteria that person uses in discussing your portfolio. Although it would be nice, this portion of your portfolio does not have to be typed or word-processed. It must simply be written or recorded. (10%)

5. Conclude by assigning a grade to this portfolio, based on its overall quality (A = supe -rior, excellent; B = good, solid; C = OK, but less than what it could be; D = poor, last-minute, hardly-worth-the-effort). Then discuss the kinds of reading and writing you would like to or are willing to focus on next fall. Try to be specific and honest, keeping in mind that this will be the plan you begin with come September. (10%)

Note: As in the past, the portfolio grade will determine 50% of your quarter grade.

are willing to treat portfolio preparation and assessment more thoughtfully and thoroughly.

For the past two years, I have included an additional section to the quarterly assessment, one that also gives students a chance to reflect on both theirs and my efforts:

Related questions:

    a.   How well have you kept up with the reading assignments, dialectical notetaking, and extended responses?

    b.   In what ways are you improving as a writer? Be candid. If you don't see improvement, say so.

    c.   Others in and beyond this class have commented on your writing. What have you found helpful? Not helpful?

    d.   What would you like me to be looking at in your writing during the second term?

    e.   Other thoughts or suggestions?

To some degree, these questions—questions about plans, the course, the quality of instruction—are there to draw students closer to their work and to me, to help them take more control and interest in their writing and reading. As I hope to illustrate shortly, students' willingness to discuss and go beyond these questions has helped make portfolio preparation and assessment a more constructive, collaborative, and valuable activity.

As John notes, the use of an initially-structured form that evolves into a framework for a student-controlled portfolio becomes a part of the instructional strategy that initiates the negotiated final portfolio. The framework recognizes the reality of grades, making periods, and school administrators, but within that framework, control has devolved to the students—audit is control in fact and not simply in name. Marian puts it this way:

Assembling the Portfolio

Deciding what to put in the portfolio may have been the stickiest point in these negotiations. It was the hardest area in which to reach compromise because it was the linchpin on which all the other *settlements* rest. If I really wanted the students to be responsible for the portfolio, then I had to let them assume ownership of it. In fact, I had promised them that ownership. In doing so, I had let loose a host of new questions: Whose goals were to be represented—only the ones students had established? the goals I had tried to address through classroom instruction? or some combination? What would constitute evidence? Should I rely solely on the discretion of students? Could I enter items into the portfolio? Or should I offer suggestions? The answer to these questions rests on the same conceptual framework that underlies all negotiation—compromise.

When I began using portfolios, I thought of them as a way to use the students' own work to prove that they had met curricular goals— basically, an annotated checklist of dates, entries, and instances of student achievement. It was a position I had to give up early in the negotiations for two reasons. From a practical standpoint I simply did not have the time to create and annotate portfolios for 100-125 students. From a more important standpoint, an annotated checklist would not help students to become more aware of their learning or more familiar with their own thinking. My next thought was that the portfolio ought to be a way to capture those moments when a student makes a breakthrough in thinking or learning about literature. However, that was still a position heavily dependent on my insight into students.

I knew the student had to own this portfolio if it was to work, but I was not quite ready to abandon the portfolio solely to the students' own goals. My experience showed me that students were not yet able to anticipate in their goals all of the different things they might learn or the ways they might grow. On the one hand, I had spent a great deal of time helping students to independently set, monitor, and work toward their goals. On the other hand, I had a need to address their attention to some of the other types of learning that had taken place as a result of class activities. The compromise we reached was this. Students would have total control over that aspect of the portfolio which related to their goals, but I also asked that they consider growth or learning they might not have anticipated with their goals. What can you do now that you couldn't do before? What do you know now that you didn't know before? Even then, it was the students' responsibility to answer those questions.

To refresh their memories I provided them with a synopsis of the curricular goals we had addressed as part of whole-class instruction. In one instance, our class had spent some time discussing both theme and conflict in books, the central part they played in books, and how they were hinged. Several students had begun to address those literary elements in their responses and were thinking about them in new ways. I wasn't willing to let that evidence of learning go totally unrecorded. I asked students to find evidence not only of their learning related to their own goals but related to class activities. One student responded:

> *Another thing I've learned about was theme. When we first started doing themes, I thought it was going to be another lesson. I didn't even come close to realizing that there is so much hiding behind that little word. Now I understand what it means and can find a theme in a piece of writing. My evidence is the* War of Twins *entry.*

Again, student-teacher conferences played a large part in helping students to think about what they have done and what it means. But in the final analysis, the portfolios belong to the students and the power to make decisions about their contents rests with them.

Judging and Grading

As we wrote at the beginning of this paper, the portfolio is a public document, a performance, a set of evidence that is to be judged by someone. Without that performance it remains inert and trivial in the mind of the student. The unjudged portfolio is a readerless text (Purves, 1993). When it is presented to an audience, the audience is there to assess it. The form of the assessment may vary and even the sorts of assessors or jurors may vary, but the fact of assessed performance is crucial to the negotiation of responsibility. The performance makes the whole exercise meaningful to the students. Here is Marian's approach to that fateful time:

> The bottom line in portfolio assessment was, in our case, the grade. It has taken a long time to wean students from their need for teacher grades and as long as the system remains the same they will never be completely weaned. For this course, grades were dependent on the student's performance. In terms of work load, there were minimal criteria students had to meet to achieve a minimum grade, but students were well aware that in order to earn any higher grade, they had to be able to prove effort and improvement. The portfolio was the vehicle through which they made their case. The students used their own work to determine a grade and then prepared a case to support that grade using their portfolios. I then validated their assessment and assigned the negotiated grade. There was perhaps no stronger bargaining chip than this in getting students to assume the responsibility for their portfolios.

> I compared portfolio assessment to the courtroom dramas we see on television. I reminded students of Perry Mason labeling the evidence *Exhibit A* and asked students when writing about their learning to refer to their evidence. As a class, we discussed the fact that, at least on television, the jury can only consider the evidence the lawyer puts before them. Then I asked students to act as lawyers in their own defense. And although in reality I assumed a dual role as both judge and legal assistant, helping them to locate and establish the proof of their case, it was up to the students to lay the evidence not only before the teacher but before themselves. Knowing that they would decide which pieces of evidence went before the court, knowing throughout the quarter that they were, in fact, responsible for creating that evidence, was a powerful motivational tool.

> To some extent, there was also security in portfolio assessment. As students learned to see themselves in their own work, some of the bewil-

dering mystery was taken out of learning. With pride they could point to their successes and with understanding they could assess what still needed to be done and the steps they would take to accomplish it.

Moving students to that point—the point at which they can set their own goals, gather their evidence, assemble their portfolios, and assess themselves—was not easy. It was a process of small steps taken by both teacher and students as we negotiated a common ground. But it was a process well worth the effort, and as with any negotiation, the result was one both parties could live with.

John approaches the time of assessment in a similar vein but with a difference; it is a time when the class functions as a rhetorical community:

As did portfolio preparation itself, the assessment procedures evolved over recent years. That evolution represents a movement toward more student-directed assessment and came about gradually as both students and I began to look beyond the syllabus of our particular English course.

The first example below, a senior's April, 1993, portfolio assessment, illustrates the method I used for several years. Students discussed the merits of each self-selected course-related piece and in turn I reacted to their discussion, based on my readings of their work. When views differed, and they occasionally did, I became the judge. I did not ask students to assign grades. The next two examples, taken from a couple of juniors' June, 1994, portfolios reflect that shift toward greater student independence and autonomy. That year, students selected work from various sources, personal and academic, and in several instances pieces from previous years. For me, this approach entailed giving up some control, reading some material for the first time, and following the students' lead. For students, it meant demonstrating their ability to assess their work critically, freshly, and convincingly. It also required their identifying the criteria on which each selection should be assessed, finding an additional reader (friend, parent, sibling, another teacher), and getting that reader to discuss *in writing* the selections. Finally, it required students' proposing grades based both on the quality of the selections and the quality of their and the other reader's discussions. I still took the last turn, assessing and responding to the selections and both parties' assessments. In most instances I agreed with the grade. Given the amount of preliminary and preparatory work, it wasn't surprising that grades were strong. If negotiating learning means giving students more of the tools and skills necessary to direct and achieve their learning goals, then this second procedure appears to be moving me and my students toward an effective and amicable relationship.

Here are the excerpts from the April, 1993, senior. My comments are italicized:

English IV

Third Term Self-Assessment [Excerpts]

Name: Karen

A.   Portfolio: Briefly discuss each of your portfolio pieces. (In addition to considering development, focus, organization, style, and mechanics, also review your goals for this term.)

1.   Imitative Piece:
     Sonnet 1: I really fell in love with E. B. White's *Sonnet* and I liked the way he compared the forming of frost to the way his lover is pictured in his soul. I compared light to God and the love and faith he restores in us. White used many lines with an extra syllable so it is different from most sonnets. Anyway, I'm pleased with the outcome. I fixed the rough parts that you had suggested I change as best I could.

     Your sonnet works well. You should set off "an everlasting" with commas. And "long elated" might also be worth a revisit. An impressive job. You avoid end-stop deftly.

     His first sentence in *Tickets, Please* was unusually long and I thought I might give it a try. The focus is there and as for development I used a good example of form fitting function.

     The Lawrence imitation works syntactically. A tighter beginning might be more effective in light of the specific "soldier" and "cabin" references. You may be mixing metaphors a bit.

2.   Literary Analysis:
     Mansfield and Lawrence: I compared their different views on the misunderstanding of people. I developed my arguments and made very close observations, citing many lines. Focus and organization stayed on track. (Also, I used the APP form for my revised draft.)

     Can't argue with anything here. Well, maybe an agreement error in the last paragraph. Excellent, thorough analysis.

3.   Other:
     Journalistic Piece: This is one of my favorite articles this year. I focus on a scholarship question and develop my arguments as I go on. I got my point across in an effective manner with an objective view.

     Agreed. This has style and substance.

4.   How well have you planned for and used writing workshop time?
     O.K.

     You seem to use your time well. Wish we could give more time to writing workshop.

B. Writing Assessment: We're moving into the last quarter of senior English. As you review your writing this year, how would you describe its development? Where have you seen improvement or change? Where would you like to see development? What do you suppose would bring about this development?

> I definitely feel my writing this year has improved from last year's. Its development has come a long way. I've seen improvement in my literary analysis (*Nature of Man* and *Mansfield and Lawrence*). I've published four articles in the paper, each one on a totally different subject. Variety is not a problem. If I just keep up the writing, my development will expand even more.

> *I'd agree with your assessment, Karen. I'd also encourage you to begin working on finer points: periodic and parallel structures, more concrete language. These will help you refine your work. You might want to look at Zinsser's* On Writing Well.

C. Course readings and reading log: Briefly assess how well you've kept up with readings and how helpful the writing response logs were or weren't.

> I've kept up with the readings. The writing responses always prove helpful. The journal is nice to have handy. (Good idea!)

> *That's good to hear. Again, you put the reading log to fine use.*

D. Suggestions and Plans: What is working for you in this course? What isn't? How can you and I work best to make the last term more effective and valuable for you?

> Everything is fine. I can't really think of anything that doesn't work for me. As for the last term, I'll just keep doing what I've been doing: improving my writing.

> *Come on, you've got to have some complaints.*
> *Karen, I'd agree with your assessments. Hope my suggestions make sense. Thanks for another fine portfolio submission.*

Here are excerpts from two juniors' June, 1994, assessments of their portfolio submissions (they are responding to the questions on form 12.4):

Modern American Literature
Fourth Quarter Portfolio [Excerpts]
Name: Danielle

Mothers' Motives: I found it very hard to think of a topic for a paper on *Women of Brewster Place*. I eventually came up with the thesis, but I was not sure how successful it would be. My first draft had a lot of holes in it and wasn't as focused as it could have been. When I revised it, I made a lot of changes that turned it into a strong piece. I feel it now has a pretty definite focus, with lots of supporting material. It holds a lot of my opinions, for I don't feel that parents should feel that their children owe them anything, be it love or a second chance at childhood. I didn't really find any concrete answers, but I explored the topic well.

Mrs. Ordinary: This was a paper that I wrote in tenth grade. It is one of my favorite papers. The book *Ordinary People* was written from the husband's and the son's views, so I switched it and wrote from the Mother's view. Although I didn't really relate to Beth, I found it pretty easy to see her side. I think I kept her thoughts pretty true to her character. I enjoyed writing the part of Grace, because although I know there is no explanation for suicide, it helped me see some logic to it. I think one of the reasons I enjoyed this paper so much was that I explored different views and characters, and got to look at situations from many angles.

Self-delusory Behavior: I feel that the strongest aspect of this paper is that it is direct. The assignment called for at least eight pages, and although this paper is only about seven, it fully explores the question and develops it. I could have made it longer, but it just would have been *fluff*. There is plenty of research that supports my paper, both primary and secondary, helping to explore the question. I enjoyed writing this paper because I like psychology and exploring different aspects and theories of it.

If I were to grade this portfolio, I would give myself an A. I feel that all the pieces included are of superior quality, and I think my critiques were to the point and honest.

Next year I would like to focus on creative writing, working on poetry and short stories. I am hoping to write for the paper, but I do not know what I want to do on that. I am also hoping to write one or two really strong college essays.

I don't know if I need to focus on anything in my reading. I feel that I am a thorough reader, so as long as the book is interesting I will finish it and usually enjoy it.

Modern American Literature

Fourth Quarter Portfolio [Excerpts]

Name: Jeff

This 4th quarter portfolio is jam-packed with nine outstanding pieces of my writing. These works range in variety from a letter, speech, book review, research paper, newspaper article, summary and assessment, a small notice from the wall of a camping goods store, literary analyzes, and finally an epitaph. Four of these pieces, the letter, speech, book review, and research paper were taken from my A.P. U.S. history class. The rest are from Modern American Literature. All of these selections in one way or another reflect my best efforts at reading, analyzing information, writing, and revising.

The Research Project: This is my first research project and I'm very proud of my accomplishment. After three months of intensive research, writing, and revising, I finally got this done. You wouldn't believe how happy I was. My experience with this project has told me that lots of work and effort are needed to come through. Lots of note cards will come in handy too. I guess 68 just didn't cut it. More important, as I said earlier, good comprehension of the topic is a must. After reading various sources with different views and information, understanding the topic is necessary to have a good research paper. Of course, no matter what you read you have to know what's going on to get anything out of it.

Summary and Assessment: Writing this assessment told me one thing, I have bad usage. It's not that bad but it could be better. My solution, administer *Writers Inc.* to everyone. Specifically to teachers and students and have them go over it. This is probably the best english book that I have ever received. Those dinky vocab. books were no good and neither were those spelling books in elementary school. This book has everything, even good illustrations. Don't think I'm getting off track by giving a book review on *Writers Inc.* I'm only assessing how to solve what I believe is a bad grammar problem. By allowing this book to become standardized in all schools, I believe everyone will have an improvement in their grammar. I like it, I've written a summary and assessment paragraph!

Literary Analysis: Love can be confusing. It has different degrees and forms. In this piece I got confused over the types of love the characters from the *The Women of Brewster Place* had in their lives. I tried to categorize love but as I said before, it has different degrees and forms. I guess confused isn't the right word for it but undeveloped may be better. I did not elaborate on the forms of love that existed in some of the character's lives. In some areas, my version of love was confusing and contradictory. However, after careful revision my piece became better developed. Just to show how much better, I have added my notes and drafts. One thing that has helped me in becoming a better writer is leaving my work for a while and coming back to it. This way, picking up errors will be more visible than trying to find them after several hours of writing. The mind tends to become less efficient and staring at a computer screen for long periods of time does not help.

I assign a grade between 87 and 97. Of course, I think my portfolio is awesome so I would give it an A but there may be some ingredients that are missing or undeveloped. I enjoyed reading all the books in english except for the *Spoon River Anthology.* I especially loved *Catcher in the Rye, A Yellow Raft on Blue Water, The Women of Brewster Place,* and *Bean Trees.* I would like to read more books like the ones I have mentioned in the future. Why? Because they are good literature. What's good literature? I believe that good literature tells how people behave. To be more specific, how they deal with life. If a book can effectively relate to our everyday lives then it is good literature. I also believe that anything you enjoy reading is good literature.

While all three students looked critically at their work, I believe that Danielle's and Jeff's submissions and assessments reveal a degree of independence that may be missing in Karen's work. That these two were strong members of a mixed *standard-level* class and Karen was perhaps the strongest member of an honors-level class further convinces me that collaborating with students in developing and applying standards of quality is a viable, engaging, and effective way to advance literacy and the language arts.

What both John and Marian have found about grading has been echoed by other teachers in the project. Through the process of negotiation, the students gather a sense of the operating criteria in the rhetorical community of the classroom and the school. Over the course of the year, they have gained a sense of what constitutes A or C+ work. As in other projects like this, the students generally can estimate their grades with a good deal of accuracy. This they do in their self-assessments, which may take the form of a checklist, like the one that John's class uses, or a narrative. It is this that forms the starting point for negotiating the grade. The students come to see that it is a combination of external standards and criteria and a sense of growth, development, or movement toward those criteria. The exact balance may vary from classroom to classroom, and in some cases from student to student within the classroom. The teachers have set forth what the curriculum expects of each student. The degree to which each student achieves those expectations is the basis for the grade. Grading thus becomes a relatively minor part of the negotiation; the lion's share has been accomplished in the first days and weeks of the class. The portfolio is not graded: rather the evidence that supports the student's judgment of the student's overall performance is then validated by the teacher.

Conclusion

What are the results of negotiating responsibility in the writing classroom and giving goal-setting and assessment to the students as part of the total approach to their learning? One result, as the list on p. 000 indicates, is that the students demonstrate how the standards of the literate society become their own, how they have become members of the rhetorical community.

We believe we have shown what was asserted in the introduction to this volume: During the course of teaching English, the teacher acts as the coach, the person who encourages the students to bring out their best, which may come out in discussions, in drafts of papers, or in rehearsals of various sorts. At the same time, however, teachers must let go of their control so as to be ready for that time when they must drop that role: when the students are showing their stuff for real, when their work will be judged, and the teacher is the judge. This is hard for many of us, and it is often hard for students, many of whom find it comforting to be dependent on teachers. But it is a shift in role that teachers must acknowledge in themselves and explain to their students. It is a shift that does not surrender the authority of rhetorical or interpretive community but, through negotiation, allows for induction into that community.

How do teachers accomplish that shift? First, as was noted in the introduction to this volume, we must be brutally honest about criteria. There must be no surprises about what we are looking for and what our criteria for success might be. We must announce these goals and standards from the first day of class. Then we must negotiate with the students how they can assume responsibility for meeting those criteria. We must appeal to their self-pride and their desire to *look good*, and we must slowly let them know that they—not we—are the ones who are responsible for their performance.

At all levels, teachers can and must at some point be the judges (unless they can get someone else to take on that role): they are the experts who can describe the performance of students and hold it up against standards that are agreed upon by teacher and student. They have to cast off the mantle of friendliness and look through the lens of the critic or the judge. This is not an inhumane act at all; it is an act of love, and teachers should try to help students realize it. Teachers can no longer be the parent/advocate, the attorney for the defense. They cannot rationalize their students' work; it must stand on its own.

That is the point at which students become independent, and it is a point toward which teachers must lead them so that they can be free and autonomous. We think it is the hardest part of teaching, but probably the most important. Teachers are seeking to have students become independent, responsible human beings who no longer need a mentor. To effect this end, teachers need to balance the tendency to do things for the students with the tendency to serve as the judge. This duality is the crux of the portfolio approach, we think; it is also the crux of what it means to be a teacher. The fact of portfolios encourages us all to face ourselves as teachers and as human beings responsible for the education (the leading out away from childhood and into the world) of our students.

Endnotes

A version of this chapter originally appeared as *Using Portfolios to Negotiate a Rhetorical Community*, Report Series 3.10 (Albany: The National Research Center on Literature Teaching and Learning, University at Albany-SUNY, 1994).

References

Kádár-Fülop, J. (1988). "Culture, writing, curriculum." In A. C. Purves (Ed.), *Writing across languages and cultures: Issues in contrastive rhetoric* (pp. 25-50). Newbury Park, CA: Sage.

Purves, A. C. (1991). "The textual contract: Literacy as common knowledge and conventional wisdom." In E. M. Jennings and A. C. Purves (Eds.), *Literate systems and individual lives: Perspectives on literacy and schooling* (pp. 51-69). Albany, NY: State University of New York Press.

Purves, A. C. (1992). "Reflections on assessment and research in written composition." *Research in the Teaching of English*, 26(1), 108-22.

Purves, A. C. (1993). "Setting standards in the language arts and literature classroom and the implications for portfolio assessment." *Educational Assessment*, 1(3), 175-99.

Purves, A. C., and G. Hawisher (1990). "Writers, judges, and text models." In R. Beach and S. Hynds (Eds.), *Developing discourse processes in adolescence and adulthood* (pp. 183-99). Norwood, NJ: Ablex.

Chapter 13

SPREADING THE WORD ON PORTFOLIOS THROUGHOUT THE SCHOOL SYSTEM

Charles Phelps
Danbury High School

When a former student, Marian Galbraith, now a middle-school language arts teacher and author of two of the chapters in this book, approached me in the spring of 1992 about joining a study of portfolio assessment in literature, the concept of portfolio assessment was new, one of those ideas that was beginning to be mentioned frequently in professional publications, but not something that the average high school teacher had seen in action. Since then, I and several of my colleagues in a large comprehensive high school have spent three years nominally as *teacher researchers* but really as learners, and we now find ourselves very involved in a systemwide adoption of some sort of performance assessment, probably with portfolios as a significant component. This chapter, then, is an account of some of our experiences and what we found in one school setting, as well as a story of the project and how, from our perspective, it developed.

For us, however, the adventure into portfolio assessment is not ending with a fully developed concept integrated into our assessment strategies. That would have been too easy. We have found ourselves propelled into the arena of district policymaking, not really a direction in which any of us particularly wanted to go, but one in which we realize we must become involved in if the concept of portfolios is indeed a valuable one that can make a continuing significant contribution to education rather than just another passing fad that will be swept away and forgotten by the turn of the century. This is the story of one project as it has evolved in one high school and school district in one state and the part it has played in introducing a concept throughout a school system. Obviously, every school situation is different, but education everywhere has enough common elements that we should all be able to learn and benefit from the experiences of others. We have certainly benefited from the experiences of our colleagues and from the opportunities we have had to share these experiences. Although this project has ended, our own work continues. We have available to us the resources of our fellow participants and their work as we continue in our attempts to institutionalize the portfolio concept in our schools in ways that will contribute positively to the education of students. If others can learn from our efforts—either steps to take and directions in which to go or steps not to take and directions to avoid like the plague—only then will we have had some real success. Throughout its life, this project was characterized by the collegial sharing of experience among teachers. May the conversations continue and expand.

First, something of my background. When approached to participate in this project, I was completing my thirty-first year of teaching; twenty-eight of those years had been spent in one building. In the late sixties and seventies I served eight years as high-school department head, but after an administrative reorganization I went back to full-time classroom teaching without regret. After having been relatively active in the National Council of Teachers of English and the New England Association of Teachers of English for a few years, I cut back on such activities but did remain as a board member and treasurer of the Connecticut Council of Teachers of English. As a result of my participation in state-level professional organizations, when the Connecticut State Department of Education began to develop a proficiency test for the ninth grade in the late seventies, I soon found myself involved in a number of committees having to do with direct-writing assessment, especially holistic scoring, as statewide testing programs developed on several levels. By the early nineties, then, I had had considerable experience with holistic scoring at all levels, from elementary-school mastery tests through examinations for prospective teachers and various other forms of English language arts assessment.

The 1991-92 school year was one in which a number of elements seem to have begun to come together. The Connecticut State Department of Education was working on a second generation of its grades' four, six, and eight mastery tests, and there were many rumors in the air of what was to become a grade-ten test far exceeding the mastery tests in scope. Terms such as *authentic assessment*, *performance assessment*, and *portfolio assessment* were appearing with increasing frequency in professional literature and even, on occasion, filtering down to classroom teachers. Grant Wiggins was loose in the land and spreading his message of authentic assessment far and wide, but most school districts, like immense ocean liners, have a momentum that carries them in the same direction for great distances long after the captain has given the command to turn the rudder.

I had become familiar with the portfolio concept of assessment by virtue of having administered the advanced placement (AP) program in my high school for many years. In the AP program, proficiency in studio art is measured and scores awarded on the basis of an evaluation of a students portfolio, which is prepared to detailed specifications and submitted to the College Board. This replaces the traditional examination format used in other disciplines and reflects common admissions and professional practice in many arts institutions. The idea appealed to me, and as I read more frequently of portfolios being used for assessment in other areas, the concept became increasingly attractive.

The curricular and demographic information we submitted to the project in the spring of 1992 mentions portfolio assessment even though in practice little was taking place. The principal device for assessment of student accomplishment in the high school was an end-of-the-year examination. Both the central office and the high-school administrations had attempted to require standardized departmental examinations, but since few resources had been provided to create such instruments in English language arts, the reliability and validity of the exams developed were questionable at best. Also, within the high-school English department there existed little or no consensus on a philosophy of assessment or on the specific content of departmental examinations. The one area in which some agreement existed—that there should be direct assessment of writing—encountered problems in that there was no time or money for consistent holistic scoring at the end of the year. The result, then, of the policy on departmental examinations was that *pro forma* exams, satisfying few teachers, were prepared and then were used by teachers inconsistently and at their own discretion inconsistently. No overall compilation of results was attempted; increasingly, these examinations were ignored.

The mention of portfolios, at least at the high-school level, seems then to have been an attempt to provide a possible alternative to the departmental exam requirement. In the junior high school and elementary grades, a few teachers may have been doing some experimentation, but their efforts were sporadic and not the result of any systemwide initiative.

In 1992, then, as a high-school English department, and as a school system, we were less than satisfied with what traditional testing could offer us. As the result of the experience of several of us in scoring the writing section of the Connecticut Mastery Test, we had found holistic scoring of direct-writing assessments to have some promise but had been unable to institute its use for year-end assessment. We also knew there was something out there called *portfolio assessment*, and that something called *performance assessment* was coming on strong.

When approached to join the project I was very definitely interested. But I did not want to go into it alone. If we, as a school system, were to gain anything from this affiliation we needed more than one teacher: we needed a variety of English language arts teachers with different backgrounds, philosophies, and amounts of experience. I was approaching the end of my teaching career; the department contained a high percentage of teachers with a great many years of experience, perhaps somewhat set in their ways, with the possibility of retirement in sight. All of us had a pretty good idea of where the others stood concerning the teaching of English; we had our own views; we had voiced our positions many times over the years; we were not likely to change.

At the time we joined this project the school district was in the midst of a reorganization from a K-6, 7-9, 10-12 structure to a K-5, 6-8, 9-12 pattern with more emphasis on middle-school concepts. Accompanying this grade-level realignment had been major construction and renovation of the secondary-school buildings, especially the high school, to accommodate the ninth grade. When the ninth grade moved to the high school from the two former junior highs, a number of experienced teachers also transferred. Although these former junior-high teachers were assigned classes in grades ten through twelve as well as nine, and the veteran high-school teachers received some ninth-grade assignments, there remained some separation between the two faculty groups with their different backgrounds. One of the high-school teachers, Richard Harris, had spent many years at the junior-high level and so had knowledge of both the junior-high program and staff. In the middle of his career, he was very much interested in learning something of the workings of portfolios, so I asked him to join us.

In the English department were also a very few relatively new teachers, still in the early years of their careers. As recent college graduates, and often enrolled in graduate programs, they tended to be somewhat more aware of current trends in English language arts education than many of the veterans. Often they felt frustration at their inability to create change and to have, apparently, any significant impact or be able to institute the practices they had become familiar with in their educations. One of these teachers was Suzanne Heyd, the youngest member of the department, for whom I had served as a mentor during the state-mandated certification process, and whom I knew to be both innovative and energetic. Suzanne, too, joined us at my request. The experiences and observations of both Richard and Suzanne appear elsewhere in this volume.

The three of us, then, at different points in our careers, represented a good cross-section of the department.

Each of us had a certain constituency in the faculty, and we were approaching the project from different levels of experience, philosophical stances, and backgrounds. If we were to have any successes, and any degree of agreement, we might be able to begin to spread the concept of portfolios to others and, just possibly, introduce some ideas on which members of the department could agree.

As we entered preliminary discussions with administration about joining the project, we discovered an interesting phenomenon that may help others working on educational reform from the ground level. Never underestimate the power of a name, especially the name of a large university. The very mention of the State University of New York at Albany caught administrative attention immediately. The prospect of such an affiliation quickly opened doors at the department, building, and central office levels. One might well wonder whether the content of a program or its public relations value is more important. In any event, all levels of administration were more than happy to do anything needed to expedite our affiliation with this project.

Each of us began the year with the idea that we would institute the use of portfolios for assessment of learning in literature in some fashion. We tried to meet frequently to compare our approaches and experiences. All three of us felt, to some extent, that we were not as successful as we had hoped, but the novelty of simply moving in the direction of change alone was probably enough to sustain us. The meetings every few months with other project participants showed us that others, too, were struggling, but the general discussion was invariably positive and stimulating, and we returned each time renewed with the realization that our efforts were at least comparable to those at the other sites. For me, however, the 1992-93 school year was something less than an overwhelming success in instituting the use of portfolios. I was given two classes of below-average-ability ninth graders, newly assigned to the high school. Having taught ninth grade several years before, I thought that I could do so again easily. I was wrong. While I had become accustomed to societal changes that had affected the upper grades simply by being with them throughout the years, I was not prepared for ninth graders coming from two years in the volatile environment of today's large urban junior high schools. I was attempting to institute an assessment methodology about which I knew very little about homogeneously-grouped classes with significant numbers of attendance and behavioral problems. My own training and background were essentially academic and traditional, and I found myself working in an environment decidedly more hostile to learning than I had experienced with tenth-, eleventh-, and twelfth-grade students or with ninth-grade students years ago.

My colleagues, too, had their problems, but less severe than mine. Suzanne also worked with freshmen, but of a higher academic level and with somewhat fewer of the nonacademic problems that my students brought from outside of school. In addition, she was much closer in age to her students than I was, and her teaching style was less traditionally academic. Richard's students were seniors and, therefore, in some sense survivors as well as more academically oriented.

Fortunately for all three of us, the project provided one element of support not available to other schools, one that gave us an outside perspective and helped us focus our efforts. While we did meet several times a year with the other participants in the project, and Alan Purves visited the school to confer with us and observe classes once or twice a year, our most frequent contact was with Mary Sawyer, then a doctoral candidate at SUNY—Albany, who studied our work and reported on it in her dissertation. Mary concentrated on Suzanne's and my classrooms but also observed and conferred with Richard and served as our day-to-day liaison with the project.

By the end of the first year my two freshman classes had produced documents that we were able to label *portfolios*. I was less than satisfied with them and with my work directing their development. To begin with, the nonacademic problems of these students, their maturity level, and their poor attendance patterns all worked against academic achievement. In hindsight, however, I believe that the most significant negative factor was homogeneous grouping and that these students had been so grouped throughout junior high school. They had few or no role models within the class, and, since we were working with new concepts, we had little or nothing to draw upon as models of materials produced by classmates.

There were other problems as well, largely of my own doing. As I have mentioned, my approach to the teaching of literature is at its core traditional, based on my own academic preparation. My experience in recent years has been largely with above-average, highly-motivated, very academically-oriented sophomores, and with seniors who, while perhaps of average or lower abilities, are still in school after the age of sixteen. By the twelfth grade those who have rejected an academic orientation have either dropped out or become chronic truants, and so I had been able to continue in my traditional ways. As a result, I had no experience with or much knowledge of reader response theory, and what I did know I tended to find suspect. Mary Sawyer recognized this in observing my classes and realized that my colleague Suzanne was working from quite a different perspective than I was. Also, I had never made any use of student self-reflection in my teaching. In this area, too, Suzanne was ahead of me, to a considerable extent because of her work in teaching creative writing. I now believe that these two elements have been significant in any successes I have had since in using portfolios for enhancing the study of literature.

At the end of the first year of the project, then, I was less than happy with what I had accomplished. In retrospect, I realize that I had very little idea where I was going, although now I am not sure that such floundering is necessarily bad. Those students who had some success, I now realize, did become familiar with the portfolio concept and, lacking models, probably did very much the best that they could under the circumstances. There were a number of positive results, however, which I believe do have some implications for the introduction of portfolios on a larger scale.

First, the opportunity to focus on regular meetings with a small group of colleagues was most beneficial. This is an activity that has not often been possible in a large school lacking a strong cohesive department organization. The first year we had problems scheduling such meetings; after that we were able to arrange a mutual planning period. While we felt less need to meet on a regular basis in the third year, the availability of and encouragement to use a joint planning period have been invaluable in becoming comfortable with a new concept.

Second, the regular presence of an outside observer, in our case Mary Sawyer, was most useful in helping us see what we had been doing. While Mary had her own motivation and agenda in preparing her dissertation, she was a very positive factor in helping us to focus our work, in providing classroom observations not linked to teacher evaluation, as a resource who could report to us what she saw us doing as opposed to what we thought we were doing, as a source for research related to our work, and finally as a liaison with the project and the English education faculty in Albany. Ideally, the function she served is one appropriate to departmental leadership, but Mary was an independent element, free of responsibility for a number of other teachers, budgets, textbook orders and inventories, evaluation of teachers, and meetings called by higher levels of administration. Her work with us was more exclusively related to pure staff development and as such was both welcome and the source of much positive reinforcement.

Third, the periodic meetings of the project members enabled us to share successes and failures, to exchange ideas, and to realize that, despite very different schools and teaching situations, we had much in common and could benefit from each other's discoveries.

Toward the end of the first full year of the project's operation, Alan Purves formulated six principles that he had found in observing and discussing our work to that point:

1. A portfolio is meant to present the student to the outside world.
2. A portfolio should seek to reflect the breadth of the student's accomplishments.
3. A portfolio should seek to justify the particular course or curriculum that the student has undertaken.
4. A portfolio should be the responsibility of the student.
5. A portfolio has a rhetorical purpose: to inform and to persuade.
6. Creating a portfolio is a form of formative evaluation; the portfolio serves as summative evaluation.

At the time Alan first presented these principles and their elaboration, they seemed to me simple. Simple they may be, but deceptively so; I now realize that they really formed the basis for my work with portfolios during the second and third years of the project.

After experiencing what I felt to be considerably less than complete success with portfolios in the ninth grade, I decided to try again at another level with students whom I knew better. Thus, in the second year I introduced portfolios to my sophomore honors English classes. Having taught this course for a great many years, I was well acquainted with this grade and ability level. Compared to the freshmen at the other end of the academic spectrum the year before, these students were much more receptive both to learning in general and to the portfolio concept. Also, I was fortunate in having in these classes a few students who had experienced portfolios the year before with Suzanne. From the beginning of the year all were well aware that they would be producing completed portfolios for evaluation at the end of the course. The first months, as in previous years, I concentrated on the development of expository writing skills without much reference to literature, but at intervals I asked for some written reflection on learning that had taken place. That, however, was not the only change that I initiated.

In Connecticut, some major new developments were occurring at the same time that we were engaged in the portfolio project. The second generation Connecticut Mastery Tests for the fourth, sixth, and eighth grades were first administered in the fall of 1993. The language arts portions of these tests were based on current research and theory, most specifically on the National Assessment of Educational Progress frameworks emphasizing a constructivist approach to the language arts.

Even more influential at the high-school level, however, was the introduction of the Connecticut Academic Performance Test (later renamed the Connecticut Academic Proficiency Test, CAPT), first administered in the spring of 1994. For the first time in this state, high-school teachers were faced with preparing students for a high-stakes assessment destined to receive very considerable public attention. The developmental stages of this test made use of the expertise of many classroom teachers; in the language arts the majority of those teachers represented a reader-response philosophy and reinforced the desire of the State Department of Education to present a test based on the best current research.

As a result, then, of the need to prepare tenth-grade students for the CAPT, I and a number of my colleagues began to make use of state-prepared sample response-to-literature tests and to develop similar instruments. Although I entered this experimentation/test preparation with some considerable skepticism, the results evident in student understanding of literature as shown in their writing and class discussion impressed me. The push that Mary Sawyer had given me, combined with the results I was finding in attempting to prepare tenth-grade students for the CAPT, together with what I was hearing from teachers elsewhere, both within and outside of the project, led me to revise considerably my classroom approach to literature so as to incorporate a reader response approach in my teaching. Other teachers in the school were beginning to do very much the same, especially those working with ninth- and tenth-grade students, because of an increasing awareness that soon the light of publicity would be focused on each high school's overall performance and especially on its passing rate as the minimum acceptable scores are applied to individual performance.

One result of this obvious example of state-level assessment-driving instruction and eventually curriculum is that the nature of much of the material beginning to be presented for inclusion in portfolios in my classes is changing radically. The more formal and more traditional plot summaries and research papers are giving way to essays that resemble more closely the answers to questions asked on the CAPT. Teachers are requiring—and students are making greater use of—response journals in reading fiction rather than the traditional *book report* format. And students seem to enjoy writing these different responses more; certainly teachers are finding the results much more interesting to read. When this writing is coupled with written reflection on learning, the student then incorporating his or her best work in a portfolio, the product can be quite impressive to a reader and the source of considerable pride on the part of the student.

In the second year of the project, activities were taking place outside of the classroom as well. Two of us, together with Mary Sawyer, who by now had spent so much time in our building that she was seen almost as one of the staff, joined other members of the project at the National Council of Teachers of English convention in Pittsburgh to present our work in a three-hour roundtable session. Through the support of both the project and the school district we were able to attend all four days of the convention and participate in enough of the program activities to have a good idea of current activities in portfolio assessment throughout the country. We returned to our school aware of a nationwide enthusiasm for more information on portfolios, recognizing that in our project we probably had as many answers as anyone, and we were ready to pass on whatever we had learned to others.

Professional development then began to assume a larger role in our work during the remainder of the second year. With Mary Sawyer, one or more members of our group presented workshops for local teachers, including middle-school representatives and teachers from other disciplines who were beginning to want to know what portfolio assessment was about, and for the annual conference of the Connecticut Council of Teachers of English. Also, we were spreading the portfolio concept in more individual ways. That year Suzanne began working with a social studies teacher in a team approach to American history and literature using a variety of performance-assessment techniques, including portfolios. Richard began a collaboration with another English teacher, Deborah Stence, who wanted to use portfolios with her classes. Deborah had a variety of experience, although she was new to teaching, and she was interested in new techniques. Her ongoing dialogue with Richard, presented elsewhere in this volume, led her to join us in the project.

On a larger scale, change was also beginning to take place for the entire school system. As the result of questions raised in meetings of the board of education, the superintendent convened a committee to formulate an assessment policy for all the schools. This included elementary-, middle-, and high-school representatives, administrators, board members, and parents. I was asked to represent English at the high-school level, presumably because of my record of involvement with state testing programs and the AP program as well as this portfolio project. With the assistance of a facilitator from a regional educational resource organization, we developed a policy and model for assessment practices throughout the school system that provided for continuing review and modification of both assessment and the programs being assessed. During the year-long deliberations of this committee, I found myself being referred to and consulted as the local *expert* on portfolio assessment. At the end of the year the committee's report was adopted without change by the board of education.

In my own classroom the development of the portfolio concept was proceeding somewhat more smoothly than the year before. Students became accustomed to writing answers to the kinds of reader-response questions used on the CAPT and produced thoughtful and well-written responses on the midyear examination when asked to reflect on their learning to date. Also, at the end of the second quarter I asked students to prepare their grade proposals, justifying them with specific references to the work they accomplished during the quarter. This was a new concept to most of them, as it was to me, and it made many of them uncomfortable, but it did encourage some reflective thinking about what they had accomplished during the first half of the year.

In the third quarter, in another attempt to make the class less teacher-centered, I launched class discussions to establish some consensus on specifications for the portfolios. This proved to be difficult. The students—and I—wrestled with the problem for several days. Finally, I closed discussion after we had reached some tentative and not particularly specific conclusions. The portfolios, ideally, would reflect the course work, with an emphasis on literature. They might well include work from other years and from other courses, as well as creative writing. They were to open with a cover letter, and they might include artwork and appropriate audiovisual materials. Such specifications did not seem unduly restrictive and, I felt, essentially followed the six principles formulated by Alan Purves. With that accomplished and the students on notice that they should be shaping these portfolios, we went on to other work.

We had been reading *Oedipus Rex*. One student approached me asking if, for her portfolio, she could make a film—or really a videotape—of the play; she had been taking a class in filmmaking. Although I had severe reservations about her project and some doubt about her ability to accomplish anything worthwhile, after discussing it with the teacher of filmmaking and establishing certain requirements, I told her to proceed. Other than making my classroom available to her after school I gave her no further assistance. Other students consulted with me from time to time about their portfolios, and I did ask for a written report on progress from everyone a few weeks before the end of the semester, but saw relatively little of what was to come.

One exception was a student who spoke with me a few times about using an automobile trip as a metaphor to introduce and organize his portfolio. By coincidence he had shown me his introductory statement on a day that Alan Purves was visiting the school; this one-page statement then found its way into print in *Creating the Writing Portfolio* (Purves, Quattrini, and Sullivan, 1993, p. 229), published the following fall. This small event, besides pleasing the student and his friends and family, attracted considerable favorable attention for the portfolio concept.

At the end of the year the sophomores handed in their portfolios. The results were an infinite improvement over those of the year before, but there was every reason they should have been. The students were a year older and of a higher ability level. They were more academically oriented and more highly motivated. Both they and I had been clearer on what we had been doing. A great contrast was to be expected; anything else would have been unthinkable. But there were, I believe, other elements at work here in addition to the experience of the previous year. First was what I had learned from my portfolio colleagues within the school. Second, the communication with the members of the project in other schools at our regular meetings and at the National Council of Teachers of English (NCTE) convention had given me a breadth of information not otherwise readily available. Attendance at the NCTE convention also had made possible the sharing of information with people from all over North America working with portfolios, helping us realize that our own resources within the project stood up well when compared with others. Third, the presence of Mary Sawyer had enabled us to see our work through the eyes and expertise of an impartial observer. And finally, the impetus of the Connecticut testing programs and the emerging standards for Connecticut English language arts teachers was providing a background for me and others to begin changing both how we approached literature and how we taught it.

The portfolios that were handed in at the end of the second year were impressive indeed. The overall level of achievement was high and the variety was considerable. The students had interpreted the specifications achieved by consensus very broadly; it might be more accurate to say that they had largely ignored them, and in looking at the results I could not object very strenuously. In some fashion the portfolios illustrated Alan Purves's six principles, even though they varied considerably. Many students showed obvious pride in their work. Joe Osnoss, the student who used the automobile trip analogy, introduced one section of his portfolio labeled *Short Story Street* in this manner:

> *Of all the works that I have produced this school year, I am most proud of my short story journal. When writing the earlier entries, I asked myself questions about the story: What was the author's purpose in writing the story? How did the author use symbolism to enhance the meaning? What is the author saying about human nature and life? After answering these types of questions, I was able to formulate the earlier entries more easily than I had thought.*
>
> *At this point I was able to shift into cruise control and enjoy the trip. I read several . . . stories for pleasure that I had not read as assignments for class. The more I wrote about the stories and listened to my peers' reactions, the more I understood them and the more I enjoyed them.*
>
> *I have included several of my reactions in this portfolio. Through writing them, I have improved my skills in both analyzing and understanding short fiction.*

Jennifer Ugalde, the young woman who had asked to include a film of *Oedipus Rex*, turned in the most unconventional portfolio. It included a selection of pieces she had written on assignment during the year illustrating the variety of her work. Half of her portfolio, however, was devoted to film:

> *Film direction is my ambition. I have taken a film course in order to fulfill this ambition. I believe that this is what I do best. In order to create a film, there are a few steps that have to be done before the actual filming can take place. For new ideas, a treatment has to be written. A treatment states the main idea of the film. Then, even if there are no words, a script has to be written. In the script, what kind of shot, what's in the shot, and how long the shot is should be stated. Finally, a storyboard must be drawn. A separate picture is drawn for each shot.*
>
> *The first film I have put in my portfolio is a piece I did in Film Production last year. I am very proud of this film. . . . The other film is the movie version of* Oedipus Rex. *Along with this I have several notes and a journal.*

Jennifer's portfolio included all of the elements she has mentioned as well as sketches of costume designs and snapshots of rehearsals. Anticipating some of the problems she would have as she developed this project, I required her to include a journal. This journal demonstrates some of the learning that occurred, on many levels, as this tenth grader came to grips with one significant piece of literature:

> *I had my first cast meeting on Saturday. . . . My Oedipus . . . has a schedule which conflicts with every day I have free. Now I need an Oedipus and a Choragos. Luckily, I found an Oedipus. . . . I hope I can count on him. I've considered shortening the play. If I do, what events occur which have been deleted, I will summarize on screen. I'm still not sure if I should do this. I'll have to ask my creative consultant. . . . She has agreed. We're going to review the script together and delete some lines. I need to find a blood-like substance.*

A third student, Adrienne Proverb, a capable and prolific writer, submitted an extensive portfolio that began with a story she, at the age of five, had dictated to her mother. She also included extensive writings from ninth- and tenth-grade English, writings from other subjects, and copies of published works. This student frequently has been honored for her scientific ability and wrote with some anguish of the problems she has had as a writer in preparing an abstract of her work for publication. Just as the filmmaker presented her unique abilities, this student too introduced her work with comments on her interests:

> *Writing has always been one of my most treasured talents. Few people are blessed with the ability to shape an idea into concrete phrases which can persevere far longer than that fleeting thought. Having the ability to write is a gift requiring constant cultivation and nurturing, however. Without practicing the art of writing, sentences become stunted, paragraphs gain unnecessary sentences, and entire passages wilt, stifled in stagnant cliches. One must find the time to till the paragraphs, weed out the excessive verbiage, and painstakingly wash away cliches in exchange for fresher phrases. Only then will a writer escape the monotony of average writing and ascend to the world of literary creativity.*

Three students, then, had produced three very different portfolios. Each had interpreted specifications established by the class rather loosely, but each had been successful in presenting himself or herself to the outside world, had presented a document reflecting the breadth of his or her accomplishments, and, I believe, had justified the course. I have since used these three portfolios both within and outside of the school system as examples of different kinds of successful portfolios that students can produce. They can serve as exemplars; they can also suggest the varieties of possibilities inherent in portfolios. In my own classes they served as examples to the students in the third year of the project and as such were on display in the classroom.

The final year of the project found us consolidating our gains. The meetings with other participants continued, often with new faces appearing from the member schools. Once again many of the project participants presented our work and learned of new developments in portfolios at the NCTE convention. Locally we collaborated in various ways with other teachers. The portfolio concept was becoming increasingly accepted in the high school; a number of English teachers other than the four of us now affiliated with the project had quietly begun to require portfolios of their students. The term *portfolio* was now familiar to most students and enough had created them so that the concept was no longer unknown and threatening. Parents, too, were becoming familiar with and enthusiastic about portfolios, both through the work of their children and because of increasing use of portfolio assessment in neighboring school districts.

In some instances the interest of students prodded teachers into portfolio assessment. The veteran teacher who inherited most of my portfolio students in an American literature course this year instituted his own portfolio program after sitting in with the students and Alan Purves on a critique of our use of portfolios last year. After their initial experience the students were better prepared for the more closely-focused portfolio assignment he devised for them this spring. The motivation and level of interest of both students and teacher have been high and the quality of work impressive. For example, Jodie Yoshimi Lee introduced her portfolio as follows:

> *Time . . . . If we have too much of it, we're bored. If we don't have enough, we're frazzled. So goes the continuing struggle of man. Since the beginning of time, people have counted it, measured it, depended on it, and lost track of it. It has been vital to scientist, dreamer, politician, and poet alike. No one ever seems to have enough of it. "Where did the time fly?" is a common lamentation of students the day before summer vacation ends. "Time flies when you're having fun," but "time drags on" when you're not.*
>
> *In this portfolio, I want to show the sometimes underrated effect time has on our lives. If we only live on this earth for a certain period of time, each second should be precious. We cannot afford to waste any time while at the same time, we must not be too busy to enjoy the time we have. The way we spend, waste, and fill our time dictates our lives. Clearly, time is not something that can be ignored or taken for granted. Equally clear, how-*

ever, is the realization that we must not allow time itself to rule our lives.
It is what we choose to do with our time that makes life worth living.

Jodie followed this with a Japanese folk tale that she justified as belonging to her as a fourth-generation American of Asian ancestry. Other works she included, with her reflections on each, were a song by Tom Jones, Longfellow's *The Tide Rises, the Tide Falls*, a quotation from Philip K. Howard in *Reader's Digest*, and her own observations and limericks. This is but one example of the spread of portfolio assessment to the classes of teachers once removed from the project.

Meanwhile, movement toward systemwide revision of assessment practices was continuing. Following the acceptance by the board of education of the report on assessment revision, the superintendent decided to proceed immediately with the development of new assessment practices in the critical areas of mathematics and English language arts. He provided for a K-12 committee with released time in each of the disciplines and made available to the English language arts committee the services of a consultant experienced with the Assessment Development Laboratory of the University of Pittsburgh. The committee now includes many of the teachers working with portfolios in the high school and several at other grade levels recognized as receptive to new forms of assessment; project member Richard Harris serves as co-chair. Administrative pressure exists to create or purchase a product, an assessment instrument or package of instruments, that can be used with some degree of reliability at various grade levels to produce scores that demonstrate progress in learning. Many committee members, however, approaching assessment from the perspective of the classroom teacher, have reservations about the validity of such an approach. They favor the development of models of assessments following certain guidelines, leaving the specific implementation to teachers, rather than the creation of a system apparently designed to produce statistical evidence rather than learning. Deliberations continue, but when all is done we will probably have some sort of K-12 performance assessment program that includes portfolios as a major component.

What, then, are the results of our three-year association with the National Research Center on Literature Teaching and Learning's project on portfolio assessment in literature? Those of us involved as teacher-researchers have learned much about portfolios and have, in some cases, significantly altered our approaches to teaching. In this school system the results have not been confined to us alone, however. Our high-school colleagues have also become involved, for a number of reasons. In some cases it has been simple curiosity, while others have seen students' portfolios and been impressed. Still others have been persuaded to begin using portfolios by the enthusiasm of the students themselves. Gradually this interest has spread to other levels of the school system, where a number of teachers who have come upon portfolios through other channels have been encouraged by reports of favorable results in the high school. Increasingly, then, there has been acceptance of the concept from the ground up. Administration has not mandated the use of portfolios, but portfolios have become common through experimentation and this acceptance by the teaching staff. Our own concentration on their use for assessment in literature learning has been different from the more conventional emphasis on writing assessment, but in actual practice to separate the two has been difficult and seems somewhat artificial. The next step, probably, is to move from the use of portfolios in individual classrooms to large-scale assessment. I, for one, am not sure that this is possible without changing the nature of the instrument and making it more confining and less spontaneous and individualized than it is now. This, however, seems to be the direction in which we are now headed in one school district. I am hopeful, but somewhat skeptical.

Finally, I offer some personal conclusions based on my efforts in the last three years. They are not necessarily original, but I see them as some of the more important concepts from the point of view of the classroom teacher:

1.   Portfolios are effective in demonstrating individual learning in the English language arts, including literature.

2.   Analysis of learning in specific components of the language arts, such as composition, conventions of mechanics and usage, reading, and knowledge and understanding of literature may at times be necessary, but in looking at portfolios it is difficult and ultimately artificial.

3.   The reflective component is what distinguishes a portfolio (as we have seen the concept develop) from a traditional writing folder.

4.   Ideally, the task of maintaining a collection of evidence of learning on a long-term basis must be the responsibility of the student. From this body of evidence the student can prepare a focused portfolio on demand to meet a specific need, such as year-end evaluation or college admission application.

5.   The use of portfolios encourages teachers to revise classroom practices, creating opportunities for more student participation, greater varieties of materials, and more individualization. The teacher becomes more of a coach and the student is encouraged to take greater responsibility for his or her learning.

6.   Whether or not portfolios can be used effectively in large-scale assessment still remains to be seen. The possibility exists, but questions remain on how to proceed without negating many of the positive aspects of the use of portfolios within individual classrooms.

I am convinced that we have—in portfolio assessment in literature, at least—found a useful educational tool when a tenth-grade student, Hilary C. Wood, includes in her portfolio this final essay. I submit this as evidence that one individual has grown in the English language arts; I suggest that it serves as an exemplar of what is possible in using the portfolio assessment concept as part of an approach to teaching the English language arts:

> *After reading and reflecting on more than twenty stories, I can definitely see a change in how I approach literature. In some ways, what I know, can do, and do make it both easier and harder for me. I find it easier to understand difficult stories because I'm better at reading, writing, and thinking about them. I have no trouble writing reactions, because I always have something to say. Looking at my first attempts, often I could not say much more than I liked or didn't like the story. In Chekhov's* The Student, *I tried to say why, but more often than not I fumbled about because I didn't understand all of the story and I just didn't know how many things there are to react to. Finding something to say is the hardest part of writing.*
>
> *I know now that most stories are not just about liking or disliking. Many are not written just to be enjoyed. Although authors create specific characters and situations, they seem to want to show us something about what it's like to be human. James Joyce's* Eveline *is so conditioned to her role that she cannot free herself when she gets the opportunity, showing how people become paralyzed by their situation. Cheever's Miss Dent shows what a person is capable of doing when pushed too far. Now I look for the larger connection. What significance does the story have beyond itself? I used to read just to find out what happened next. Now I read more closely and carefully, knowing there will be clues and patterns for understanding why, not just what. In many of these stories, what the characters do seemed to be less important than what motivated them, such as Carter's* Lizzie Borden.
>
> *I knew that plot, character, setting, theme, irony, tone, etc. were elements of literature and used in writing stories. What I didn't know was that thinking, talking, and writing about a work not only makes us comprehend it better but even enjoy it more sometimes. I always thought having to analyze stories spoiled them. This might be true for simple works, but some of the stories we did this year I didn't enjoy or really understand until we analyzed them. I hated* The Jolly Corner *when I first tried to read it, but after the pieces started fitting, I really began to like it. I even liked the way James uses long, complicated sentences to show Brydon's personality and thinking process as he struggles to confront his alter ego.*
>
> *I also learned that it is not enough to be able to summarize the plot, describe the setting and characters, etc. Besides, some stories have almost no plot as such or have unusual structures that make it difficult to apply traditional approaches. Carter's* The Cabinet *and Walker's* Roselily *both are non-traditional. To interpret means to draw conclusions about many things. To draw conclusions means to make connections, and to make connections means asking the right questions. I think finding the right question is the key. It's easier to answer questions than ask them. The reactions make it easier for me to start asking questions. Everything I wrote about in a reaction always led to something else I had to find out more about. And each answer usually led to another question. Looking back on my*

reactions, I noticed how many questions I asked. In The Worn Path, *in just three paragraphs I asked at least seven or eight questions about the meaning of the title, the significance of the journey, how Phoenix came to be taking care of her grandson and what would happen to him. Although I did not try to answer them in the reaction, I consider asking them the first step to finding an interpretation.*

What I know now that I didn't know before is that there are many valid ways to look at a story. Before, I thought there was only one right *answer. I didn't really understand how more than one answer could be* true. *I stopped looking for* proof *and started looking at what was probable or even possible. I stopped looking for* truth *and started looking for what was partly or maybe true. I considered that most things are too complex to have an easy answer. Poe's* Ligeia, *for example: was she ever a real person or only an ideal dream woman? Did Ligeia come back to life in the second wife's body or was the narrator just hallucinating? The first answer often is not the final one or even the best one. I started to think of many possibilities before deciding, knowing I might change my mind as I thought some more. Listening to classmates' reactions always made me re-think what I had said. Sometimes, even when I thought they missed the point, something they said made me think of something I hadn't thought of or sometimes they used an example that I hadn't considered. I really found Christina's and Amanda's reflections very interesting. They always gave me new things to consider. The variety of reactions showed how many ways there are to think about literature.*

Literature doesn't reveal itself in one reading. Even reading very carefully, there's always more you see when you reread it, even if the second reading takes place soon after the first. After I reread Everyday Use *just a few minutes after the first reading, I noticed how the opening and closing scenes paralleled each other but reflected the changes in the characters and their relation to one another. It's even more revealing when the second reading is a long time from the first. I read* The Necklace *last year. We talked about it and answered study questions. I had a very different opinion of the Loisels this year. I still sympathized with them, but this time I saw that Maupassant was also criticizing them.*

For years we learned about the writing process, but now I know that writing is a process for discovering what you think, not just conveying it. The more complicated the idea, the harder it is to express it clearly and precisely. It takes two drafts just to know what I want to say and at least one more to decide how to say it. Before, I did not rewrite as much. Usually I can do really well if I have enough time. Unfortunately, I think I'm not doing as well as I used to on assignments where I can't do several drafts, such as essay tests. I have come to depend on having time really to rethink what I'm trying to do, not just correct spelling and grammar. This is one area where what I know has made it harder for me. On balance, though, what I know has increased the things I can do and do do.

References

Purves, A. C., J. A. Quattrini, and C. I. Sullivan (1995). *Creating the writing portfolio*. Lincolnwood, IL: NTC.

Chapter 14

ASSESSMENTS AS AWARENESS

Suzanne Heyd
Danbury High School

> When I teach a beginning class, it is good. I have to come back to beginner's mind, the first way I thought and felt about writing. In a sense, that beginner's mind is what we must come back to every time we sit down and write. There is not security, no assurance that because we wrote something good two months ago, we will do it again. Actually, every time we begin, we wonder how we ever did it before. Each time is a new journey with no maps. (Goldberg, 1986, p. 5)

When I first decided to try portfolios as a new and important way to teach literature and writing, I tried to *fit it in* to my existing repertoire. By April of that year, my classroom was purposeful with teaching and learning, but the use of portfolios didn't seem terribly new or important. Then I had an experience that reminded me that the only way to newness is through *beginner's mind*, the willingness to let go of any *map* I had for teaching literature and writing and venture into uncharted territory. This was uncomfortable at first because I had invested the term *teacher* with the concept of *knowingness*. A teacher was one who *knew* what she was doing and *knew how* to do what she was doing! Beginner's mind threatened my definition of teaching because it required that I relinquish my notion of knowing how to teach and what to teach and begin again—for the first time. This experience has made me a student with my students, and it has allowed me to travel with them on a journey of discovery, exploration, and transformation.

That same April, I went on a seven-day silent meditation retreat that had an enormous and unexpected effect on my research. The emphasis of the practice of meditation is cultivating a moment-to-moment awareness of the world and relating to it from that point of awareness. There is a very different quality to this kind of experience: an openness, a receptivity, an appreciation not often found in the classroom, but potentially very desirable. I left the retreat resolved to bring what my retreat leader called "a meditative spirit" and what Natalie Goldberg called "beginner's mind" to my research on portfolios. This has informed and re-formed my ideas about teaching and learning and assessment.

As a note of definition, although in my writing it may appear that I separate the concepts of teaching and learning, I feel that they are inseparable and, in practice, one and the same. When I am in a classroom, there is a seamless continuity between the two. This is evident, for example, when I ask a question to a student and the student gives me an answer I have never thought of before. Here I am simultaneously teacher and student: the experience is one, but we use two concepts to define it. In fact, it seems that the two concepts are separated from each other in practice only when I interpret teaching as one-way transmission. Then I am neither open nor receptive, nor can I leave any room for wonder or original thinking in myself or in my students.

Traditionally, the role of the teacher in assessment is that of judge. My approach during my first two years of teaching was often to rank and grade according to a set of criteria that was sometimes negotiated with my class, sometimes not. I would evaluate a paper according to my knowledge of its comparability to other works by the student or to other work in the class. I more or less equated assessment with grading, and furthermore, I felt that without grades, standards would be difficult to uphold in the classroom. I also believed that grades were the vehicle for upholding a certain commitment to society. As Peter Elbow (1983) puts it:

> Our commitment to knowledge and to society asks us to be guardians
> or bouncers: we must discriminate, evaluate, test, certify. We are invit-
> ed to stay true to the standards of what we teach, whether or not that
> standard fits the particular students before us. We have a responsibil-
> ity to society . . . to see that the students we certify really understand
> or can do what we teach, to see that the grades and credits and degrees
> we give really have the meaning or currency they are supposed to have.
> (p. 328)

Often, I felt uncomfortable with this guardian or bouncer role when my commitment to the student required me to play the opposing role of coach. As Elbow points out, a student often fears or is defensive in the face of a content-committed teacher, and will shut down, be unwilling to take risks, and often not develop.

While my first years of teaching were spent fulfilling my role according to what I perceived to be society's expectations, this year I began to focus on what has been for me the unsettled issue of assessment. Like a beginner, I did not know what to do when I received that first set of papers from my students this year. I felt I didn't want to grade them for fear of them shutting down or becoming overly competitive, but I didn't know how else to set standards so that my students would not perceive me as an easy teacher or my course as a *blow-off.* My compromise was to give two grades instead of my usual holistic one. I gave a grade for *process*, which included evidence of multiple drafts, following directions, and completion of a self-reflective commentary on the piece that I called a *learning analysis.* This grade rewarded all students who worked diligently on the assignment, whether or not their product was certifiable. I also gave a product grade for the final outcome. This way, I reasoned, I was rewarding and differentiating between the outcomes of the two roles I played as a teacher: process grade for the coach and product grade for the judge.

As time went by, I became uncomfortable with this system because it seemed to me that putting two grades on something instead of one did not open the possibilities up for my students to see their work as learning in process; the grades were still the final word. I also found that following a certain process often became an end in itself for the students, that multiple drafts were done without revision or that a learning analysis was written without any analytical thought. Similarly, when I evaluated their work, I often found it difficult to separate the elements of process from the product. And finally, I found that students often reacted to receiving two grades no differently than they would react to one, and therefore did not learn anything through them.

My feelings of frustration about grades and their limitations were taking hold. Even though my students were going through the motions of reflecting on their learning and collecting their graded work in portfolios, they still seemed to be fixated on the letter or number they found on their work; they would feel good or bad according to that grade and often would make their classmates feel good or bad through the infamous "Whadjaget?" interrogation. Worse yet, I was keenly aware of how subjective these numbers and letters can be—too often a grade is simply a momentary impression of what I judged to be good or not-so-good about an individual piece of a student's work. As Robert Probst notes:

> The problem is not simply that the grade doesn't inform; rather, it misinforms and deceives. It imitates the precision of mathematics, though it is at best only impression and judgment. In so doing it conceals information that might be useful to students and parents [and teachers], and trains them to accept an empty symbol as surrogate. (224)

I sensed not only my students but also myself shutting down once a grade was assigned to something. When I began reading a piece with the intention of giving it a grade, I was open to its possibilities, but by the halfway mark, I had already formed a judgment about it, and I often read the rest of the piece to confirm or change that judgment. This judgment was then translated into a grade, which was justified by my written comments. Students would in turn receive their judged papers (and perhaps even read the comments), but they would rarely rethink their work or learn from the grade. The grade was not an opening into new understanding, but the end of an assignment.

It was the problem of judgment that became a central focus of concern as my study of portfolios in the classroom developed. Interestingly, the effect of judgment on our lives was also one of the main themes of the meditation retreat I attended. Through the course of that week in silence, I began to see how judgment affects the teacher's openness to learning and teaching. We make judgments of quality when we look at how students perform day in and day out; we many times say, "This student is better than that" or "This work is better than we would have expected":

> For many students as well as for others involved in education, the question, "How am I doing?" is a valid question that deserves an answer. The student has a vested interest in getting an external judgment to validate her sense of success or failure. The policy-maker and the taxpayer have a vested interest in knowing the value of their investment in education. We cannot deny these legitimate concerns. Nonetheless, we should not give them a simple answer but one that respects both their legitimate interest and our sense of the complexity of what we do as teachers of literature, whether in our classroom or as a community of teachers at large. (Purves et al., p. 4)

Here, again, concern about standards seems to emphasize the importance of judgment in the process of assessment.

If judgment is indeed important, how then do teachers make it authentic and truly meaningful instead of an unsubstantial assignation of letters and numbers? My first impulse is to share some of the responsibility of judgment with my students, since ultimately I want them to achieve the intellectual independence it takes to evaluate their own ideas, performance, and progress:

> The teacher's help in evaluating beliefs, ideas, and judgments is extremely important. But the responsibility for evaluation must lie primarily with the student, since she is the only one with access to the necessary information. She alone knows whether she has thought carefully and honestly; she alone can know what issues matter most to her, what she believes, or what memories are triggered by a literary work. (Probst, 1988, p. 223)

The idea that only individual students themselves know if their work is done with the care and attention it deserves and whether or not they have learned something strikes me. I have had many students who were capable when they came into my class (i.e., who got good grades) but seemed to be simply going through the motions. So often I find myself wondering what, if anything, this kind of student is learning. Ultimately, that knowledge lies within the individual students themselves, and only they can truly assess the depth and breadth of their growth. Where does this leave my role in evaluation and assessment? How do I help students become aware of the complexity of their work as learners and to be able to assess that work meaningfully? These two questions shaped the work I did with portfolios.

The learning analysis was my first attempt at infusing a formal component of self-evaluation into the assessment process. For every piece my students submitted to me, they included a cover letter in the form of a learning analysis. The directions for this analysis read:

> In narrative form, explain the *process* you went through to get from an idea to this final piece. How did you get your idea? How did you expand on that idea? What changed in each draft? What was difficult to do? What was easy? What advice did you get from others as you were doing this piece? What did you decide to use/not to use? Why? Point out what you perceive to be the *strengths* and *weaknesses* of the piece. Tell me what you feel you did well, and what you wish to improve upon. Write down everything you learned by doing this assignment. Connect this with what you have learned in the past and/or what you still want to learn.

This met with good results insofar as it satisfied my concern that the students had a chance to reflect and think about their own work. I found the learning analysis provided me with a much richer view of a student's work. I read a student's learning analysis before I read his or her piece itself, and would often refer to it afterward. I would then put a process and a product grade on the piece and give it back to the student, who would add it to his or her works-in-progress folder.

But the bottom line still seemed to be the grade, both for me and for my students. If I had that string of numbers and letters in my grade book at the end of the quarter, I relied on them to tell me about the student as much as the students relied on the grade at the end of the quarter to tell them about themselves! Because this seemed to me to be investing an awful lot of power into one person's (the teacher's) momentary impressions (a fixed grade), I began to question my reliance on grades and their use in learning. My students and I had many conversations about grades as the year went on. We discussed the inability of a grade to teach us what we do well and what we need to do better. We experimented with new forms of grading: we would come up with the criteria for grading an assignment together; students would grade each other, sometimes in groups, sometimes individually; sometimes we wouldn't use grades at all, but we would write notes to each other about our impressions. With time, my students became aware of the intricate nature of assessment. They also began to see that a grade is based on one individual's judgment, which may not be the same as another's.

In a final evaluation of my class, Kristen writes:

> *Grades are more complicated than I thought. . . . Sometimes I wished we had grades because it was easier. Grades are totally different now than they*

were at the beginning of the year. I found I really didn't want grades, just the comments to see what people thought, not just some superficial letter that everyone gets.

And Jim writes:

I like the grading portion that we did in class, where we don't put a letter grade just comments. That helped me out because people said what I did wrong, and I was able to see that and work on it, so I can improve it. I don't think grades mean the same to me as they did back then. I mean, the teacher would give you a C, and not tell you what you did wrong.

My students and I were asking ourselves what possibility there was for growth when one has already defined oneself or one's work by a letter or a number. We began to see traditional grades differently—they became conclusions, endings, or closings, instead of invitations to learn and grow.

Here is a story from my meditation teacher, Christina Feldman:

I have a friend, a woman I've known already many years. One day she's mad at me, and I have no idea from where it comes. I have insulted her, she tells me. How, I don't know. Why don't I know? Because I don't know her. She surprised me, that's good. That's how it should be. You cannot tell someone, "I know you." People jump around, they're like a ball, rubbery, they bounce. A ball cannot be long in one place; rubbery, it must jump. So what do you do to keep a person from jumping? The same as with a ball. You take a pin and stick it in, make a little hole and it goes flat. When you tell someone "I know you," you put a little pin in. So what should you do? Leave them be! Don't try to make them stand still for your convenience. You don't ever know them. Let people surprise you. This likewise you could do concerning yourself. (1992)

It seems a wise story, with much advice for us as teachers. James Moffet says that "the reminder is to stay as a small child who keeps his antennae out and still feels awe and wonder because he hasn't yet put a grid over reality" (1981, p. 167). If we want to help our students to do this—and I think that if we want them to have the most meaningful interactions with literature, it is crucial—then we must ourselves cultivate a habit of openness, or nonjudging. The role of teacher as judge is limited because "judges do not rate objects or people but perceptions. They rate what they perceive" (Purves et al., [DATE?], p. 14), and our perceptions of others are not necessarily complete or helpful for them.

Tricia was a case-study student this year. She often came to class without her homework or her book. She handed in assignments that were incomplete or late, if done at all. She ignored required formats and procedures and would ask when we were going to be through with any book we read for homework because she didn't like it. In class, she was usually engaged in class discussion and participated in activities, but this never seemed to carry over to her work outside of class. I perceived Tricia to be a lazy and careless student, and judged her work according to my perceptions. In her final interview, I learned that Tricia had an unstable home life, shared a room with two of her siblings, and had parents who did not expect anything from her academically. This changed my perceptions of her, and it shed new light on her work.

John Dewey's ideas about perception may inform our understanding of the uses and limitations of judgment as a form of assessment. Dewey explains that cognition is not a primary experience but a secondary one. We think abstractly to gain insight into what we directly experience through the senses:

> All thought, according to Dewey, relies on the potential of the mind to make discriminations within experience. Thinking proceeds, for example, by making a distinction between subject and object, or between human culture and natural phenomena. Sometimes, however, the products of our thoughts are mistaken for reality itself. When this occurs, reality comes to be understood as constituted by hard and fast dualisms, such as subject and object, or humanity and nature [or teaching and learning, or good and bad]. Because we like to believe that what is of greater value to us is somehow rooted in the very nature of reality, we often forget that a value choice was involved in isolating the mind from the body or the human from the natural. (Shields, 1986, p. 45)

As I understand it, then, primary experience is not one of cognition, but a fluid event in the present moment. Cognition is secondary experience—abstracting for the sake of reconstructing primary experience and gaining insight. When we judge or evaluate and place one thing over another, we are trying to pin down in certainty something we have experienced. This is abstraction, or engaging "in a process of mental selection" (Shields, p. 43). Dewey posits that we engage in a quest for certainty because the world is a troubling mixture of the constant and the haphazard. And that "since it is impossible to eliminate the uncertainties of reality, . . . our desire to do so often leads us to believe in a pretend world [our world of abstractions]. The precariousness of life often leads to a quest for certainty' that frequently eventuates in elaborate false solutions to the problem of existence" (Shields, p. 41). This pretend world happens when we mistake our mental constructs for reality. When we mistake the products of our thought for reality, we are led to look at the objects of our experience as divided and unequal. It is what we appear to live with in the world of school: there are good and bad, right and wrong, fact and opinion, student and teacher, smart kids and average kids and remedial kids.

I have a hunch that very often when we judge our students' work, behavior, and growth, our judgments take on an illusion of solidity and we limit what is possible for us and for them. Tracking helps us to categorize and label our students. Grades help even more. We can talk about the good students and the lazy students and the bad students. (So, too, can these students label themselves and live up to their labels.) But do these labels become the lens through which we see the work and behavior of a student, a class, a grade-level, or even our colleagues? We might do well to remember that our labels and judgments are not truth (primary experience), so that we can stay open to all that might contradict them.

James Moffett refers to our reliance on secondary experience as a way of knowing the world as living in a "verbal-conceptual cage." He points out that:

> what mostly gives us the feeling of richness, beauty, and originality . . . owes precisely to our managing to escape a while from the cage. We would best regard fresh perception and original thinking as *unthinking* prior thought that were not so or were too partial, as *removing limitations that we previously took for granted*. (1981, p. 167)

In the arena of learning, this secondary experience is learning that is filtered through our ideas, opinions, and conclusions. The student who holds to the conclusion that he or she "stinks at English" will come in contact with the learning through those darkly-tinted glasses. And how often in our teaching do we hold to an impression of a student and in the process miss what doesn't seem to fit with that impression? In the quest for certainty in an uncertain world, we cling to our conclusions and our opinions and our judgments because they tell us about the world and make it familiar to us. We think we know another person, their work, ourselves, or the world around us because we know our opinions about them all. But what do we sacrifice when we accept our conclusions as true and they become our reality (Feldman, 1992)? Do we limit what is possible for them and for ourselves?

These questions led me to rethink some of my classroom activities and the assumptions behind them. The idea of valuing fresh perception and original thinking prompted me to value openness and awareness. I found that when I used this to define learning, the content of my teaching changed. For example, helping students to reflect on their learning and set goals for their progress was very important to me when I began this research. To this end, in September I created an *English Skills Inventory* in which I asked the students to assess their proficiency in each of the skills listed on the school's grade-appropriate curriculum. After students took this inventory, they set learning goals for themselves for the quarter, explaining what they would like to improve upon and why. At the end of each quarter, they assessed their progress in each of the goal areas, using the material gathered in their portfolios as evidence to substantiate this progress. They would then take another inventory, and they would set new goals for the next quarter.

My sense was that I could help the students gain awareness of their learning by taking them through the process of setting, achieving, and assessing learning-related goals. This seemed to work. My students went through each procedure I asked them to, and as a class they seemed to be improving and growing. The approach to learning and growth seemed to be a fairly linear, rational, and methodical process, one where we worked step-by-step toward our goals.

This went along fairly well until April vacation, when I spent seven days in silent meditation. Each night of the retreat, the teacher of the course would give a talk on some subject of meditative life. I found a kernel of truth for my own teaching each night, and with all of the next day spent in silent contemplation, I had lots of time to consider each one! One of the first concepts that struck me was the idea that thinking of ourselves as if we are in process can be very harmful. Returning for a moment to the idea of mental selection, this kind of abstraction sets up a hierarchical understanding of ourselves, one that devalues who we are now in favor of what will be in the future. We say, "This is who I used to be," and "This is who I am now," but "*This* is who I want to be." In the proper context this kind of abstraction can be very useful; we can set goals for ourselves, and we can see the potential for change and transformation within us. But Dewey warns that if our abstractions are not reintegrated in practice with our primary experience, then we mistake our thinking process (in the form of judgments and concepts) for reality.

In this way, "who I am now" can become something not worthy of our attention and awareness; we focus on who we want to be and ignore who we are and then no growth or change is possible (Feldman, 1993). In-process thinking puts a value on our sense of ourselves, so that we think that we are better than we used to be, but that in the future we will be better still. Where then is the possibility for truly opening to our present experience, if we cling to the notion that who we are now is somehow not acceptable or not completely worthy? The whole of meditative thinking centers around the idea that learning can only take place when we are present, open, and aware—when we put our ideas, opinions, and judgments aside and wholeheartedly engage in our experience right now.

What happens when we are open, receptive, and curious? Each one of us knows that feeling—it is the beginner's mind referred to at the start of this chapter—and it evokes in us a sense of possibility. Openness, as opposed to defining, grading, or labeling, connects us to the present moment, giving us the power of awareness and the freedom from our preconceptions and our judgments. Christina Feldman says that this changes the quality of what we do from intensity to passion:

> *Passion is something different than intensity. Intensity is about goals, intensity is about destination, intensity is about the future. Intensity is about arriving somewhere that is not present right now. Passion has to do with our relationship to this moment. To how wholeheartedly we listen, and feel, and open. (1992)*

Can we teach awareness, openness, and receptivity? How can we rethink teaching and learning to encourage the kind of openness and receptivity that allows us to know ourselves and to grow from there? And how might we assess this growth? How can we help our students give up the habit of limitation brought about by the myriad of ideas, opinions, and preconceptions they bring with them to our classrooms? These questions led me to question the view of assessment as judgment. If we define self-inquiry and awareness as tools of learning, then perhaps we need to redefine assessment: "Evaluation has become something the teacher does *to* the students, rather than with them, something imposed rather than shared. But at its best it could be a cooperative venture in which teacher and student share impressions and help each other understand what has happened in the reading of the literature" (Probst, 1988, p. 225). If our purpose is to help our students become more self-aware, self-directed, and self-confident learners, then what would happen if we conceived of assessment as a tool of awareness instead of a tool for judgment?

I have just begun to explore these questions, and there have been interesting changes in my classroom as a result. Instead of grades and goals in the fourth quarter, each student kept a daily observation log. Students spent the last five minutes of each class writing in their logs, which were a vehicle for them to record the things they noticed, learned, and were aware of in the classroom. I asked them to work on bare awareness and beginner's mind and record what they actually observed without coloring it with value judgments of good, bad, right, wrong, and so forth. I kept one, too, in which I recorded those fleeting—yet very telling—impressions and noticings I had in the forty-one minutes. I observed the students mostly, and sometimes the lesson or myself, always striving for clean awareness (observation unencumbered by value judgments). During class time, I often played the role of observer and recorder, and I let the students facilitate the discussions or activities. During our log-writing time, they would make notes about the discussion and their part in it. Often at the end of class, after individual log writing-time, the students would share observations about the dynamics, activities, or content of the day's class. I generally stayed out of these debriefings, but I did find a way to use my observations on a day-to-day basis. When my students came into the classroom, I greeted them with a handshake or just a "hello" and eye contact. This gave me the opportunity to interact with each one of them every day. Before class began, I would check my log from the day before so that I could informally share my observations with individual students as they came into class.

Instead of traditional exams, my students created portfolios at various points in a semester. At the midpoint of each quarter, I filled out the school's interim progress report to be sent home. This time, they evaluated themselves and chose the items they felt should be listed in their interim report. (The questions and format of the evaluation are given in Appendix A.) I reviewed and commented on this report, and changed items if I felt it necessary before sending the evaluation home. This gave both of us an awareness of the work and an opportunity to meaningfully and constructively discuss the student's learning. Similarly, at the end of the quarter, students created a grade proposal in which they reviewed, evaluated, and compiled a portfolio of all of the work they had done during the quarter and submitted it to me for review and approval (see Appendix B). When I reviewed these, it was quite easy for me to make comments about what I had seen over the course of the quarter and to explain why I agreed or disagreed with their proposed grade. In most instances, the students' self-assigned grades corresponded quite closely to my sense of their grades, and when they varied, it was not difficult for me to point out how and why I felt they differed. At the end of the year, I again used a self-awareness approach in my final exam. I gave the students a series of self-evaluative questions to answer, using a portfolio of their work as documentation (the exam is reprinted in Appendix C). This was the culmination of all of the work we had done, and although it was not content-based in the traditional sense, it was based on the culmination of their growing awareness of themselves as students of literature and writing. When I assessed these final exams, I had a hard time at first knowing what to assess. I found I was interested in what the students were able to notice about themselves—and in most cases, that was quite a lot.

If it is the case that portfolios are a vehicle for students to internalize a sense of who they are as students, as well as a record of their ability to know and recognize their growth and learning, it would seem that the teacher plays a very vital role in helping the student develop this sense of self and this ability to reflect on and record growth and learning. When the teacher embraces this role, what happens to Peter Elbow's concept of a teacher's commitment to knowledge and to society? I found that my concern broadened beyond being a gatekeeper of knowledge. My knowledge of what my students knew became less important than their own understanding of what they knew and could do. This seems right for two reasons. First of all, I knew that we would part company at the end of June and, more importantly, that my perceptions and impressions of them could never be as complete and truthful as their own could be. In my estimation, this in no way negates or lowers standards in the field of English education. To the contrary, it seems to me that it is taking them one notch higher by giving our students an internal awareness of them.

This may be what portfolios are most useful for. Perhaps this type of assessment shifts our focus away from something that can be quantified and evaluated by others toward something that can be evaluated and internalized by the student. Perhaps a portfolio is a tool to help students be more fully aware of who they are and what they can do. This kind of thinking adds a new facet to the concept of assessment, based on the belief that observation and awareness can teach our students the lessons they need to learn, that their portfolios are reflections of that awareness, and that the more fully we awaken a sense of passion in our students, the better they will perform. Perhaps assessment isn't about judgment, but about knowing ourselves intimately, about deepening into the kind of wisdom that only we can know: the wisdom of self-awareness. It would seem that this turns the notion of assessment around on its heels.

References

Elbow, P. (April, 1983). "Embracing contraries in the teaching process." *College English, 45*(4).

Feldman, C. (April 19, 1992). *Learning.* Lecture.

Feldman, C. (April 15, 1993). *The spirit of freedom.* Lecture.

Goldberg, N. (1986). *Writing down the bones.* Boston, MA: Shambhala.

Moffett, J. (1981). *Coming on center.* NJ: Boynton/Cook.

Probst, R. (1988). *Response and analysis.* NH: Heinemann.

Purves, A. C., N. Bryant, M. Ciarnello, L. Haddow, E. Looije, J. Rutage, A. Sakai, E. Smith, T. Sinclair, L. Stender, and S. Ward. *Setting standards in the language arts and literature and the implications for portfolio assessment.*

Shields, D. L. (1986). *Growing beyond prejudices.* CT: Twenty-Third Publications.

Appendix A

Interim Evaluation

This worksheet is meant to help both of us reflect on and assess your work so far this quarter. This reflection will help us in various ways: it will allow us to see the areas in which you have progressed as well as those in which you have not. It will also help you to set your sights on what you want to have happen in your learning before the quarter ends and communicate this to me. Be as specific as you can!

1. Discuss the two to four assignments that have been the most meaningful to you this quarter and what you have learned from each.

2. Discuss your participation (in class and homework) and what you have learned through your involvement.

3. What have you observed about yourself as a reader/writer/thinker this quarter?

4. What would you like to improve upon at this point and why?

5. Which of the three interim comments do you feel are most appropriate, based on your above analysis?

Appendix B

Grade Proposal

For your fourth-quarter grade, you will need to propose a grade to me, based upon your performance this quarter. In this proposal, you must take into consideration both the quality and the quantity of your assignments, participation, and your commitment to your growth and learning in this class. You will need to defend your proposal with proof from your portfolio, your journal, class logs, etc. The grade you propose must be an honest assessment of your work as you see it. I will consider your proposal, make my assessment of its accuracy, and make modifications as I see fit.

Follow these directions carefully and completely.

1. Begin by checking off the class assignments (O = on time and complete, L = late and/or incomplete, N = not at all).

    ____ *Gatsby* Essay

    ____ *Gatsby* Study Guide

    ____ Read *Grapes of Wrath*

    ____ *Grapes* Responses

    ____ Class Journal Submission

    ____ Read *Manzanar*

_____ *Manzanar* Responses

_____ Read *Night*

_____ *Night* double entry

To prove that you have done all of the above, go back to your folder and journal and assemble these materials in order. If you have checked all of the above, then go to step two, if not, go to step three.

2.   To receive above a C+, explain how you have excelled in any of the following areas, referring me to the work in which you can prove this.

   a.   My written responses to the literature are exceptional. Explain:

   b.   My in-class listening and speaking skills are exceptional. Explain:

   c.   My formal writing skills are exceptional. Explain:

   d.   I have shown extra effort by:

   e.   I have shown significant improvement by:

3.   Explain which minimum requirements you did not meet and explain why.

PROPOSED GRADE:

ACCEPTED GRADE:

COMMENTS:

Appendix C

Final Assessment: Who Are You Now?

Your final-exam grade for this course will depend on how honestly and completely you can reflect upon what you have discovered, how you have grown, and where you have been this year as a reader, writer and thinker. There are five areas to examine: Range, Flexibility, Connections, Conventions, and Independence. You will need to answer each question in narrative form, referring to pieces in your portfolio as proof.

Remember: There is no right or wrong here, nor is there good or bad. You are not competing. You are exploring yourself and your work deeply and honestly and completely.

RANGE

1.   a. Do you read a wide range of topics and subject matter?

   b. Do you read a wide range of genres and forms?

   c. Do you read from a variety of cultures?

2. As the year goes by, do you undertake texts that are more and more challenging?

3. a. Do you read for information and knowledge?

   b. Do you read for appreciation and enjoyment of the beautiful?

4. Do you respond to what you read in a variety of ways (sometimes to explain or question, sometimes to connect with your own life, sometimes to write practically?

FLEXIBILITY

1. When you respond to your reading, do you consider the text in the context (time, place, experience) of today's world?

2. Have you approached what you read from a variety of critical and cultural perspectives (as an American, as a boy or girl, as a student, as a member of a certain ethnic group, etc.)?

3. When responding to what you read, do you choose the kind of writing that seems suitable to what you have to say?

4. Do you change the diction, voice, level of usage, and evidence to match the kind of writing you are doing (genre, purpose, audience, and context)?

CONNECTIONS

1. Do you apply concepts you've learned in school and through personal experience to what you read?

2. Do you make connections between texts (common themes, similar characters or plots, conventional forms or structures)?

3. When you read something that has situations, language, or settings that are unfamiliar to you, do you have a strategy for *decoding* (or understanding) them?

4. Do your responses fully reflect and convey your deeply-held, personally-meaningful impressions and interactions with the text?

CONVENTIONS

1. Do your responses to a text show an awareness of the conventions of the genre and period of that work?

2. Do your poems and creative writing show an awareness of the conventions of the genre?

3. Do your essays, reports, and theses reflect conventions appropriate to that genre, purpose, and audience?

4. Have your pieces of writing been edited to eliminate surface errors?

INDEPENDENCE

1. To what extent are your own views, imagination, language, and style dominant in your portfolio?

2. What evidence is there of your ability to use other resources to accomplish your purposes?

3. How effectively do you synthesize material from other sources to support or illustrate your own thinking?

4. What do your reflections on the pieces in the portfolio indicate about your understanding and control of your own learning?

5. What questions do you want to pursue in the future: about yourself, the subject matter, and the worlds between the two?

Chapter 15

A DEPARTMENT INSTITUTES PORTFOLIOS

Anne Kuthy

Shaker High School

Can portfolios be a key element in a departments writing program? What essential activities should take place in a portfolio plan? And, most importantly, how do portfolios change both instruction and learning?

Our department is currently in the midst of adopting a portfolio requirement as part of the composition strand of our curriculum for grades 9-12. While we have always emphasized the teaching of writing and have a strong writing program, portfolios have clearly added a new dimension. The portfolio plan we found most workable involves certain specific steps, and it has changed the way both our students and our teachers think about writing.

Identifying Writing Objectives

One of the most important benefits of the portfolio is that it encourages self-analysis. Students learn to assess their current skills in terms of their own projected goals. In the past, even the most dedicated writing teachers have not always empowered students to work toward individually defined and specific goals.

Getting students to identify personal objectives, however, is no easy task. Initially, we explained to our students what objectives were and asked them to write down two or three goals. The students had difficulty articulating specific and workable objectives, and they wrote such vague and general statements as "I want to punctuate better." We found that spending additional classroom time on the topic and extending the actual deadline for creating objectives to the end of September were beneficial. During the month of September, teachers discussed and presented models of student objectives. They also gave students an opportunity to establish objectives after a graded paper had been returned to them. Finally, teachers used peer partnering and one-on-one conferencing to focus students on appropriate objectives.

Working through the Process of Writing

Developing objectives is a natural segue to the writing process. With long-term goals in mind, students come to see each paper as a step toward achieving their goals and are more willing to make corrections and changes.

Our teachers found the computer to be a very valuable tool in the revising process. The students were more willing to make changes when such alterations could be accomplished with ease. Our teachers also devised a variety of revision lessons based on traditional techniques. For instance, students worked with peers to evaluate each other's papers, and they were guided in this task by a teacher-created worksheet. Additional revision activities included asking students to highlight what would be changed, requiring that all students revise at least one paragraph in their paper, and asking students to highlight and change vague or nonspecific words.

The portfolio process emphasizes and teaches revision. Students may edit a paper before it is completed and then revise selected pieces again when they are preparing their final portfolios.

Reflecting on the Writing

The portfolio's reflective aspect encourages student ownership. Throughout the year, we asked our students to discuss their individual writing processes. This culminated in a *letter of metacognition* written for the final portfolio, but we found that it was important to make reflection an ongoing practice during the year.

As usual, teachers tried a variety of techniques to help students self-analyze. During the early part of the year, we used checklists that students completed after a paper was graded. Later on, students wrote short reflection pieces based on specific questions that focused on a particular part of the paper. Another reflection exercise asked students to record the various steps used in creating the paper. By year's end, students were given more open-ended reflection assignments.

To conclude the year, we asked each student to write a metacognition letter in which he or she discussed each piece selected for the portfolio. Students were asked to explain why each piece was chosen, what its strengths and weaknesses were, and what it showed about them as writers.

The letter of metacognition brought closure to the year's work and specifically showed what the students had learned. We were encouraged to see that our students had begun to evaluate their own work and direct themselves toward specific future goals. Below are unedited excerpts from tenth-grade student letters:

> *In* Growing Up in Auschwitz, *the strongest aspect was the structure of the essay. I had an impressive creative opening, good transition sentences, and a clearly stated thesis sentence. One weakness of this piece was that I carelessly overlooked the fact that I should have explained how the thesis affected Elie Wiesel mentally, physically, and spiritually.*

> *The first piece of my writing that I included is the essay on the play* Julius Caesar. *I included this play because I thought it was a mature play and my essay could be more mature and sophisticated. Looking over my writing I noticed some of my sentences were short and most of the words were plain. I wanted to change the plain words into words with real meaning. I learned that good and sophisticated writing is all about revising, thinking, and changing. Looking over the essay, I noticed that a lot of the words used once were found again and more often, so I changed the words.*

> *I truly believe that my skills as a writer have become immensely better since September of 1994. In my first paper about* The Canterbury Tales, *I used broad and vague sentences. I wrote, "the prioress is shown to be a very flirty, coy, and a sensuous woman." I now realize that this would be a good topic sentence for a paper on physiogamy, but I placed this sentence in the middle of a paragraph. I did not follow this statement with any specific examples. Later, I wrote that "the prioress is not a very holy and devout woman." I then brought in a quote about her possessions, but did not discuss it. I left it up to the readers to figure out the connection for themselves.*

> *The first creative paper in my portfolio is one of my favorite pieces of writing this year. What makes this piece of writing stand apart from many of my other creative papers in the past is my strong attention to descriptive details. In this paper, I specifically describe summer as I saw it as a young child. For example, I refer to the frogs that I captured as "slimy yet wily beasts," and the fireflies as "flashing spots of light which fluttered in the air."*

> *When I handed in my final draft I was quite certain that it was descriptive and well written. When I got the story back, I saw there was a lot to improve on. It was not that hard to revise because I just expanded on most of the sentences, such as, "Their lips moved closer and closer." I expanded on this to read, "The man stopped playing. He turned his head to look directly into her eyes as his head tilted a little to the side at about a thirty degree angle. Her blonde curls flipped to the side as her head tilted. Their lips moved closer and closer together."*

The portfolio has been very beneficial to our department. It has changed the way we teach writing; it has changed the way students respond to the evaluation of their writing; it has given students ownership of their work; and most importantly, it has improved student writing.

Many teachers were reluctant to begin portfolios at first. They felt that the process would be cumbersome and would rob them of valuable teaching time. In the end, however, these teachers saw the growth that took place as a result of the program. They did become believers, and they accepted the benefit of spending classroom time on the writing process.

Chapter 16

THE USE OF A CENTRAL PORTFOLIO TO UNIFY A MIDDLE-SCHOOL TEACHING TEAM

Carol Mohrmann
Oneida Middle School

Oneida Middle School is one of three newly-organized middle schools in the city of Schenectady, which is located in upstate New York. Schenectady has a population of approximately sixty thousand, and Oneida draws its students from the city's socioeconomic extremes, serving students who are the sons and daughters of college professors and doctors as well as also students whose families are on welfare. There are approximately six hundred students in grades 6-8. The school is organized into heterogeneously-grouped teams, and this chapter is about how portfolios became a unifying force for the eighth-grade team.

The team consists of four teachers, one in each of the four academic areas, with additional teachers serving as remedial support in English and math. There are ninety-six eighth graders in the team. All students keep a journal and a portfolio, which are located in the English teacher's room but are accessible to the students at all times. The portfolio is a work in progress, and the journals are handed in quarterly. Each student is expected to have at least ten entries in each quarterly journal, and each entry is expected to be approximately a page in length. Students are given prompts for each entry but are also encouraged to write on topics of their own choice. All four academic subjects contribute to the one central portfolio.

At the beginning of the year, each teacher has each student write a plan for for that subject. The student discusses what he or she learned the previous year, outlines his or her strengths and weaknesses, and makes some suggestions about how the subject can help him or her achieve long-range objectives. The student identifies career goals and discusses how success in each of the academic subjects could help in achieving those aims. (As an example, the prompt the math teacher gave his students is given in the Appendix.)

The students then continue to write journal entries relating to what they are reading and learning in each discipline. The general theme for the first month for all four academic subjects was *Jurassic Park* by Michael Crichton. The students in science researched topics relating to their reading, such as chaos theory, fractals, DNA, amber, and so on. The novel was read during English class along with a number of other related science fiction short stories such as *The Birds*, by Daphne du Maurier; *By the Waters of Babylon*, by Stephen Vincent Benet; and *All Summer in a Day*, by Ray Bradbury. Some of the students had difficulty reading the original novel of *Jurassic Park*, so they read the screenplay instead. All the students felt they were doing the same work, but it was individualized according to their abilities. The students wrote journal entries discussing their choice of topic for the science research. Similar activities continued during the year based on other readings and projects. For instance, the students read *Slave Dancer* in English while they were studying the slave trade in social studies. A culminating activity to this unit was a workshop conducted by Nego Gato that showed the students some of the culture connected to slavery in Brazil. The students learned some of the dances and how to play the musical instruments. At the end of the week-long workshop, the students produced an assembly for the rest of the school. They then wrote journal entries clarifying their thoughts about the readings and the project.

Periodically, the students were asked to refer back to their original plan and analyze how they were progressing in each subject. As I stated before, the team aimed for at least ten journal entries in a ten-week period of time, with at least one entry for each subject. Students were encouraged to write more than the minimum requirement, and many began work on novels, their own original poetry, or simply made "Dear Diary" entries. The main emphasis of the journal, however, was as a reader response journal—mostly to literature, but also to the material students read in other subject areas.

Frequently, the four teachers would sit together and read the journals and discuss the individual students. The journals provided great insight to what each student was like, and this gave us ideas on how best to work with each of them. They had been told that there was no guarantee of confidentiality, so the teachers felt free to discuss what the students had written and share it with one another. On one occasion a student wrote about suicide, and we were able to get her the help she needed. Frequently, problems such as hunger, abuse, or potential conflicts came to light, and we were able to address those situations. At one point, a student was moving to a different school district, and there was a question of whether or not he should be admitted to the Honors English class. When the district was shown the student's portfolio, he was accepted into the program.

The four quarterly sets of journal entries were placed in the student's portfolio. In addition to these journals, the students selected other projects developed during the year. They had many from which to choose, including a science fair project, a social studies research paper, the program showing their participation in the school play, an intensive study of a novel of their choice, a resume, any creative writing of poetry and short stories, and a number of projects worked on in all of their classes.

The science fair project was developed jointly by the science and English teachers. The science teacher developed the original experiment and the English teacher did the related research and bibliographical references. The science teacher helped the students produce the display and the English teacher helped the students write the hypothesis and abstract. Some of the students developed much of their project in technology class, including interactive computer presentations containing sounds and pictures. Both teachers gave the final product a grade.

The social studies teacher and the English teacher worked together to produce a research paper. The students chose their topics and did much of the research in their social studies class, and they put the information together in English. They were taught how to write a content outline, an introduction, a conclusion, a main body, a bibliography, a citation of references, and an appendix. Again, the final paper was graded by both teachers. This gave it importance and most students attempted to do the work. Often, middle-school students do not see the importance of doing homework, but with the weight placed on these projects, and with the grading being done by multiple teachers, the team was successful in getting almost 100 percent participation on these assignments.

In April, the entire team participated in the annual school musical. The music teacher and the English teacher, with support from all the eighth-grade teachers, produced *You're a Good Man Charlie Brown*. Students were released from various classes to rehearse. They also practiced after school and at night. The play was performed for friends, neighbors, and parents, and it was also videotaped and shown on the local television station. The music teacher taught the music, the technology classes made the scenery and produced the sound and lights, the home and career classes made the costumes, and the English classes staged the production. It was an all-team project. The students wrote periodic journal entries discussing their participation and what they learned from the experience, and they placed copies of the program in their portfolios.

Another of the projects they could include in their portfolio was a program developed by the English teacher called *A Novel Approach*. For six weeks, in English class, the students studied a novel of their own choosing. They were encouraged to choose one they were interested in but that was challenging as well. The choices they made ranged from *A Separate Peace*, *The King Must Die*, and the play *Inherit the Wind* to *The Shining*, *Doc Holiday*, and *The Web of Dreams*. The students purchased their own copies of the novels if they could; students who could not were given a copy of the book they had chosen. If they purchased their own copy, they highlighted significant passages and wrote responses to what they had read in the margins. If they were given the book by the teacher, they took notes and wrote reader responses within their notes. They began the project by setting up a calendar and planning how they would divide the available time in order to accomplish the task. They wrote a journal entry discussing their plans for successfully completing the study of the book. As they read, they wrote journal entries quoting significant passages and discussing what these passages meant to them. They summarized the book and made up a fifty-question test. They also did a project based on their novel. Many students chose the same book and were allowed to work in groups on their project. They chose several different methods for their demonstration. These included skits based on segments of the book. One group audiotaped a group of students reading dialogue from the play *Inherit the Wind.* These audiotapes were then placed in the portfolios. Other projects included models (the student who read *The Shining* made a model of the hotel), mobiles, interpretive readings from the books, life-sized drawings of major characters, book jackets, cartoons, and board games. This project was well suited for the needs of a widely diverse classroom. Since the classes are grouped heterogeneously, and there is such a wide range of abilities and cultures, this program appealed to the interests of most of the students.

As the year progressed, each student began developing the cover for his or her portfolio. Students made drawings that represented themselves as individuals. They also pasted on photographs, pictures, cartoons, and anything else that demonstrated their self-concept. They included text either from their own writing or from significant passages they found in their reading. These covers were continually developed both in class and during free time. The students were extremely anxious to work on their portfolio covers and were constantly asking if they could do so.

At the end of the year, each student made a table of contents for his or her portfolio and wrote a cover letter discussing what was included and why each item had been chosen. In their journals, the students discussed their *best piece* and why they thought it was the best work they had done all year. They also discussed their progress over the course of the year and made suggestions as to how they would perform the next year in order to be successful. They described the progress they believed they had shown in all of their subjects. They used the covers they developed as covers for photo albums, scrapbooks, or any other method of unifying their portfolios.

The students were then asked to present their portfolios to small writing groups. During the year, students had frequently met in groups and shared their writing with each other. They would listen to suggestions, make changes, and then present their portfolios to the group again. The groups changed frequently. At the end of the year, the groups were formed arbitrarily through a random choice of numbers. In these random groups, each student showed his or her entire portfolio to the group and was then graded through the use of a rubric. The following questions are some examples of the types of questions used on the rubric using the choices of *all, most, some,* or *none.*

_____ of the items in this portfolio represent the student's best work.

_____ of the portfolio is complete.

_____ of the items were done in a timely manner.

_____ of the projects are neatly done.

_____ of the items in the portfolio demonstrate improvement in writing.

_____ of the projects represent time and effort.

_____ of the items are free of spelling and punctuation errors.

_____ of the portfolio is well organized.

_____ of the portfolio illustrates creativity.

_____ of the portfolio cover demonstrates time, effort, and originality.

The grade received on this portfolio represented one-third of the final-exam grade. The students then presented their portfolios to the entire class. They were to read their cover letter and demonstrate the materials they had included in the collection, indicating what they thought was their best work and why. These presentations were videotaped and shown to the rest of the class. As part of the end-of-the-year evaluations, the following questions were answered in their journals:

- What were your plans for the year in each subject?
- Did you accomplish your goals? Why or why not?
- What does your portfolio say about you as an individual with hopes, dreams, beliefs, and values?
- What have you learned about your ability to read and write this year?
- What was your *best piece* this year. Why was it your best? What steps did you use to develop it?
- How does your *best piece* compare to your other writing?
- What causes you to do your best writing? When your writing has not been your best, why was that?
- Name some of the books you read this year. Why did you choose these? What do your choices say about you? Have your tastes in reading changed?
- What do you find difficult about reading? How could you improve this?

- How does your writing at the end of the year compare with the beginning?
- How have your study skills improved this year?
- How does your portfolio as a whole help you to understand your self as a student? What are your strengths and weaknesses?
- How was your homework effort this year? How did this affect your progress?
- How was your class participation?

Once the portfolios were completed, presented, and graded, they were all placed on display in the library. The English teachers in the sixth and seventh grades brought their classes to the library to view the portfolios of the eighth graders so their students could get an idea of what was ahead for the next year.

The common portfolio is certainly a strong point for team teaching. All four academic teachers and the remedial teachers began to work much more closely together. The goals became more common among everyone concerned with the team. For instance, when the English teacher was teaching the writing of complete sentences, the other teachers would only accept answers written in complete sentences. When the students were working on research, everyone agreed on the format for citation. The English teacher supported social studies by having the class read novels on the same subject matter.

The results of this approach to learning are amazing. On the 1995 Preliminary Competency Test in Reading, 109 students were tested, including students in special education classes. Thirty-nine students tested at the ninetieth percentile or better. The previous year, 124 students were tested, and only thirty-eight students tested at the same percentile. That same year, seventeen students tested below the state reference point, compared to fourteen in 1995, a figure that includes eleven students in special-area classes; thus, only three students in mainstream classes scored below the state reference point of forty-four out of seventy-seven questions. The Preliminary Competency Test in Writing results were even more dramatic. In 1994, thirty-four students tested at the ninetieth percentile or better. In 1995, fifty-seven students tested ninety or better, and no student scored below the state reference point of sixty-five. In fact, eighty-eight students out of 109 scored at the eightieth percentile or better.

There are more subtle signs of success with this program. The science teacher reported how one student had said that something he had written was good enough to go into his portfolio. In other words, the student had recognized what material of his own was quality work and was able to make a positive self-evaluation. When the students took the New York State Social Studies Program Evaluation Test, most students, if they finished early, took out books and began to read, instead of drawing pictures, playing Tic Tac Toe, sleeping, or just gazing around the room, as had occurred in previous years. In addition, their writing was not found wadded up and thrown around in the halls, and they actually asked to work on their portfolios in their spare time. Because of the reader response journals and the work relating to their reading, our eighth grade had become a class of readers and writers. Our students took pride in their work. They knew the meaning of excellence and quality and strove to apply these concepts to their writing.

Perhaps the best judge of the effectiveness of any program is through the eyes of the participants. The students wrote many compelling arguments for the effectiveness of the program in their cover letters. Here are some evaluations in the students' own words:

> *I enjoyed breezing over the entire year's work. A feeling of satisfaction emerged as I congratulated myself for the hard work, and other times feelings of disappointment when I knew I could have done better quality work.*

> *This portfolio is full of my work from this year. I have put all of my best work in it. My work shows signs of how my writing has improved since the beginning of the year. . . . I never before would have believed I could write like I do now. Our portfolios are, in a sense, us in writing form. They express our feelings, our opinions, our lives, and our dignity.*

> *You may ask why I have a portfolio and why I am allowing you to read it. That is a question which is very simple to answer, pride. One word is all I need. I have pride in my work, and I am confident enough to let you see some of the quality work of which I am very proud.*

> *We've read many short stories and novels, but I've learned more than just complex sentences and John Steinbeck and polynomials and the Gilded Age and volume and Einstein. I've learned that education is more than that; more than just facts and notes and tests and grades. I think that is the most important thing. You won't see that in my portfolio, but you'll see that in me, which is the most important thing.*

> *This present year has been quite successful for me. I have learned so much about my self identity, my self worth, and most important of all, my values. It's amazing what you can learn from reading school books.*

> *My portfolio is a representation of who I am, and what someday, I will be.*

As I noted earlier, the classes at Oneida Middle School are heterogeneously grouped. Those students who need remedial services get them through the efforts of a remedial teacher in the same classroom as the mainstream students in both English and math. In addition to bringing the efforts of the team closer together, the portfolio experience provides an answer to the questions of how to deal effectively with the wide range of interests and abilities found within a heterogeneous class. The portfolio has the power to help students make changes and demonstrate progress. It presents the student to the world, to the best of the student's capabilities. Even students for whom English is a second language progress in both reading and writing when portfolios are used. Furthermore, students continue to develop their organizational and study skills, and take pride in their work. This focal point of all their work can change attitudes, crystallize values, develop individual goals, promote successful behavior, and help the young adolescent formulate a philosophy of life. There seems to be something magical in a student's writing down on a piece of paper that he or she is going to try harder. This comes to be regarded as a contract or a promise, and very often he or she will try to live up to it. The journal is an avenue for students to make promises to the teacher and to themselves. What other avenue is there for this type of self-evaluation? As one student said in his cover letter:

> *This portfolio is a collection of all my best work. When people look at it, they can see just how much I can do. When I look at it, I see how much I have changed and improved. . . . Portfolios are a way to improve our skills along with making us think about what's going on in our lives.*

Another student wrote:

> *The value of the portfolio to me was that I had the power to choose whatever I wanted to put in it. I could also decide how I wanted to arrange it. Most of the time teachers tell you how to put things in order in a special way, but this time it was our choice. I like the idea of being in control.*

This statement demonstrates how important it is for students to have a feeling of ownership toward what they do. If students feel they have some control over some part of their lives, then the motivation is there to do quality work and to do it in a timely and complete manner—a definite advantage with middle-school students.

Finally, one student actually referred to her portfolio in a very poetic manner:

> *It looks as though the end,*
> *Of the eighth grade is near.*
> *I have survived,*
> *Another busy year.*
> *Now is the time,*
> *To show off my success,*
> *Look at me world,*
> *Look at all I've learned.*
> *Look at my portfolio,*
> *I don't mean to brag,*
> *Or let out a crow.*
> *But you'll understand,*
> *If you see my portfolio!*
> *This folder contains,*
> *All that I've done in this grade.*
> *It has papers I've written,*

And projects I've made.
Just look at what I've got,
It really is a lot!
I have projects that I did,
In science and in social studies.
I wrote journal entries,
About my family and buddies.
Go ahead, browse through it and see,
Everything in it was done by me!
It has poems and pictures,
And packets galore,
But really this portfolio,
Was so much more!
We did packets on novels,
To be exact, two.
This year, my skills in letter writing grew.
This portfolio is a way
For my very best to show,
A way for everyone,
To see how I glow!

Appendix

Because the math teacher had difficulty in designing topics for journal entries, the team developed questions for the first math entry.

My Plan for Math

To the student:

Use the following questions to devise a plan for your success in math. These questions are only meant to help you develop ideas. You need not answer them all, but use them as suggestions for your journal entry.

- What do I know about math?
- What one particular thing do I remember about math from last year?
- What are my strong points in math?
- What are my weaknesses?
- How are my math study skills?
- What do I need to work on regarding my study skills in math?
- How was my attitude in math? How could it be improved?
- What grade would I like to receive in math on the first report card? What do I have to do in order to achieve that grade?
- What do I hope to accomplish in math this year?
- What do I need to learn this year in math?
- How is my behavior in math? How can I improve it if needed?
- What do I hope to accomplish in math in high school?
- How is math important to my adult life?
- How might I use math in my career?

Chapter 17

How a Five-Year Program of Portfolios Raises the Learning Standards in an Urban High School

Gertrude Karabas

The Bayard Rustin High School for the Humanities

There is a wonderful irony in the fact that the impetus for our school's involvement with portfolio assessment resulted from frustration with the tyranny of the New York State Regents' Examination in English, which now, five years later, allows for the inclusion of portfolio assessment. It should be noted that passing this exam is currently a graduation requirement at our school, and that the significantly less challenging competency exams in reading and writing are administered only to students with learning disabilities or to English as a Second Language (ESL) students who entered our school system at the end of the eighth grade. However, the ESL students have recently taken to using portfolios, and for the 1996 Regents' exam, twenty-four ESL students submitted portfolios in fulfillment of the same requirements asked of native speakers.

Five years ago, only seniors in specially-designated classes were allowed to take the rigorous English Regents' exam. Today, all juniors must take and pass this exam as a prerequisite for admission into our senior elective program. We have come a long way. In looking back, it seems that the catalyst for all the sundry changes that took place in our English program at the Bayard Rustin High School for the Humanities can be tied to our involvement with portfolios.

How Did We Begin?

During the 1990 school year, our school's passing rate on the New York State Regents' Examination in English dropped to an all-time low of 78%, which sparked heated discussions as to the value and purpose of this exam. While several of the members of the English department felt that the exam was irrelevant to our language arts program at Humanities High School, we all concurred that this exam was infinitely preferable to administering a competency exam in reading and writing. Thus, we decided to continue using the Regents' exam as a way of evaluating our English program. We also made a strong commitment to experiment with portfolios in order to develop viable alternatives for our diverse student body. In the meantime, we took a long hard look at our changing student body and restructured our language arts program to meet their needs. Within the last three years, the demographic structure of the school had changed dramatically. Second-language learners accounted for about 15% of the total population, and 13% had immigrated to the United States from one of fifty-five countries within the last three years.

Additionally, since students entering our school are not screened by test scores, each entering class reflects a range of academic strengths. Over the previous three years there had been a noticeable decline in the reading and writing abilities of each entering class. Currently, 38% percent of the entering class reads below grade level.

Portfolios As Instructional Tools

A few teachers began experimenting with portfolios in 1991, and the results of our first year with portfolios were so powerfully persuasive that we felt that portfolio practices might be the way to get students to achieve better scores on the English Regents' exams. As we had noticed, our students had no sense of their own history as learners. Everything was short-lived. An assignment was given, it was written, and then it was tucked away and forgotten. Students never seemed to be able to connect what was taught in the ninth grade with work done in the following grades. Schoolwork was seen as random and discrete and meaningless. We saw the portfolio as an ideal way to integrate what the students had learned, what was happening in all their classes, and how they were developing as young men and women. Armed with this assumption and a faith in the efficacy of portfolio practices, we presented our ideas to the members of the English department. Following is an excerpt from the minutes of the September, 1992, meeting:

> After discussions on the scheduling of the new computer room, the remainder of the meeting was spent in an exciting and fruitful discussion of the portfolio process.
>
> Ms. Karabas and Ms. Paley conducted the meeting. On the blackboard were three questions: What are portfolios? Why are portfolios useful? How do we get started?
>
> The members of the department looked through a random sampling of portfolios that had been produced last semester by youngsters in Ms. Paley's, Ms. Karabas's, and Ms. Steinberg's classes. The young-

sters' work was spectacular. The portfolios included examples of every kind of writing and were illustrated creatively. Some of the students were perhaps more gifted than others, but all the portfolios showed hard work and sincere effort. The first question was answered.

The members of the department then answered the second question with statements like:

- self-conscious reflections on the self and on writing
- linking the real world to the self
- packaging the term's learning
- an instrument for conveying values
- student-student or student-teacher collaboration in establishing order
- intellectual compendium
- dynamic process that causes change not only in the young people but also in the instructor
- can be regarded by young people without cynicism since they reflect effort and there is a result rather than a mark
- allow youngsters to own instruction rather than remain passive recipients of pieces of information

The members of the department eagerly moved on to the third question. Ms. Paley, with thanks to Ms. LaFave for the material, gave each of us a copy of a handout from Arts PROPEL entitled *Suggestions For Creating Writing Portfolios*. . . .

The question of grading the portfolios came up. This issue has not been completely resolved, but both Ms. Karabas and Ms. Paley felt that a student's portfolio could easily count as 40 percent of his final mark. Ms. Paley had had her senior AP class grade the portfolios of sophomores and freshmen.

Ms. Gleichman suggested that youngsters could be involved in the grading process if they were given a single piece to evaluate and to discuss. They could arrive at a consensus for a grade.

Mr. Teitelbaum noted that while many things may not be within a student's control, the amount of effort expended on the portfolio was indeed within his or her scope and that the portfolio has a payoff.

Ms. Gleichman noted that the pressure to do well was therefore internal.

Ms. DeCardy suggested that the tape made last June of the portfolio presentations be shown to classes as a beginning lesson.

Other department members asked whether the students' portfolios on display during the meeting could be used as samples. It was agreed that they could be made available.

Ms. Karabas continued to answer questions about the portfolio process. She suggested several ways of inspiring writing on the part of the students. Among the most successful methods she'd used were retelling stories as children's stories, memoir writing, and writing poems of praise. The suggestion was made that assignments related to class reading could be included in the portfolios. Materials produced for other classes could be included, making the portfolio an exemplar of interdisciplinarity. Materials could be looked at before their inclusion, but this might well be in the form of *checking with* the teacher rather than receiving specific recipes for a product.

Ms. Karabas suggested that each student should include one completely original piece that had never been seen by the teacher.

The meeting was concluded on a particularly positive note. Everyone left the room feeling charged with the energy and enthusiasm of the presenters and hopeful that the portfolio process could make a difference.

After the September meeting, other teachers joined the team, and in 1992 we gained a citywide reputation as a school that used portfolios in classroom instruction. Regents' examination scores rose to 85% the next year, and teachers felt that the portfolio experiment was working. One year after our initial portfolio conference, we held a workshop on portfolio assessment. The minutes of that meeting are included:

Mr. Brinkerhoff, the facilitator, began the meeting by playing the role of devil's advocate. He claimed serious pedagogical objections to the use of portfolios in his classroom. He reasoned that (1) it takes away the focus of the organization of the class from what the students have already been doing; (2) it takes away the ownership of their work from their control so that they only work and write towards the portfolio endeavor; (3) some students might be intimidated if they know their work will be evaluated and judged by their peers. He invited the group to comment.

Ms. LaFave disagreed, saying that the use of portfolios allows the students to take control of the writing process. The portfolio process allows young writers to develop analytical tools to help them evaluate and plan the progress of their writing.

Ms. Gleichman thought that portfolios are a tool for student creativity because students give their own suggestions on how to proceed. This helps encourage creativity.

Ms. Karabas said that people have personal reasons for using portfolios and each teacher may use the portfolio in an individual way that best meets the needs of the class.

Ms. LaFave emphasized that writing is meant to be read and portfolio writing helps students imagine their potential audience, and hence in the long run implements a sense of communication and power.

Mr. Anderson mentioned that portfolios are good for students who cannot share their ideas openly. They can examine the process of their own writing and hopefully come to share it with their peers.

Mr. Brinkerhoff in his devil's advocate role disagreed and stated that portfolios are difficult to implement because the process has to be a regular part of the classroom schedule and hence takes away from other activities, such as group work.

Ms. Karabas suggested that portfolios should be used by teachers as a natural part of the pedagogical process, a kind of running summary of classroom work.

Ms. DeCardy mentioned that students like to share their writing with each other. She showed her colleagues models of student's writing from various classes. The students, apparently, did not want to give the papers back to the teacher because they enjoyed reading their peers' work.

Mr. Brinkerhoff mentioned that one of the problems with portfolios is that the student who has done the portfolio work thinks he or she should pass the class on that basis alone, forgetting that studying for class examinations is also a necessary and integral part of the academic experience. The group then discussed the weight of the portfolio in the overall grade for the term.

Mr. Randle said one of the dangers of being criticized by peers is that a student might lose the impetus of creativity, feeling inferior to others.

Ms. Karabas ended the meeting saying that teachers have to teach students to learn to be critics of their own and other students' work. They should learn the structure of criticism from the beginning.

In 1993, the teachers of the English department shifted their focus from using the portfolio as an instructional tool and decided that portfolios should be a requirement in each class and that scores on these portfolios would be included on student transcripts. Thus students would graduate after having compiled an eight-volume set of portfolios. Not content with this department-wide requirement, teachers went on to suggest a senior-project requirement. Each graduating senior would complete a department-approved project—a senior thesis, a manuscript of plays or short stories, a cycle of poetry, a photo essay, or a video or audio project. It took two years to work out the details, but we were able to launch this requirement in the spring of 1996. This final requirement represents a maturity in our vision for our students that came as a byproduct of portfolio assessment.

Perhaps the most significant change that has resulted from our portfolio practices over the past five years is that our students have emerged as instructional resources within our educational community. As students became more reflective, more confident, and more evaluative, they demanded more of classroom instruction. In essence, they challenged us to provide a more meaningful education, one in which we were joint collaborators with our students. Thus, we shifted from teacher-centered classrooms to learning-centered classrooms. Students participate in developing guidelines for the portfolios, determining the performance standards, and trying out the authentic tasks developed by their teachers. Our students' involvement underscores the dynamic nature of the portfolio process.

Portfolios and the English Regents' Exam: First Year

In 1994, the New York State Department of Education invited schools from around the state to participate in a three-year pilot program designed to investigate performance-based assessment. Our school was allowed to design components worth up to thirty-five points for inclusion with the Regents' examination. The performance-based component for the English Regents' exam at Humanities was the submission of a writing portfolio. We were happy to participate in the project since we saw the state's movement toward portfolio assessment as a validation of our own program at Humanities. In addition, we wanted the *experts* in Albany to review our work and give us feedback. Our decision to participate in this large-scale assessment brought changes to our original portfolio program that have since shaped our thinking, teaching, and beliefs about literacy.

After two years of designing portfolio items for this exam, we have improved the quality of teaching and learning at Humanities. The passing percentage on the English Regents' exam has always been the standard for determining the effectiveness of the high-school language arts programs across the state. In most New York schools, including ours, this exam is more important than any exam except the AP English. The exam has the following purposes:

- To assess students' ability to understand and interpret text that is read to them
- To assess the effects of students' reading and writing on their knowledge of vocabulary
- To assess the effects of students' reading and writing on their knowledge of spelling conventions
- To assess students' ability to use known strategies for understanding and interpreting narrative, exposition, and poetry
- To assess students' ability to use the literature they have read to respond to a literary prompt
- To assess students' ability to apply known composing strategies to a choice of topic

Whereas before we had worked in isolation and with complete autonomy with portfolios in our classrooms, we were now required to design a system that met the needs of the five teachers on our Regents' Committee. The team had to adhere to state and local standards as well as fulfill the mission of our school's program. We attempted all of these and still remained friends at the end of the school year. In fact, all members of the original team opted to participate for the entire three-year pilot. The state offered some helpful guidelines for designing a portfolio system, and they worked well for our school. We did not attempt any fancy footwork that first year, but followed these design questions:

- Who will be involved in planning?
- Who will have primary control over the decisions to be made?
- What purposes are of particular importance for the portfolio system you are developing?
- What are the major instructional goals for your program?
- What problems do you anticipate?
- What issues need to be resolved? List four categories of evidence that should be included in the work students select for their portfolios. How many samples of each should students select?
- Who will you get to assist you in finalizing these decisions?
- What criteria will you use to assess the portfolios as a whole? Who assesses?

These questions allowed us to be systematic about the process, yet they were flexible enough for us to draw upon our own experiences with portfolios.

Pilot Description

In the first year, beginning with the June, 1994, Regents' Comprehensive Examination in English, we eliminated the reading comprehension, vocabulary, and spelling sections of the exam, and we awarded the points from those sections to a portfolio of work that demonstrated the students' abilities to use language skillfully in these four areas: literary response and expression; information and understanding; critical analysis and evaluation; and social interaction.

The portfolio included works based on responses to the reading of nonfiction, fiction, and poetry. While we sought to maintain high standards, we tried to resist the temptation to make the portfolio substantially more difficult than the original sections of the exam it replaced. We felt the forty-five minute multiple-choice test should not be exchanged for a more arduous obstacle for students so close to graduation. In fact, this project was used to help students graduate by keeping our evaluation of them more in line with our teaching and by helping our ESL population to avoid the kind of testing for which they were least prepared.

The first-year pilot was targeted for all juniors, and it involved English

classes with a total register of approximately 280 students. Five teachers participated in the project. The parents of all students involved were notified in writing of the pilot and all students were given an outline of the basic items required
for the portfolio with a copy of the scoring rubric attached.

Description of Portfolio Items

Since we wished to deal with nonfiction, fiction, and poetry, we had students design and complete four-item portfolios, with each item being dedicated
to one of the three modes. Students had the option of handing in more than four
items, but nonfiction, fiction, and poetry had to be represented. The list below
suggests some of the possibilities for writing that were a direct outgrowth of our
curriculum and teaching methodology at the point in our use of portfolios:

1. *Tasks that deal with non-fiction*: to demonstrate use of language for informa-
   tion and understanding.
   - Real-life letters to newspaper editors, congressional representatives,
     or business people, perhaps submitted with received responses
   - Research-based writings, complete with footnotes and bibliogra-
     phies
   - College application essays
   - Ironic essays, modeled on Swift's *A Modest Proposal* or Syfers's *Why
     I Want A Wife*

2. *Tasks that deal with fiction (or drama)*: to demonstrate critical analysis and
   evaluation of a work.
   - Journals or logs that collect responses to reading
   - Critical or analytical essays on literary works, perhaps expanding on
     ideas discussed in journals
   - Letters to the author
   - Book reports

3. *Tasks that deal with poetry*: to demonstrate response to aesthetic expression.
   - Essays on tone, diction, style, imagery, and symbolism in a poem
   - Collections or anthologies of three or more poems that belong
     together (students choose and explain their choices, based on simi-
     larities of structure, theme, and literary devices)
   - Essays on the work of a favorite poet
   - Essays on a poetic school, such as Romanticism
   - Original poems modeled on other poems, such as *New Songs of
     Innocence and Experience*
   - Original poetry, with critical commentary

These works and the portfolio were evaluated according to the following criteria: First, did the writing present and deal with real issues, and did it consider ideas and topics in depth? Second, was it written in an authentic *voice* and with a sense of audience? Third, did it show evidence of varied, competent writing strategies? Fourth, were strong thinking skills demonstrated in the drafts and final pieces? Finally, how many errors in mechanics were evident? These judgments were made based on such evidence of reading behaviors as high levels of comprehension, integration of what was read in various sources, running records or tape recordings (to indicate fluency), and awareness of reading strategies and the inclination to use them appropriately. The criteria with respect to content-area learning included understanding and using terminology, grasping and using necessary concepts, integrating information from texts and other sources, and assuming different perspectives in writing about social studies, literature, or science.

Evaluating Humanities Regents' Portfolio Project: First Year

After the first year of the project, the five teachers in the project reviewed the portfolios with an eye toward figuring out what had worked, what hadn't worked, and what we might consider for the next year. In terms of what worked, we found that students had addressed a wide range of topics in a wide range of styles, and that they clearly understood the importance of mastering the four important modes of thinking and writing that had been stressed. We were also pleased with our assignments, which we believed stressed the importance of educated opinions as well as reinforced skills for the on-demand essays on the Regents' examination. The authenticity and importance of portfolios were enhanced, and students generally treated the portfolio as a high-stakes endeavor, which was reflected both in terms of a rise in student output and a rise in the average Regents' examination grades. In terms of our teaching, portfolios raised teachers' expectations, and teachers got to know a wider range of students after evaluating portfolios. We felt that our teaching had improved through focus on important tasks, and that teacher cooperation had been stressed in all aspects: setting rules, establishing grading procedures, sharing workloads, sharing lesson plans, and discussing texts and assignments. This last outcome was widely felt to be the most important.

Not everything was perfect, however. In reviewing the portfolios we came to the conclusion that students needed more time to assemble them after the assignments were essentially complete, and that firmer, earlier deadlines needed to be set in order to allow for more time to assemble the portfolios later on. In addition, we felt that we needed to establish more avenues for positive reinforcement, and we also felt that the portfolio grade should be included on the report card. A question that came up was whether students who did not hand in a portfolio deserved an opportunity to take the entire Regents' examination. Finally, we found that poetry assignments were difficult to integrate into some classes.

We also had plenty that we wanted to work on for the next year. For one thing, we wanted to work on making the grading process easier for teachers as well as to more formally involve the classroom teacher in the process of grading the portfolios for the Regents' examination. Thus, we felt the portfolios should be read twice: once by the classroom teacher and once by another teacher. In terms of poetry, we wanted to develop more specific guidelines and lessons for poetry assignments, and we considered using an agreed-upon group of poems for all eleventh-grade classes. We also wanted to develop consistent vocabulary lists for poetry analysis, and we decided to use the Advanced Placement examination question on *tone* as a model for poetry assignments. We also felt that creative writing should be included in the portfolio, and we considered using the Regents' portfolio as a final exam for the junior year. Finally, we decided to continue the process of sharing assignments and lessons on a more formal basis.

Impact of Regents' Portfolio Project: Second Year

Using portfolios for large-scale assessment proved exciting, challenging, and revitalizing for the Humanities High School community. Five years with a successful portfolio program already in place could have caused us to settle into complacency and satisfaction with the status quo. When we embraced the Regents' Option Program in 1994, we found that we embarked on a risky and rocky journey to design and to investigate portfolio assessment. We had to take what we already knew about portfolios and reshape this knowledge in such a way that we could meet state and local standards in a manner that did not conflict with our educational mission at Humanities. The reshaping process showed us exactly what we valued as educators. The process also showed us what we needed to do in order to improve teaching and learning for our students.

We found that as we shaped assessment design, we were simultaneously reworking it for the next year's group of students. For example, when we used New York State's English Language Arts Standards to plan the curriculum and assessment for the Regents' Portfolio Project, we tried to focus on (a) *activities* (reading, writing, speaking, listening, and viewing), (b) *functions of language* (informational, literary, critical, and social), and (c) *qualities* (range, flexibility, independence, connections, and conventions). However, after reviewing the portfolios of our 280 students for the June, 1995, exam and finding one audio-cassette submitted by a student who had reworked the ending of Conrad Aiken's short story *Silent Snow, Secret Snow*, we realized that while we included speaking and listening in our instructional program, we had not included it in our assessment design. We all agreed that evidence of listening and speaking must be included in the design for the 1996 exam.

On the local level, the 1994 New York City Curriculum Frameworks gave us the following set of components to help us further strengthen our instructional program by including them in our teaching and in our assessment:

- Personal satisfaction: the knowledge, skills, and abilities enabling students to become life-long learners

- Listening, Reading, Viewing: the knowledge, skills, and abilities attained through reading, listening, and viewing

- Speaking, Writing, Performing: the knowledge, skills, and abilities attained through speaking, writing, illustrating, and performing

- Nature of Language: the knowledge, skills, and abilities enabling students to appreciate both formal and informal language and its importance in social, academic, and professional life

- Research: the knowledge, skills, and abilities enabling students to gather, synthesize, evaluate, and use information in social, academic, and professional activities

- Self-Assessment: the knowledge, skills, and abilities enabling students to internalize standards of excellence and habitually apply them to their own performance

- Diversity: the knowledge, skills, and abilities enabling students to understand and value their own and other cultures

- Social Responsibility: the knowledge, skills, and abilities enabling students to practice responsible citizenship

- Cross-Curricular Participation: the use of all the language arts knowledge, skills, and abilities in all social, academic, and professional settings

To integrate these components into our program, we designed an anchor task for the portfolios, which was administered to each student. This task begins with a freewriting activity. The student then reads the poem and is asked to respond to it (using words and pictures) and to explain his or her response. Students then pair up to create an understanding of the poem. After this, each student writes an essay. When they have completed the assignment, they are asked to evaluate the task.

We also reshaped fundamental parts of the portfolio, such as the *Dear Reader Letter*, which each student included as an introduction to his or her portfolio. Before working with the Regents' Portfolio Project, we wanted the *Dear Reader Letter* to do too many things—introduce the student and the portfolio, demonstrate the student's metacognitive strategies, and discuss or annotate the contents of the portfolio. This was simply too much for one letter, and much of what we received from the students was stilted and artificial. In our second year with the project, we agreed on the need for students to name what they were doing and to find a metaphor for their work, and we gave them the following prompt:

Prompt for *Dear Reader Letter*:

- What extended metaphor have you chosen to portray yourself as a reader and writer?

- What are your strengths and weaknesses as a writer and reader?

- How have these strengths developed?

- How have you attempted to improve your weaknesses?

- What were your goals for the term as a reader and writer? Have you achieved them? Explain some of the successful strategies employed.

- What common themes have you observed in these pieces? What do the pieces in your portfolio have in common?

We embraced the idea of the metaphors in the *story* of the portfolio after reading Denton's definition of *metaphor* as "a set of terms that permit one to speak of experience and possibilities and the mystery and hiddenness of their fundamental reality" (Denton, 1974; quoted in Jordan and Purves, 1994, p. 12). Students are now required to find a metaphor to describe themselves as learners and writers and to give shape to the ordering of materials in their portfolios. It was a marvelous conceit! Students came up with such metaphors as "lock and key," "museum of the mind," "an oil painting," "battlefield," and "exploration." As a result, the students' work showed greater evidence of ownership, more accurate and meaningful self-assessment, and more interesting use of language.

Finally, on a schoolwide level, we were happy to note that most of the portfolios read in the second year of the pilot showed that our mission as a high school focusing on the humanities is being accomplished. Our department believes that through the vicarious living experiences provided by literature, the student learns to relate directly to the best that mankind has thought and written about the experience of being human. It is through reading and discussing that literature that students become more human: gentler, more generous, more curious, more tolerant, more willing to use their intellect, more capable of understanding the thoughts and feelings of others, and more respectful of all people— their problems as well as their accomplishments. It is through exposure to the humanities that the student becomes a fully functional member of the human community. We were able to see evidence of this in our student portfolios.

References

Jordan, S., and A.C. Purves (1994). *The metaphor of the portfolio and the metaphors in portfolios: The relation of classroom-based to large-scale assessment* (Report Series 3.9). Albany, NY: National Research Center on Literature Teaching and Learning, University at Albany—SUNY.

Alan C. Purves, formally Director of the Center for Writing and Literacy and project leader in portfolios for the National Literature Center, is Professor Emeritus of English and Education at the University of Illinois, and Professor Emeritus of Education and Humanities at SUNY—Albany. Currently, he is President of The Scribes, Inc., a company specializing in editorial and curriculum consulting in English Language Arts. A specialist in literature, composition, and assessment; he has taught English in elementary and secondary schools as well as in colleges and universities. He recently edited the two-volume Encyclopedia of English Studies and Language Arts, and is currently at work on books on assessment in

English, on the history of literacy, and on the education of the soul.

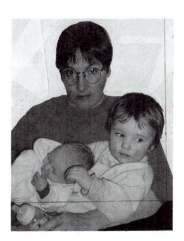

Sarah Jordan received her Ph. D. in Education from the State University of New York—Albany. She has been invited by the government of Finland to give presentations on portfolios, and is Associate Editor of the two-volume Encyclopedia of English Studies and Language Arts. She has published a book on multicultural literature, and currently works in the Alternative Education Department of Wachusett Regional High School, MA, teaching English, math, and civics.

James Peltz received his M.A. in Expository Writing from the University of Iowa. He has taught writing and speech at the University of Iowa and at the College of Saint Rose in Albany, NY. He served as Publications Editor for the National Research Center on Literature Teaching and Learning at the State University of New York—Albany, and has had extensive editing experience in the fields of education and literature. Currently, he is an Aquisitions Editor for State University of New York Press. He resides in Albany, NY.

INDEX